An Illustrated History of the

An Illustrated History of the

GESTAPO

RUPERT BUTLER

Motorbooks International
Publishers & Wholesalers ®

This edition published in 1996 by Wordwright Books,
25 Oakford Road, London NW5 1AJ, England.

© Wordwright Books, 1992

Previously published by Ian Allan Publishing, Shepperton, England

The information in this book is true and complete to the best of our
knowledge. All recommendations are made without any guarantee
on the part of the author or Publisher, who also disclaim any
liability incurred in connection with the use of this data or specific
details.

ISBN 0-95271-280-6

Printed and bound in the United States

Frontispiece (page 2): A wartime view of the Gestapo and
Sicherheitsdienst in occupied Europe
by L. Jordaan for the Dutch weekly, *De Groene*.

Contents

Foreword

Rupert Butler has written a book which traces the establishment and growth of the Gestapo in all its horrifying detail. He shows how it developed into an organization covering every aspect of German life – a machine of mass murder, torture, and genocide.

The book's publication coincides with the 50th anniversary of the destruction of the Czech mining village of Lidice (full story in the text). There were many such acts of destruction in World War II. Lidice stands out, not because of the cold and cynical planning, but because the Nazis chose to announce their deed to the world.

Hitherto the Gestapo had tended to cover up its operations but, by the third year of the War, the world had begun to realize the full evil of Hitler. Public announcement of his order that Lidice be "wiped from the face of the map" provoked a shocked reaction worldwide. Within days a "Lidice Shall Live" Committee was formed and this became a slogan taken up all over the free world. After the War, Lidice was rebuilt on a site overlooking the old village and it has become a symbol of rebirth and reconciliation.

Rupert Butler has done a great service in cataloguing the work of the Gestapo. His book is a timely reminder that the concept of evil can emerge anywhere, anytime. But now the new Lidice is threatened by all the economic and ecological problems of the post-War world. Pollution has ravaged the country around Lidice and, as we approach the 50th anniversary, the Committee thought it appropriate to ask for the gift of trees to be planted there. The generous (and continuing) response to this call is an affirmation of the reply we all must make to such evils as the Gestapo. Good shall prevail; new life will emerge.

If you would like to support the future work of the Committee, please send your contribution to:
The Lidice Committee, 7, The Tiltwood, Acacia Road, London W3 6HG, England

Lou Kenton
Honorary Secretary of The Lidice 50th Anniversary Committee

Introduction

In its day the Gestapo was the most feared and the most efficient police organization in the world. Twenty thousand secret policemen kept intact the Nazis' grip on the German population and, after 1939, on the conquered populations of Europe. Though the western states firmly believed that Hitler might be overthrown by internal revolt, or his war machine be undermined by European resistance, the Gestapo saw to it that the Nazi machine kept going to the end.

The Gestapo was the key instrument of Nazi terror and of Nazi power. It could direct its attention to anyone, however important. No-one was immune, and everyone knew this. It was as equally at home hunting down the generals and aristocrats who tried to blow Hitler up in July 1944 as it was searching out work-shy labourers and subjecting them to 'work education' weekends. The German people soon came to realize that the smallest hint of dissent – the odd remark on a bus, a rough day at work – could bring the knock on the door in the middle of the night. The Gestapo organization worked so well because it encouraged a climate of obedience, conformity, and denunciation.

Keeping the political peace was only part of the Gestapo's work. As the Nazi regime began to pursue systematic anti-semitism, the Gestapo became involved in Jewish persecution. For Europe's Jews, obedience and conformity were of no use. Hitler's and Himmler's race policy branded all Jews as enemies of the German state by definition. The Gestapo helped provide the personnel for the dreaded *Einsatzgruppen* which followed German troops into battle to hunt out and murder 'enemies' of the regime. The Gestapo rooted out all those who sympathized with the Jewish cause, or those brave Europeans who sheltered Jews, or brought Jewish children up as their own. Being a Jew or helping a Jew became in the warped world-view of the Nazi security apparatus a political crime.

How did the Gestapo come to play such a rôle in the Third Reich? In 1933 it employed a mere 300 people in a small Berlin office, keeping index cards on known Communists. At the end of its sordid existence it had offices everywhere and effectively controlled Hitler's political empire. In twelve years the Gestapo established an unenviable reputation for state terror and political persecution on a vast scale. Historians treat this transformation in very different ways. The traditional view saw the Gestapo as a uniquely evil phenomenon, bound up with the imposition of Nazi totalitarian rule and Hitler's ambition to destroy the Jews. More recent historians, particularly in Germany, have come to see the Gestapo not as a unique expression of state barbarism but as one of many examples over the century of the unscrupulous use of state power. The new generation of 'revisionist' writers has rejected the view of a smooth-running totalitarian system imposed on Germany. They see the development both of the Gestapo apparatus and the anti-semitic strategies as a gradual process, responding to circumstances and opportunities, helped by the complicity and co-operation of important sections of the

German community, but in no sense pre-planned.

These new views have dangerous implications. Nationalist apologists and neo-Nazi writers now argue that the Gestapo was no worse than the Stalinist secret police, that Germans do not hold the monopoly of evil in the modern world. They argue that Hitler did not plan to destroy the Jews, even, in the most extreme cases, that the Holocaust never happened. They blame instead the circumstances of war, or the threat that Stalinism posed to Europe. By this devious route the Gestapo has become an instrument to keep Communism from destroying 'European culture.'

This kind of history is largely spurious. The fact that state terror and mass murder has happened in other countries and at other times does not in any sense justify it. State terror is deplorable wherever and whenever it has manifested itself. Defence against Communism need not involve the wholesale persecution of dissidents and the slaughter of a whole race. The lawlessness and barbarism displayed by the Gestapo can be explained but it can never be excused.

The emergence and early development of the Gestapo must be understood in the context of German politics before Hitler. There was nothing new about political policemen. Even before the First World War the government operated police surveillance and harassment of political opponents and radicals. During the war pacifists, communists, and political 'undesirables' were imprisoned and maltreated. In the 1920s a political secret police based in Berlin was established whose powers were gradually increased to allow them 'to prevent, and prosecute. . .all penal offences which have a political character.' In practice the secret police directed their attentions much more enthusiastically against the left wing political movements. When the Nazis came to power in 1933 they simply took over the existing political police department, recruited much of its personnel, and strengthened its rights to root out what the Nazi regime defined as subversive activity. For many ordinary Germans, brought up all their lives to see the extreme left as a genuine threat to the German people, the initial Nazi persecution of political opponents was either welcomed or was not regarded as anything too out of the ordinary.

From then on the Gestapo began the slow build-up of a secret police organization with all the apparatus of card-index, filing-cabinet, interrogation centres, spies, and *agents provocateurs* which are the stock-in-trade of all police states. The critical turning point came in November 1933. That was the point at which the rule of law was effectively dispensed with by the Nazi regime. The Gestapo got the right of arbitrary arrest and 'protective custody' without any legal restriction or accountability, except to Göring and, later, Himmler. From 1933 the Gestapo became effectively a law unto itself and the German tradition of the *Rechtsstaat*, the state rooted in law and respect for the law, was torn aside.

Even then the Gestapo might never have become the centre of Nazism's terror empire without the ambitions of its leaders. In the chapters that follow Rupert Butler introduces us to the men who shaped and led the Gestapo and made it into the familiar symbol of terror. First Hermann Göring, the ambitious ex-pilot who joined Hitler's first cabinet in January 1933, and who ran the Prussian police force and the political police until 1934. He was utterly unscrupulous in his use of force and terror but had difficulty controlling the wave of popular Nazi violence unleashed after the seizure of power. He was followed in April 1934 by Heinrich Himmler, who gradually acquired responsibility for all the police forces in Germany, and who made the Gestapo, under the ruthless direction of Reinhard Heydrich, the centre of his security and terror empire. On the surface Himmler was an unlikely figure to run the apparatus. He neither behaved nor looked a monster. He was modest, unassuming, orderly. There was no showmanship, no mad rages. His portraits betray a very ordinary, almost genial clerk.

Beneath the surface there lay a very different personality. Himmler was deeply insecure, obsessive, prudish, and fundamentally amoral. He took out all the anxieties and obsessions of his fragile personality on those weaker than himself – on all the political prisoners, homosexuals, mentally ill, gypsies, and Jews ensnared by his police and SS system. It is difficult to imagine that without Himmler the Gestapo would have developed in quite the way that it did. Himmler's obsession with racial purity and moral cleansing, his hatred of all 'deviants' – political, racial, or sexual – gave the Gestapo a character quite distinct from other secret police forces. Himmler did not just want power and the means to hold on to it. He wanted a race of Aryan supermen who would cleanse Europe for him. He turned Hitler's anti-semitic diatribes into practical reality. He listened to Hitler's rages against traitors and dissidents, then hunted them down and tortured and executed them, all in the name of a warped, self-indulgent idealism.

If the rôle and character of the Gestapo was shaped by the personal ambitions of its leaders, its success as an instrument of terror must be explained in other ways. The political opponents of Nazism were divided among themselves and were poorly experienced in fighting police terror. The Gestapo succeeded in infiltrating and breaking every opposition group or movement in Germany. The state defined all opposition or criticism, however mild, as treachery. This made it difficult for any kind of opposition to flourish and exposed political dissidents not only to the tender mercies of the Gestapo but to the hostility and resentment of ordinary Germans who were persuaded by propaganda to treat opponents of the regime as social outcasts. By the late 1930s it was a brave German who risked his career, his family, even his life, for speaking his mind. We might wish that more had opposed Nazism; we should recall the fate of those who did.

The success of the Gestapo also rested on the development of a psychological climate that made its job much easier. In the first place it thrived on fear. Though its activities were secret, enough was known about its methods and the consequences of getting caught to make ordinary Germans wary and fearful. These fears were real enough, but it produced in people a kind of inertia, making it easier to obey and pay lip service to the regime and its orders. Many Germans indulged in what was called 'inner emigration,' keeping their real thoughts to themselves while going through the form of obedience and conformity. This produced the outcome desired by the Nazi regime of effective social control with the minimum of political supervision. Germans became non-political for fear of what might happen to them if they thought differently.

Under these circumstances it did not take long before broad sections of the population not only stopped thinking differently, but began to endorse the regime, to identify with its goals and to comply with its requirements. It was easier to join in than to oppose. And not only easier, it could be rewarding too. The Gestapo succeeded in controlling a very large population with relatively small numbers because it depended on the active support of ordinary Germans in giving information, acting as secret police spies, reporting on neighbours and workmates. This could be a result, of course, of genuine enthusiasm for the Nazi ideals; but it was just as often the result of careerism, malevolence, revenge, and conformism. In an atmosphere of police terror it is usually the case that the police depend on the support and active co-operation of at least a part of the population, and this was no less true of Germany under Hitler.

The final psychological prop on which the Gestapo relied was the popular perception of the legitimacy of what it was doing. Those Germans who co-operated with the police, or endorsed the police state, were able to persuade themselves that there was nothing wrong with what they were doing and that there really were enemies of the state which they had to help bring to justice. It was easier to believe this than to contradict entirely the prevailing political climate. Evidence from Stalin's Russia in the 1930s shows how, in the absence of any alternative information, people genuinely believed the propaganda lies. The same was true in Germany. When Bernd Engelmann wrote his memoirs of life in the Third Reich he went back to his home town to interview people he had known then. He met the Gestapo officer who had arrested and bullied him when he was seized as a suspected Social Democrat resister. To Engelmann's amazement the man showed no remorse. More than that, he could not see that he had done anything which was not entirely legitimate. To him, Gestapo work was just a job. He ended his career as a respected policeman in Adenauer's West Germany.

None of this excuses the crimes committed against the 'enemies' of the Nazi regime, or against those whose only fault was to be a different race. But it does help to explain how, through a combination of terror, inertia, complicity and endorsement the Gestapo was able to impose its savage grip on the German people, and recruit the torturers and terrorists who ran it. The same processes can be seen at work since the war throughout eastern Europe. The state security police in what was until recently East Germany have a sorry pedigree. The Gestapo men who ended up in Latin America after the war carried on their trade for different masters. Wherever state terror is practised there will always be the thugs and cranks to put it into operation.

In all this the Gestapo has a special rôle to play. It has come to symbolize since the war the potential for barbarism in the midst of the modern trappings of civilization. It is the bleakest chapter in the sorry story of human oppression and brutality this century. In the pages that follow Rupert Butler takes us through the history of Hitler's secret police force dispassionately and thoroughly. From whatever perspective it is viewed, the Gestapo deserves its symbolic reputation.

Doctor Richard Overy
Reader in History, University of London

1
The Gestapo
is
Born

Berlin, first city of Hitler's Reich, wore a welcoming, festive air that first day of May, 1933. The Nazis had come to power after the March elections and the country's new masters intended that their first Day of National Labour should be celebrated in style. Trades union leaders who had been invited to Berlin were fêted as honoured guests and paraded through streets decked with Swastika banners. President von Hindenburg and Dr Joseph Goebbels, the Reich Minister of Public Enlightenment and Propaganda, addressed a large gathering of children in the capital's Lustgarten. Later came the set piece: 100,000 workers packed Tempelhof Air Field where an emotional Goebbels paid tribute to seven miners who, along with members of the SA (Sturm Abteilung – Storm Troopers), had been killed during their Führer's fierce struggle for power.

Dr. Joseph Goebbels, the Reich Minister of Public Enlightenment and Propaganda.

May Day, 1933. 100,000 pack Berlin's Templehof Airfield to mark the Nazi's first Day of National Labour.

Then it was the turn of Adolf Hitler to speak. This day, the Führer announced, would be marked with the motto "Honour work and respect the worker." Furthermore, May Day would be celebrated in honour of German labour "throughout the centuries." Here, on this first of Nazi Germany's May Days, was a message of hope for German workers hungry for vision; above all, for a leader who would feed them more than dreams.

But what of tomorrow? One man at least had no doubts about that. Dr Goebbels, alone that night with his diary, gave an excited account of the day's events. Anyone looking over his shoulder would not have had any cause for anxiety – except for one significant sentence. "Tomorrow," Goebbels wrote, "we shall occupy the trades union buildings. There will be little resistance."

The next day, the *Deutsche Allgemeine Zeitung* newspaper carried the headlines: "THE NATIONAL SOCIALISTS TAKE OVER THE TRADES UNIONS / THE LEADERS ARRESTED / ACTION THROUGHOUT THE REICH." At 10:00 a.m. detachments of the SA had swept down in mass raids on the headquarters of those trades union leaders they had lured to Berlin. The sight of hordes of brown-shirted SA bully boys under their pig-eyed, scarfaced, homosexual commander Hauptmann Ernst Röhm was no novelty in Berlin. But now there was a sinister addition. The arrest of fifty-eight trades union leaders was carried out by contingents of Prussian police who, sanctioned by official decrees signed by their chief, Hermann Göring, operated for the first time under a new name. This name was the GEheime STAats POlizei (Secret State Police), a title soon to be shortened with brutal brevity to Gestapo.

Five months previously, on the evening of 30 January 1933, Berlin had been caught in deep delirium. From dusk until long past midnight, Nazi Storm Troopers, numbering some tens of thousands, had marched in a gigantic torchlight parade to celebrate the most remarkable spectacle in all that city's long history. Forty-three year old Austrian-born Adolf Hitler, the former derelict of the Vienna doss houses, the unknown Gefreiter of the trenches, had become Chancellor of Germany. It had indeed seemed like a new dawn. But by no means everyone that day viewed the birth of the Third Reich favourably. Certainly not the elderly and rigidly conservative Generalfeldmarschall Paul Beneckendorff von Hindenburg, veteran of the Prussian wars against Austria and France, and commander of the German forces on the eastern front in 1914.

As recently as 26 January, he had told Freiherr Kurt von Hammerstein-Equord, the Chief-of-Staff of the Army, that he had no intention whatever of making "that Bohemian Corporal" either Minister of Defence or Chancellor of the Reich. And General Erich Ludendorff who, during the war, had become Chief-of-Staff to Hindenburg, was to write to his old chief, "I must warn you most solemnly that this sinister individual will lead our country into the abyss and our nation into an unprecedented catastrophe."

The loss by Germany of the war in 1918 had brought a collapse in living standards. The democratic parties in the Reichstag had to pick up the pieces that followed the collapse of Imperial Germany. While the Communists clamoured for revolution, the right smarted in cold fury at what it saw as nothing less than betrayal by the Government of the Republic when it signed a Peace Treaty in the following year. Agitation and conspiracy soon became open violence on the streets of virtually every German city; democracy in Germany

Berlin, 30 January 1933. The birth of the Third Reich. Storm Troopers march in a giant torchlight parade to celebrate the Nazi's victory at the polls.

was terminally ill even at the very moment of the creation of the Weimar Republic, which had been intended to give the country a watertight liberal constitution.

During the twenty-one years which separated the two world wars a number of movements sprang up, all of them demanding violent political change. There were the members of the Stahlhelm (Steel Helmet), a militant right wing, nationalist ex-serviceman's organization. One of the more notorious right wing adventures of the Weimar Republic, the so-called Kapp Putsch of March 1920, was undertaken for the purpose of overthrowing the Reich government of Berlin by force. It was spearheaded by a brutal contingent of the Freikorps consisting of various paramilitary units. One of these Freikorps was the Erhardt Brigade, the first to adopt the ancient Swastika symbol. The jackbooted columns of the brigade, newly painted Swastikas gleaming on each green-grey "coal scuttle" helmet, poured into the capital. The language of their leader, General Walther von Luttwitz, foreshadowed the crudity that was soon to become all too familiar: "We need two things. Order and work. . ... Only compulsion makes people work. He who doesn't work, won't eat. Secondly, a complete ban on strikes. . .agitators will be exterminated without compassion." The reaction of the workers was swift and co-ordinated – a general strike crippled all attempts by Luttwitz and Dr Wolfgang Kapp, the ardent nationalist who had given his name to the coup, to govern. The coup collapsed in farce.

Such manifestations of aggressive nationalism were not confined to Berlin. In Munich, the Bavarian capital, Gustav von Kahr headed a right wing state

General Erich von Ludendorff who wrote of Hitler to his old chief, President Hindenburg, "This sinister individual will lead our country into the abyss and our nation into an unprecedented catastrophe."

Below: *Dr Wolfgang Kapp, the ardent nationalist who gave his name to the abortive 1920 coup.*

Opposite above: *Munich on the first Nazi Party Day, 28 January 1923.*

Opposite below right: *The Kapp Putsch, 1920. "We need two things. Order and work...He who doesn't work, won't eat;" the words of General Walther von Luttwitz, leader of the Erhardt Brigade.*

Left: *Freikorps volunteers outside the Munich Bierkeller where it all began.*

Above: *Distribution of weapons to Party members.*

government, strongly out of sympathy with the policies followed by the central administration in Berlin. In Munich also was the former Gefreiter Adolf Hitler, who had remained on the strength of his old unit, the List (16th Bavarian Infantry) Reserve Regiment. His superior officers had been impressed by his talents as a fiery speaker – invaluable for whipping up nationalist sentiments in the ranks and controlling vexatious radicals.

Hitler had gained control by February 1920 of the political party that his army superiors had sent him to spy upon: the German Workers' Party. This party was racist and anti-Semitic; it repudiated the hated Versailles Treaty, rejected the Republic, and scorned capitalism. Above all, its programme proclaimed that it stood for "the little people" – the ruined, the defeated, the dispossessed.

About this time Hitler made a valuable contact. This was the formidable Hauptmann Ernst Röhm, whose task in Bavaria was to organize what was termed "the black Reichswehr," a highly secret and illegal reinforcement of the l00,000 strong "official Army" permitted under the terms of the Versailles Treaty. In particular, Röhm had, with the full support of the official Army, the task of channelling Army funds and support to paramilitary and right-orientated groups which could, in time of trouble, be of use to the Army as reserves. It did not take Röhm long to decide, on meeting Hitler, that "this was the man for Germany." More important to Hitler than approval, however, was his realization that Röhm had access to potential manpower.

Hitler had another crucial meeting at around this time: Hauptmann Hermann Wilhelm Göring was one of Germany's prominent war heroes – the last commander of the legendary Richthofen fighter squadron and holder of the Pour le Merite, the country's highest wartime decoration.

Göring, with an uncertain future and at first slender means, had come to Munich after the war to study economics at the university. Late in 1922, a demonstration had been called in Munich's Königsplatz to protest the latest Allied demands on a defeated Germany.

Göring, on the edge of the crowd, was intrigued to hear shouts for a certain Adolf Hitler whom, he learnt from other bystanders, headed the small Nationalsozialistische Deutsche Arbeiterpartei (National Socialist German Workers

Early days. Ernst Röhm and Hermann Göring lead a Party Day parade. Göring was later to play an important rôle in the assassination of Röhm.

Party or Nazis). It was an inauspicious encounter: Göring saw a callow, ill-dressed man in his early thirties who, on this occasion, refused to speak. A few days later, however, Göring did hear Hitler hold forth on "The Versailles Treaty and the Extradition of the German Army Commanders," screaming such phrases as "You've got to have bayonets to back up threats," and, "Down with Versailles." Göring was wholly won over.

Hitler himself was preoccupied with finding a measure of respectability for his infant movement. For a father figure he wheeled out a powerful totem of the old order: no less than General Ludendorff, the military hero of the First World War, who was living near Munich and, as an avowed nationalist, not averse to furthering the designs of the right by force.

The Brownshirts on Parade. Ernst Röhm's Sturm Abteilung (Storm Troopers) display the new NSDAP (Nazi) standard.

Relations between the governments of Berlin and Bavaria at this time were hostile. Prussian voters inclined to the left or centre, whereas the complexion in Bavaria was aggressively to the right. The ruling triumvirate in Bavaria personified the mood: Gustav von Kahr, the elderly, stiff Kommissar; General Otto von Lossow, commander of the Reichswehr (Army) in Bavaria; and Oberst Hans von Seisser, head of the state police. Hitler viewed this triumvirate as the basis for a bold gamble: muster supporters under Ludendorff as front man and sweep out the old order by force. On 8 November 1923, while Kahr was addressing a patriotic meeting at the Bürgerbräukeller, a fashionable rendezvous on the outskirts of Munich, Hitler struck. With the aid of Göring and with forces from Ernst Röhm's Freikorps-style Reichskriegsflagge and 600 steel-helmeted SA men, Hitler surrounded the cellar, burst in on the meeting and fired a shot into the ceiling. In florid language, he declared a national revolution and the deposing of both the Bavarian and Berlin Reich governments.

Hitler took Kahr and others to a back room and forced them to declare their co-operation. Hitler would direct political affairs in a new regime and Ludendorff (who had only been told of the attempt at the last moment) would command the Army. It was sheer intimidation; Kahr, playing for time, agreed, but once free of SA threats, he renounced his promises. At this point, the putsch should have collapsed. Instead, at around noon the next day, with some 2,000 followers, the Nazi leaders marched towards Odeonplatz in the centre of Munich, where state police, under the orders of the triumvirate, blocked the streets. The marchers refused to dissolve; the police opened fire. Sixteen party members and three police were killed. Hitler and Göring were wounded, the former only slightly. In the confusion, Hitler was whisked away in a waiting car to the house of an associate. The bullet which struck Göring had pierced the groin close to an artery. He was given first aid by the Jewish proprietor of a nearby bank and then smuggled into Austria.

Nazi Art: An idealized Hitler speaks in the Munich Bierkeller from which he launched his unsuccessful putsch in 1923.

Seemingly, the putsch was an ignominious failure but Hitler's cause still had many supporters in Bavaria. Equally important, the putsch had made both Hitler and his movement headline news. The future Führer, who was eventually arrested along with Ludendorff and Röhm and brought before a sympathetic court, received the lowest possible sentence: five years' fortress detention. Röhm was ordered to be held in Stadelheim prison. Ludendorff was given a clean acquittal, leaving the court to enthusiastic shouts of "Heil Ludendorff!"

After his early release on 20 December 1924 from the fortress of Landsberg, Hitler vowed there there would be no more putsch attempts. The methods he would henceforth use for attaining power would be within a framework of legality.

Nevertheless, the Kapp and Bierkeller adventures had depended on illegality and violence to achieve their ends; each foreshadowed how Germany would go down the path of repression to ultimate dictatorship. In the uprising against Bavaria, Hitler had already in place two figures destined to rise high in the Nazi hierarchy – and above all in the Gestapo.

In addition to Hermann Göring who went on to found the Geheime Staats Polizei, there was present on the edge of the putsch one of Röhm's disciples from the Reichskriegsflagge. A photograph survives of an owlish, bespectacled figure holding the traditional Imperial standard and gazing over the flimsy barricades and barbed wire. The name of this standard bearer was Heinrich Himmler.

The year 1924 marked the lowest point for the Nazis. Although the star was in the ascendant for the parties of the left, Hitler's followers nevertheless made

The Munich putsch, 9 November 1923. The bespectacled figure holding the Imperial Standard is Heinrich Himmler.

progress at the polls. During those years, Hitler sharpened his talent for political horsetrading, seeking backstairs deals with the right and centre.

The final phases of the Nazi struggle for power came on 30 May 1932 when Generalfeldmarschall Hindenburg abruptly dismissed Chancellor Heinrich Brüning of the Centre Party and appointed as his successor Franz von Papen who had the support of the Army – the Reichswehr – and the industrial barons. Papen had been in office barely two weeks when he raised the ban on the SA and the wearing of Nazi uniforms which had been instituted by Brüning. A month later, the governments of various provinces were removed and replaced by those less likely to stir opposition. When the Social Democrat government of Otto Braun in Prussia protested, Papen dealt with the matter by disbanding it.

These were measures appreciated by the Nazis and their followers. In the elections of July 1932, the National Socialists captured 230 seats and became the most powerful party in Germany. On 30 August, Hermann Göring was elected President of the Reichstag. Kurt von Schleicher, who in World War I had been a general on Hindenburg's staff and was a founder member of the Freikorps, succeeded Papen as Chancellor. Nevertheless, the in-fighting between Papen and Schleicher for political power continued. Schleicher offered to support a Nazi government provided Hitler gave him a cabinet post and allowed him to direct the Reichswehr. Papen, not wanting to be outdone, promised Hitler the financial muscle of the Rhineland industrialists. Papen emerged the favourite with Hitler and at midday on 30 January 1933, President Hindenburg appointed Adolf Hitler Chancellor with Papen as his Vice-Chancellor.

Once he had been confirmed in the job, it was necessary for Hitler to move fast. The Bavarian Gregor Strasser, an early rival of Hitler for the leadership of the National Socialists, had been a believer in "undiluted socialist principles." He believed that National Socialism should hasten the destruction of capitalism by any means, even co-operation with Bolshevik Russia. The two men had quarrelled violently and Strasser had resigned from the Party leadership, but Hitler knew that he would have to overcome any residual left/right split within the Party if he was to survive.

At the first cabinet meeting, held in the afternoon of Hitler's appointment, Göring, acting under the new Chancellor's prerogative, lost no time in banning a Communist protest demonstration planned for the same evening. The surviving cabinet minutes also record that Hitler received the full support of Göring in suggesting that there should be a new general election. It was essential to gain the two-thirds majority granting the Nazis the constitutional power to pass the so-called Enabling Law (Ermächtigungsgesetz) – the "Law for Removing the Distress of People and Reich," a sweeping measure which in five short paragraphs would enable the new government to make laws without the approval of the Reichstag.

On 1 February, Hitler secured from President Hindenburg a decree to dissolve the Reichstag. The elections were fixed for 5 March, but Hitler and Göring realized that to achieve an electoral triumph was one thing, to ensure firm government by means of dictatorship, quite another. Göring used his new-found power as virtually uncrowned King of Prussia. And he did so through the most powerful instrument to hand – the police.

Adolf Hitler at a Massing of the Standards ceremony in 1934.

Hermann Göring's credentials for senior office appeared irreproachable. He was also President of the Reichstag, a member of the Landtag (Regional Government), and was in charge of aviation. It was the Prussian connection, however, which most interested Hitler for this enabled Göring to control the police. Prussia was by far the largest state in Germany, and included the capital, Berlin, within its boundaries, as well as the industrial centres.

Göring was determined that, whatever type of police force would evolve, it should be responsible ultimately to the Ministry of the Interior in Prussia – in other words, to himself. The creation of the Gestapo is often ascribed to Himmler: understandably so, since he was to take over with deadly effect the ultimate control of the Secret State Police alongside the SS. But the prototype organization was born as a product of the ruthlessness and energy of Göring.

On the matter of the creation of his Gestapo on 26 April 1933, Göring wrote in his short book *Germany Reborn*: "To begin with, it seemed to me of the first importance to get the weapon of the police firmly into my own hands. Here it was that I made the first sweeping changes. Out of 32 police chiefs, I removed 22. Hundreds of inspectors and thousands of police sergeants followed. . .. New men were brought in, and in every case these men came from the great reservoir of the Storm Troopers and the guards."

On 5 March, the final election of the Weimar Republic took place. The campaign was raucous: the streets were bedecked with Swastika flags and echoed to the tramp of Stormtroopers. The result terrorized many voters into placing a cross for the Nazis – but not enough of them. The Nazis led the polling with 17,227,180 votes, an increase over previous figures of some five and a half million, but it comprised only forty-four percent of the total vote. Hitler had been denied a clear majority. The Centre Party held up well, actually increasing its vote from 4,230,600 to 4,424,900, while its ally, the Catholic Bavarian People's Party, secured a total of five and a half million votes. Even the Social Democrats held their position as the second largest party with 7,181,629 votes, a drop of only 70,000. The Communists lost a million supporters but nevertheless had managed to secure 4,848,058 votes. The Nationalists, under Hugenberg and Papen, crashed to 3,136,760, a mere eight per cent of the votes cast.

Still, the fifty-two seats of the Nationalists when added to the 288 of the Nazis, gave the government a majority of sixteen in the Reichstag. However Hitler needed a two-thirds majority to carry his Enabling Law. At a cabinet meeting on 15 March 1933, the minutes of which have survived, it was suggested that part of the problem could be solved by the "absence" of the eighty-one Communist members of the Reichstag – who in fact were already in hiding and in fear for their lives. Communist meetings had been banned since early in February, along with Communist newspapers. At the meeting Göring propounded a solution that was characteristically brutal and direct: Communists and Social Democrats would be refused admittance to the chamber. And they were. When the time came for the vote, the leader of the Catholic Centre Party caved in, rising in the ornate Kroll Opera House to announce support for the Bill. Outside, Stormtroopers were chanting "Full powers – or else." The Enabling Law conferred on Hitler's cabinet exclusive legislative powers for four years. Thus, the Nazis acquired at least a nominal legality, but there were problems with the SA. The Brownshirt battalions roamed the streets of Berlin, seemingly able to loot and terrorize with total freedom. Their increasingly outrageous behaviour had the sanction of the police who took no action when the rowdies strolled on and off streetcars without paying or threatened shopkeepers whose premises they then looted.

Göring's legendary energy, fuelled in part by his addiction to morphine, (which had originally been administered to relieve the pain of his wound acquired during the abortive Bierkeller putsch), had been much in evidence in the weeks leading up to the 1933 election. Late in February, he had set up a 50,000 strong police (Hilfspolizei) which had been drawn largely from the forces of the SA and its rival, the black-garbed SS under Himmler. The men of the Hilfspolizei had been most persuasive in guiding voters towards the correct polling booths during the election. Those who favoured the booths of rivals were apt to find themselves consigned to one of the two concentration camps already set up by Göring at Oranienberg and Papenberg. These establishments were blandly dismissed to questioners as being centres for re-educating political malcontents.

There were other sinister centres which also became familiar to dissidents. Those who had known Berlin's police headquarters on the Alexanderplatz before the advent of the Nazis were aware that some frightening changes seemed to have taken place overnight. Familiar warders had been replaced by unpleasant brown-shirted youths sporting white armbands – most of whom looked as if they should have been on the other side of 'Alex's' prison bars. The interview rooms, dungeons, and corridors were the stuff of nightmares. Arrested suspects of both sexes arrived under SA guard at all hours, were unloaded and driven into the buildings with kicks and blows. Occasionally, individuals who considered that they had been arrested with no cause by over-zealous policemen were sufficiently influential to gasp out a name that might vouch for them. If they were successful they would be subjected to an interview with the one man who could ensure their freedom from the Alexanderplatz – Rudolf Diels. Diels has his dubious niche in history as the first chief of the future Gestapo. Previously, Diels had been a young Oberregierungsrat (Senior Police Official) at the Prussian Ministry of the Interior. Diels won favour with Göring for his avowed anti-Communism and gained promotion. The cynical Göring, as creator of the Gestapo, did not much care if a protégé was a party member or not. He preferred to pick people with whom he knew he could work and, within strict limits, trust.

Rudolf Diels (1900-1957), first chief of what became the Gestapo, was both capable and cunning. His specialty was ferreting out Communists.

Diels, the object of Göring's confidence on this occasion, had been born in 1900, the son of a prominent landowner. He had taken up studies in medicine and law at the universities of Giessen and Marburg. His preoccupations, however, would seem to have been anything but academic. As well as fighting duels, he was said to be a prodigious drinker and (so rumour had it) glass-chewer. He was quick to appreciate the considerable value of the voluminous Prussian State Police secret files on political personalities that passed through his hands. Naturally, these included those National Socialist leaders who had come to the attention of his department; all had their personal dossiers, Hermann Göring included. Far from being affronted at such diligence, Göring actively encouraged Diels' zeal. There was, not unnaturally, an element of self-interest in all this: Göring was able to inspect at first hand such skeletons as were rattling in the cupboards of the Nazi hierarchy. For his part, Diels – "the eloquent and efficient schemer" in the words of an SS contemporary Wilhelm Hoetl – insinuated himself by stages into Göring's favour.

The latter had considerable cause for satisfaction. After all, he had by now purged the Berlin police. Fifty thousand armed auxiliaries, wearing the Swastika armlet, swaggered on the streets at a salary of three marks a day. Moreover, Göring had previously signed a decree which enrolled members of the SA and the Stalhelm as police auxiliaries.

A further decree on 26 April 1933 established the Geheime Staats Polizeiamt (Gestapa, Secret State Police Office), which was later to be renamed the Geheime Staats Polizei (Gestapo, Secret State Police). The initials GPA or GPS, originally considered for the new organization, were reckoned to resemble too closely those of the Soviet State Police, the GPU. The distinction of creating one of the grimmest acronyms in history is popularly said to belong to an impatient Prussian postal official looking for a handy shorthand that would fit comfortably onto a regulation rubber stamp. The police structure inherited by Göring was many-faceted; in this respect it was not to change when it became, as the Gestapo, the ultimate in bureaucratic obfuscation. In Prussia, the plain clothes branches had consisted of the Kriminalpolizei or Criminal Police (Kripo), a sort of detective bureau, and the Political Police (Stapo). It was this organization that was to be taken over by Diels and turned into the Gestapo. The uniformed police consisted of the Order Police, or Orpo, who were barracked in the larger cities and used as mobile squads to quell civil disorders.

Göring's main concern was with the Kripo. From it he hived off its specifically political sections, together with the Stapo, which dealt with high treason, and the counter-espionage police (Abwehrpolizei). These were all amalgamated into the new organization called the Gestapo. There was much for this new Gestapo to do but the power and influence of the Communists remained the greatest single anxiety. The precise extent of the Communist threat needed to be demonstrated before the Gestapo could go about its work under the cloak of legality.

On the evening of 27 February, events played into Göring's hands. The building that housed the German Reichstag was engulfed in flames. A passer-by had caught sight of a figure at a second-storey window waving a flaming brand. Göring was quickly on the spot and publicly accused the Communists of arson: a weak-minded Dutch Communist idealist, Marinus van der Lubbe, arrested while running from the building, was accused by Göring of being a Communist agent and subsequently interrogated by Diels. Three other leading Communists were arrested with him and more than 4,000 others were rounded up by the Prussian police. Van der Lubbe was subsequently convicted and executed.

Speculation as to who was responsible for firing the Reichstag has been rife for over half a century. Whether or not the Communists were guilty or the Nazis themselves put the building to the torch to discredit their opponents will almost certainly never be established conclusively. There were those who, at the time, believed that the Reichstag fire had been started by an SS team from Munich. Many present-day historians, however, incline to the view that Marinus van der Lubbe, who had previously tried unsuccessfully to burn down three other buildings, including Berlin's City Hall, was acting alone and making a sole protest against the regime. This was a view, incidentally, which had been shared by Diels after his interrogation of the prisoner.

To Göring it made no difference. Repression of all dissident elements started immediately. The so called "Emergency Laws of February 28" were promulgated "for the defence of the people and the State." This amounted to total abolition of personal freedom. The police were armed with full authority to search and arrest without warrant and were empowered to take people into "protective custody" indefinitely without filing charges or bringing them before a judge. In addition, the decree authorized the government of the Reich to take over complete power in the federal states when necessary and imposed the death sentence for certain crimes, such as "serious disturbances of the peace" by armed individuals. The enfeebled, near-senile President Hindenburg signed the decrees without a murmur.

The Communists – for the moment at least – appeared tamed, but there remained the running sore of the SA whose activities of unbridled thuggery on the streets of German cities continued unabated. As part of his preparations to deal with Röhm's followers and establish his own power base, Göring moved Diels' anti-Communist branch of the Berlin police into an abandoned arts and

The half-witted Dutch bricklayer, Marinus van der Lubbe, was found in the Reichstag building at the time of the mysterious fire. Did he set fire to the Reichstag or was he set up by the Nazis? This was a secret van der Lubbe took with him to the executioner's block.

crafts school at No 8 Prinz Albrechtstrasse; here it was to flourish until the end as the Gestapo.

So far this account has not mentioned two other supremely loyal, obsessively ambitious servants of the Third Reich. These were Heinrich Himmler, that same bespectacled nonenity of Röhm's Reichskriegsflagge who had held the Imperial standard and gazed over the barricades during the ill-fated Munich initiative a decade before. The other man was Reinhard Eugen Tristan Heydrich, a ruthless, and ambitious former naval officer. Both regarded Göring as a formidable obstruction to their ultimate aim of appropriating the infant Gestapo for themselves.

Himmler, by 1929, at the age of only twenty-eight, had achieved full command of the SS with the grandiose title of Reichsführer-SS, a title which he

The burning Reichstag at around 10.00pm on 27 February 1933. The Reichstag fire gave Hitler the pretext for passing the Enabling Act which provided the constitutional foundation for his dictatorship.

Firemen survey the interior of the burned out Reichstag the morning after the fire.

Upper left below:
*Medical certificate
confirming Göring's
treatment for mental
illness in a Swedish
hospital in 1925.*

Lower left below:
*Hauptmann Hermann
Wilhelm Göring, one of
Germany's most
glamorous war heroes;
holder of the Pour le
Merite.*

Right below: *Göring, the
family man, with his
wife and infant
daughter.*

held until nearly the end of his life. Even so the SS in 1929 was a pygmy, scarcely beyond company strength of some 200 men. This meant that genuine power, as Himmler conceived it, still eluded him. Even when SS strength had risen to 30,000 men by 1932, it still remained firmly subordinate to the massive SA army of Röhm with its 2.3 million followers. Himmler received, on Hitler's assumption of power, only the relatively minor office of President of the Bavarian Police (BPP).

Despite this, Heinrich Himmler, the pale bureaucrat and (in Göring's phrase) "little pawn," who was barely known outside his native Bavaria, was determined that his office should be a springboard to greater things. The creeping Nazification of Germany came to his aid. The parliaments of all the Länder (States), with the exception of Prussia, were abolished. In their place were created Reichsstatthalter (Regional Governors) appointed at the behest of Hitler. For the moment, Himmler could do nothing about Prussia, but he was content to wait. In the interim his subordinates were sent touting for business. They were told to look for police jobs likely to fall vacant. When they found one, it would be suggested that perhaps the Chief of the Bavarian Political Police was the man to fulfil a certain desirable position.

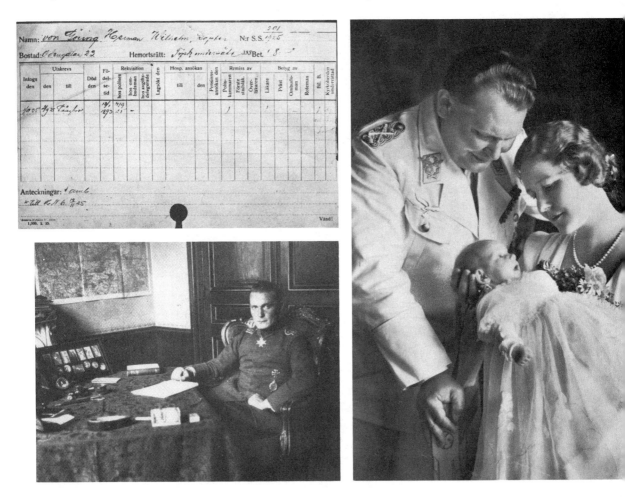

Hermann Göring addresses a crowd of 15,000 in the Berlin Sports Palast on 29 October 1936.

Such methods proved their worth. Within months, Himmler was controlling the police of Hamburg, the second city of the Reich. Then came Mecklenburg, Lübeck, Thuringia, the Grand Duchy of Hesse, Baden, Würtemberg, and Anhalt. At the start of 1934, Bremen, Oldenburg, and Saxony came under Himmler's control. By the spring, Himmler was the police supremo of the Third Reich – with the obstinate exception of Prussia. As it turned out, a variety of factors were to secure this most succulent plum of all for the SS.

Hermann Göring by this time had his mind on new horizons. Police work, he conceded, had its attractions. It was plainly necessary to have an organization that would keep an eye on Röhm's louts. But once the Gestapo had been set up, Göring, as restless as Himmler was patient, seemed to lose interest.

The man who had been the flier hero of the war had always cherished the dream that the German Air Force would one day rise again. That ambition was fired anew when in August 1933 President Hindenburg promoted him General der Infanterie. Somehow, it all seemed more glamorous than being a glorified policeman. Göring had no intention, however, of losing total control of the Gestapo – his Gestapo. He was also sensible of the threat to his own position which the sly, insinuating Himmler represented. The Reichsführer-SS, covetous for the Gestapo in Prussia, had been pressing his suit with Hitler – pleading that it would be "just, opportune and necessary to pursue the enemy in the same manner throughout the Reich." Rudolf Diels was especially uneasy about the threat Himmler posed. Diels knew he had created many enemies among subordinates, many of whom would welcome his job. It would not be too difficult to compile a dossier about Diels' own excesses. This in fact was done and forwarded, with suitable protestations of moral outrage, to President Hindenburg by Diels' opponents. Diels was sacrificed. By way of compensation, there was the position of Deputy Director of the Berlin Police. Diels, however, was not deceived. Berlin had the smell of danger and he deemed it wise to withdraw for a while. He crossed the frontier into Czechoslovakia and settled down to play a waiting game.

Göring appointed as Diels' successor a Nazi of the old guard named Paul Hinkler. Although Hinkler's loyalty was cast-iron, he happened to be a hopeless drunk. At the end of October, after less than thirty fuddled days in office, he was dismissed. Göring recalled Diels by telegram; the latter agreed to resume his old post. Diels held his job until the arrival of Himmler and Heydrich in Berlin. His removal on 1 April 1934 was final. As a parting gesture, he was given the job of Regierungspräsident (Head of the Regional Goverment) in Cologne.

Göring by then had made up his mind: he would relinquish direct control of the Gestapo. Himmler would become leader. The latter, docile and impassive as ever behind his metal spectacles, accepted his appointment as leader on 20 April 1934. It could not have been anything but an equal cause of satisfaction

The Kroll State Opera House, used by the Nazis as the seat of government after the Reichstag fire.

*On 20 April 1934,
Göring handed over the
leadership of the
Gestapo to Heinrich
Himmler.*

to his byzantine associate, Reinhard Heydrich. The next day, the Party newspaper the *Völkischer Beobachter* (*People's Observer*) carried the banner headline: "REICHSFÜHRER HIMMLER TAKES OVER THE LEADERSHIP OF THE PRUSSIAN SECRET STATE POLICE." Göring, as both Minister-President (approximating to Prime Minister) of Prussia and Interior Minister, issued a decree which extended Himmler's authority as Director of the Secret State Police Office. It was prefaced by a note from Himmler drawing the attention of all departments in "the house" to its contents.

The decree elaborated: "Technical reasons impel me to deputize the Reichsführer-SS Himmler to handle all affairs of the Prussian Secret State Police without further participation of the Prussian State Ministry. Himmler will be completely in charge and responsible only to me directly. All correspondence will go under the heading 'Prussian Secret State Police/The Deputy Chief and Inspector,' and will henceforth be directed exclusively to the Secret State Police Office, Berlin S.W.11, Prinz Albrechtstrasse 8. Signed, Göring."

In his address on accepting the appointment, Himmler came as near to warmth as he was capable, promising to Göring, "I shall always remain faithful to you. You will never have anything to fear from me."

Göring's reign as police overlord of the Third Reich was over. That of Heinrich Himmler was just beginning.

Heinrich Himmler
and the
SS

Heinrich Himmler, as a young student at the Technical High School, Munich University.

Walter Dornberger, a veteran of the Reichswehr who was ultimately to be responsible for the development of Nazi Germany's V-2 rockets, stared in puzzlement at the man who sat opposite him for a crucial meeting.

Heinrich Himmler, chief of the SS and Gestapo, appeared to be "like an intelligent elementary schoolteacher, certainly not a man of violence. I could not for the life of me see anything outstanding or extraordinary about this middle-sized, youthfully slender man in grey SS uniform. Under a brow of average height two grey-blue eyes looked out at me, behind glittering pince-nez, with an eye of peaceful interrogation. The trimmed moustache below the straight, well-shaped nose traced a dark line on his unhealthy pale features. The lips were colourless and very thin. Only the inconspicuous, receding chin surprised me. . .. His slender, pale and almost girlishly soft hands, covered with blue veins, lay motionless on the table throughout our conversation."

Himmler's origins could scarcely have been more respectable. His father Gebhard received – and indeed accepted as his right – the unstinted respect of his Bavarian neighbours. At the turn of the century, we find the irreproachable Professor Himmler complacent and secure at the age of thirty-five in his position as a Munich schoolmaster.

There had been the patronage of the royal household of Wittelsbach which had followed his education at the University of Munich where he had studied philology and languages. He had been appointed to no less a position than tutor to Prince Heinrich of Bavaria. Only after this period, Gebhard would remind everyone, did he become a mere teacher. Surviving photographs of the "Herr Professor " indicate a personality that was studious, prim, and pedantic – qualities which were to be handed down to the second child born to his wife Anna on 7 October 1900 in a comfortable apartment on Munich's Hildegard-strasse.

The first child, Gebhard, had been named after his father. The second, Heinrich, was a tribute to the Bavarian prince. A third son, Ernst, was born in 1905. Heinrich, who at birth weighed six pounds, was a sickly child with poor sight. It is to Gebhard the younger that we owe the assurance that the young Heinrich was "kind to old ladies and once ran errands for them and carried their shopping."

He was, by all accounts, as a boy, conspicuously amenable to discipline, to the need to obey rules. It was hardly surprising therefore that he longed for a career in the Army. He had to wait until 1918 before he achieved service in the llth Bavarian Infantry Regiment but this scarcely satisfied his ambition. The armistice of November 1918 came too soon for him to be commissioned; his service record was merely that of an officer cadet. Robbed of his dreams, he turned to a shoddy substitute – the ranks of the discontented, furtively-armed, Freikorps volunteers. From this he hoped to seek a commission in the peace-time regular Army, the Reichswehr. But father Gebhard intervened: what was the use of a career in the Army of a bankrupt, inflation-ridden country which, in his view, had been betrayed by its politicians and led to defeat in war? Heinrich must seek a more stable profession. The boy was by nature pliable; it probably never occured to him to go against the orders of his father. Next to soldiering, the greatest fascination of the young Himmler was farming. As a boy he had kept a collection of plants with a passion for garden herbs. It is perhaps instructive to relate that later in his career Heinrich Himmler was to place a particular emphasis on herbs. Each of the concentration camps over which he had jurisdiction was under permanent instruction to produce a collection of every conceivable form of herb which he considered efficacious.

Himmler was destined not to be left alone with his cranky, seemingly harmless form of farming and agriculture, however. He went to a farm near Ingolstadt to learn the business; he had scarcely begun before this dream, too, was shattered. A bout of paratyphoid fever left him too weak for military service. He was told that he must rest from physical labour, although academic study was permitted. On 18 October 1919, he enrolled as a student of agriculture at the Technical High School, Munich University.

He was a singularly solemn student, buried in his books on plant biology, soil fertilization, and chemistry. There was, however, a strong Puritan streak in him when it came to money and he was an excellent manager. The man who, as Reichsführer-SS and arguably the most powerful individual in Hitler's Germany, was to deduct conscientiously from his salary the cost of petrol used on personal business, became an expert at ekeing out the allowances he received from his father. He submitted accounts conscientiously, keeping all receipts and ticket stubs.

His reading also included the absorption of a code of principles outlined by Richard Walter Darré, one of the earliest National Socialist adherents whose views on agriculture and selective breeding were to accord with Himmler's own. In his book *Blut und Boden* (*Blood and Soil*), Darré advocated the protection of the peasantry as the "life source of the Nordic race." The Latin people, Darré argued, were among the inferior races which notably included Negroes and Asiatics.

Himmler, as unquestioning as a child, absorbed this farrago of racialist prejudice; above all he concentrated his hatred on the Jews. His preoccupation with his studies was allowed but one deviation: an obsession with his health and physical fitness. His efforts to achieve it were laughably inadequate – he could not even reach the parallel bars in the university gymnasium. In his risible pursuit of his own conception of manliness and physical perfection, Himmler was a conscientious attender at the Munich students' duelling and

*Gebhard Himmler,
Heinrich's brother, was
recruited by Röhm to
join the Reichs-
kriegsflagge in 1922.*

shooting section. Eventually, after many months of pleading, he managed to secure a duel for himself. He was well satisfied with his own subsequent performance, noting afterwards, "I certainly did not get agitated. Stood very well and fought technically beautifully. My opponent. . .struck honest blows." Himmler was disabled in the thirteenth of fifty scheduled bouts. The stern test came when the duellists were led away by their seconds to be stitched up. Himmler had suffered five cuts and received five stitches and a ligature. He noted, "I really did not flinch once." He reckoned that he had proved himself.

It was in these circumstances, in January 1922, that he met Hauptmann Ernst Röhm who was talent-spotting for adherents to the Nazi cause (for whose meetings he was already supplying Storm Troopers). Röhm was equally assiduous in seeking out homosexual partners. If he was attracted to Himmler on this basis, Röhm was doomed to disappointment. Himmler's own sexual proclivities, however limited, were indisputably heterosexual. ("Accompanied Fräulein von Buck home. She did not take my arm which, in a way, I appreci-

From left to right: *Kurt
Daluege, Himmler, and
Ernst Röhm.*

ated," he recorded in his diary). Indeed, Himmler was a rabid homophobic. It is likely that Röhm eventually realized this and was astute enough to change tack. Himmler's primary value would be as a political partner. In this respect, Röhm's seduction was successful. Himmler was soon enrolled, along with his elder brother Gebhard, as a member of the Reichskriegsflagge contingent with its Freikorps antecedents and which, as we have seen, was to join forces with Hitler in the ill-fated Munich putsch.

Himmler graduated on 5 August 1922. His studies had included chemistry as well as how to produce new varieties of plants and crops. His job as laboratory assistant in the agricultural firm of Stickstoff-Land GmbH in Schleissheim was doubly convenient. It gave him a salary and Schleissheim was a mere fifteen miles from Munich. It was therefore possible to keep in touch with the hub of political life and to study the activities, not just of Ernst Röhm, but of Adolf Hitler whose own brand of nationalism had already led to the formation of the National Socialist German Workers' Party.

Himmler did not apply formally to join the Nazi Party until August 1923, four months before the unsuccessful Munich putsch. As his part of the putsch, Röhm had agreed to march on the military headquarters of the Ministry of War on the Schoenfeldstrasse, where he would barricade his men behind barbed wire and set up machine-gun defences. The events of the next day, however, had forced Röhm to surrender and he was incarcerated in Stadelheim prison. Himmler recorded in his diary that he rode out on his prized secondhand Swedish motorcycle to visit Röhm who discoursed on politics, and was grateful for a present of oranges and a copy of the *Grossdeutsche Zeitung* newspaper.

On Röhm's release from jail, Himmler vowed that he would direct all his energies to working for the "good Hauptmann." While Hitler was confined in Landsberg, Röhm went ahead with his own plans for founding a revolutionary organization which embraced nationalist and anti-Semitic groups and was known as the Völkisch movement. Among its leading supporters were two figures who later gained prominence in the Nazi movement, one as a loser and the other as a survivor – at least until he found himself in the dock at Nuremberg at the end of the war. Gregor Strasser owned a chemist's shop at Landshut in Bavaria. This hard, good-living blond Bavarian believed that Nazism should emphasize its Socialist character. Alfred Rosenberg, was the violent, anti-semitic Estonian whom Hitler had met in Munich in 1920 and who had performed a caretaker rôle for the Nazi party during Hitler's imprisonment. Rosenberg held that "liberalism" had wrecked the proper ascendancy of the Nordic people, that lesser races had taken power, and that it was Germany's sacred duty to subdue them. Collectively, the Völkisch clique became a powerful pressure group in the Bavarian government. In 1924, it managed to secure sufficient support in the Reichstag election to gain thirty-two seats. Strasser, Röhm, and Ludendorff were among those who became members of the Reichstag.

By the time Hitler was released from Landsberg, only Gregor Strasser had kept his seat; an election had swept away the others. Hitler must have felt considerable satisfaction; he had no love for potential rivals. His interest, however, was in re-establishing his Nazi party which had fragmented dangerously during his time in jail.

Gregor Strasser (1892-1934) in 1932. Former Nationalist Director of Party Organization of the NSDAP. Strasser was an early rival of Hitler for the leadership of the National Socialists.

Hitler was not worried about Rosenburg as a rival. He was devoted to the Nazi racial creed and became one of its most vocal adherents. The two rivals who *did* worry Hitler were Strasser and Röhm. The former had his uses, not least as a charismatic platform speaker and as an energetic organizer. To Hitler, Strasser was possibly *too* brilliant. He made it clear that his devotion to Hitler would be by no means total and unquestioning. The bullet-scarred, roistering Röhm made no secret that he saw himself ultimately as military dictator of Germany. Röhm then received an offer to go to South America with the rank of Oberst to train the Bolivian Army.

He told himself that such a position would be only a stepping stone to a triumphant return; meanwhile, it would be a marvellous boost to his prestige. Ernst Röhm's resignation from the Party in April 1925 left Hitler with only Gregor Strasser as a serious rival.

What of Heinrich Himmler, the eager convert? The fortunes of the Nazis were reviving; Gregor Strasser, and his brother Otto, were able to give Himmler modestly paid secretarial work. Himmler was seemingly content to serve Strasser as a dogsbody, a dutifully submissive drafter of letters and carrier of files. Strasser appointed Himmler as a district organizer in Lower Bavaria, working, naturally, under Hitler's shadow in Munich and doing so, moreover, at a parsimonous 120 Reichsmarks a month.

Himmler however did not crave money. He wanted power. Strasser gave him at least its semblance – the high-sounding position of Abgeordneter Ortsgruppenleiter, (Locally Elected Branch Leader). Himmler also became second-in-command of the small corps numbering some 200 and known as the Schutzstaffel, or SS – that same group which had started life as Hitler's Stabwache or Headquarters Guard. Himmler himself had joined in 1925, receiving the SS number 168. There came in 1925, another significant encounter: this time with Joseph Goebbels, the crippled Rhinelander who was a passionate nationalist and keen admirer of the Strasser brand of radicalism. Each had his own distinctive talent to put at the service of a revolutionary movement. Goebbels was the brilliant speaker and publicist, while Himmler, who had no such aspirations, was at his happiest buried in innumerable files and dossiers, to say nothing of narcissistic contemplation of his racialist convictions. Hitler was not slow to recognize Goebbels' obvious talents; increasingly, he had need of him in Berlin and, during 1926, flattered him into accepting the post of Gauleiter (District Leader) there.

Himmler was now free to consolidate his own position in Lower Bavaria which was still, in essence, that of dogsbody. He was expected to increase the number of Party members, to collect subscriptions, and to generate advertizing for the Party newspaper, the *Völkischer Beobachter*. In 1926, the post of Deputy Reich Propaganda Chief was created for him. Himmler, with some stature at last, began scooping up a number of subordinate offices and collecting, incidentally, a modest increase in salary.

In that same year, on a trip to Berlin, Himmler met Margaret Concerzowo, a blonde nurse of Polish origins and dominating demeanour. She was eight years Himmler's senior. Marga, as she was known, owned a small Berlin nursing home but of at least equal interest to Himmler, was the fact that she shared some of his unorthodox ideas on medicine, notably in the field of homoeopathic treatments. She also expressed enthusiasm for such specialisms as mesmerism, astrology, and curative hypnosis. Here it seemed was an ideal marriage of minds: both were fanatical admirers of efficiency, thrift, and a rigorous, parsimonious lifestyle.

It was in pursuit of this spartan ideal that Marga sold her nursing home and put the money towards a smallholding for the sale of produce and agricultural implements at Waldtrudering, some ten miles outside Munich. The couple married in July 1928 and the following year Marga gave birth to a daughter, Gudrun. The child incidentally had been conceived outside wedlock. The occasion, apparently, had coincided with the loss of Himmler's virginity.

Social unrest during Himmler's student days: Students burning and destroying books. The slogan on the truck reads 'German students march against the un-German intellect.' Inflation became so high that money was hardly worth the paper it was printed on.

Upper left: *Food ration card.*

Heinrich Himmler and his wife 'Marga.' Himmler met Margaret Concerzowo, a nurse of Polish origins, in 1926. They married in July 1928 but the marriage was not destined to be a happy one. Shortly after the birth of their daughter Gudrun in 1929, the Himmlers began living apart.

Gravely, Himmler had confided this moral lapse, as he saw it, to Gregor Strasser who had riposted: "And about time, too."

The year 1929 was to be significant for Himmler in other ways. The first holder of the office of Reichsführer-SS had been Joseph Berchtold. His successor was a former police informer, Erhard Heiden, with Himmler as his deputy. Along with his new office, Heiden had inherited the raucous nuisance of the SA. Its members considered themselves the aristocracy of National Socialism. It became necessary for Heiden and eventually Himmler to contend with the rivalry of the infinitely larger, but loosely disciplined Stormtroopers. Heiden saw the SS as "super-efficient but certainly arrogant." Himmler, on the other hand, proclaimed, "The SA is the infantry of the line, the SS the guards. There has always been a guard: the Persians had one, the Greeks, Caesar, Napoleon, and Frederick the Great, right up to the world war; the SS will be the imperial guard of the new Germany."

Such fervour, to say nothing of the intense self-discipline and organizing ability which Himmler possessed, had already been brought to Hitler's attention. 6 January 1929 was a fateful day in the history of National Socialism: on it, Heinrich Himmler succeeded to the post of Reichsführer-SS. This pompous title may have flattered Himmler but at this stage impressed few outsiders. In fact, to be Reichsführer-SS meant a command of less than 300 men at 50 Schellingstrasse, Munich. There were some very real worries for Himmler: the centre of radicalism, due largely to the propaganda and public relations skills of Joseph Goebbels, had shifted to Berlin. The local SS there, under the command of another Freikorps veteran, Kurt Daluege, acted independently of the Reichsführer-SS and was feared accordingly. And, of course, there remained the incubus of the SA.

In addition, Himmler's personal life was distressingly drab. He was twenty-eight years old with a dubious future and a slender salary. There was an older pregnant wife and a small holding financed out of his earnings and which barely paid its way. Furthermore, Marga was becoming increasingly fed up with her husband's neglect of his family in favour of politics. If the marriage had ever possessed any genuine passion, that was coursing out as rapidly as the money. The nervous and neurotic Himmler was no proof against Marga's constant nagging. The relationship deteriorated and soon after the birth of Gudrun the Himmlers began living apart. Hitler had charged his Reichsführer-SS with building up an utterly dependable body of carefully selected men; nothing was going to deflect Himmler from that task.

He received scant encouragement from another source. Franz von Salomon, the SA Supreme Commander (OSAF), did little to conceal his hostility. Himmler reacted with his most effective weapon: the office memorandum. He now produced one, with the Führer's blessing, which was slapped down on Salomon's desk as an instruction. In effect, it constituted the Order of the SS. It was all there: how the SS man must be a racial paragon, how candidates for membership could only be drawn from those filling the criteria of the Nordic warrior hero.

By June 1931, the Reichsführer-SS was pronouncing, "Our enemies' efforts to bolshevize Germany are increasing. Our information and Intelligence service must aim to discover, and to suppress, our Jewish and Freemason enemies; this is the most important task of the SS today." As membership of the SS increased through Himmler's assiduous "poaching" policy from the SA, he set up SS Abschnitte (Districts) and, within these Abschnitte, secret Intelligence sections who had been given the task of spying on all enemies of the Party.

At this point a new and terrible figure enters the saga of the SS and, ultimately, the Gestapo. Reinhard Heydrich, blond, arrogant, icy, and ruthless, sprang from the ranks of displaced intellectuals adrift amid the collective economic misery of the 1930s, many of whom sought a haven within the Nazi movement. He had some knowledge of Intelligence and, as a born opportunist, was not slow to put his gifts at the service of Himmler. Heydrich's timing, as it turned out, was impeccable.

The Nazis were obsessive about spying. Enemies were seen everywhere. Relations with Gregor Strasser and his brother Otto, also a representative of the Party's left wing, were, for example, known to be strained. Gregor declared his view that Hitler was inclining too much to the right by courting the German National Conservative bloc. The SA continued to give trouble; the potential loyalty of even the most avowed Nazi adherents repaid watching. Himmler thus entrusted Heydrich with the building up an IC service (Intelligence Service) with Information Officers (informers). This was ultimately to grow into the Sicherheitsdienst (SD, the SS Security Service) which in due course would incorporate the Gestapo.

Gudrun Himmler, aged six.

Above: *In 1933, all Reich police forces - civil, political, and secret - were put in the charge of Himmler and the SS. Himmler moved to Berlin, bringing with him three battalions of well-disciplined SS.*

Heydrich undertook the transformation of the SD into the Party's main secret service. The diligence of the new disciple gained Hitler's full approval. On 25 January 1932, Himmler was nominated Head of Security in the Brown House, Party headquarters at 45 Briennerstrasse, Munich. An order issued by the SA, which was still the superior body, stated: "Control of the security services throughout Party headquarters (the Brown House and adjacent building) is hereby transferred to the Reichsführer-SS." Himmler's personal powers were kept deliberately vague. The Reichsführer-SS was responsible for measures "to repel Marxist/Communist attacks and prevent police interference." It was Himmler's aim to exploit his remit for all it was worth. But precisely what *was* it worth?

From the perspective of that all-important 30 January 1933, the answer would seem to be: not much. For Heinrich Himmler, the Third Reich, the "National Revolution" for which they had all schemed, opened in disappointment. Everyone in Berlin was seemingly falling over each other to grab the most tempting jobs, but no one invited the small-time farmer of Waldtrudering to share the pickings. Hitler was prepared only to advance Himmler one step – to the position of Police President of Munich, then promoting him in stages to be head of the entire Bavarian Political Police.

The all-too-willing Reinhard Heydrich was entrusted the task of compiling and refining the dossiers on the Reich's political enemies. A Party Intelligence network was created, its servants happy to receive any information concerned with economic developments, social life, politics and, above all, the private life of Party members. Himmler spelt out the fundamental purpose of the network in an SS order of April 1933: "A great deal of potentially useful information can be extracted from suspects. Even if suspicion of their treasonable activities proves to be unfounded they can often be persuaded to give the SD information that will lead to other suspects. Such information is usually readily given under duress, threat or promise of release."

Himmler proceeded further. Aware of what had been going on in Berlin with the Gestapo under Diels, he decided to follow Göring's example and institute his own concentration camps. For the site of the first, Himmler opted for a couple of old stone huts in the precincts of a disused powder factory at Dachau, situated about twelve miles northwest of Munich. It served as a reception area for those taken into protective custody. A victim would be informed, "Based on Article 1 of the Decree of the Reich President for the Protection of People and State of 28 February 1933, you are taken into protective custody in the interest of public security and order. Reason: suspicion of activities inimical to the State." Such bloodless, bureaucratic terminology characterized Himmler's entire approach when constructing his police state.

Reinhard Heydrich

Heydrich's SD, seen as the matrix of a police state, remained a miniscule department within the scarcely larger SS which, in turn, was subordinate to the SA. To make matters worse, the SA was under the control once again of Ernst Röhm who had returned from Bolivia and been reinstated by Hitler as Stabschef (Chief of Staff) of the SA. In addition, the leadership of the Berlin section was in the hands of Edmund Heines, Röhm's homosexual lover and one of the most powerful men in the SA. Himmler and Heydrich were anxious to establish the Berlin-based Gestapo nationally and awaited their opportunity.

Providentially, their chance was provided by one of Heydrich's V-Leute (confidential agents) who claimed to have wind of a Bolshevik plot to kill Göring. Whether or not such a plot in fact existed cannot be determined for certain, even though the SS made it their business to carry out some arrests in Munich. True or not, Himmler seized his opportunity. His tone to Hitler, was, naturally, of deferential reasonableness: what, he wanted to know, was to be made of an existing police organization that was not even aware of a plan to assassinate its chief?

· The remedy was to put all the Reich police forces – civil, political, and secret – under the command of the SS. Hitler, after some hesitation, agreed. With Göring's consent, the Prussian Ministry of the Interior, and its political police, including the Gestapo, was placed under Himmler. At long last, the Reichsführer-SS came to Berlin. He brought with him three battalions of well-disciplined SS men, their power buttressed by the talents of Heydrich's SD – the latter headquartered at the newly constituted Security Head Office of the Reichsführer-SS at 103 Wilhelmstrasse.

Henceforth the SS and Gestapo would form the centre of Heinrich Himmler's entire existence. It was by no means unusual for his day, starting at 8 o'clock in the morning, to last sixteen hours. He invariably travelled with a secretary, keeping in touch by radio with his office. The drafting and dictating of memos went on ceaselessly in train or aircraft. Bundles of files accompanied him everywhere; all of which were, once read and approved, signed in the margin meticulously with a pencil of green lead – a colour permitted to be

At Dachau concentration camp, near Munich, a group of political prisoners who had agitated against the state. This photograph was published in Hitler's own publication Illustratrierte Beobachter.

used by no one else. Since Himmler allowed himself virtually no private life, his relationship with Marga deteriorated even further. His innate sense of Puritanism, however, did not prevent him from taking a mistress: a girl named Hedwig (nicknamed Häschen) Potthast who was his personal secretary. But a solid streak of respectability remained – there could be no question of the scandal of a divorce.

Above all, there was Himmler the bureaucrat, taking refuge from domestic unhappiness in the contemplation of his eternal dossiers. Walter Schellenberg, a student of medicine and law at the University of Bonn who became one of Reinhard Heydrich's brightest young men and who was in a position to study the Reichsführer-SS at close quarters, considered: "He was like a schoolmaster who graded the lessons of his pupils with finicky exactitude, and for each answer would have liked to enter a mark in his class book. His whole personality expressed bureaucratic precision, industry and loyalty. . ... It really went against his nature to express an opinion; it was safer for someone else to be in the position of having been at fault. If time proved that some criticism had been wrong or blame misplaced, a subordinate could always be found to have erred. This system gave Himmler an air of aloofness, of being above ordinary conflicts. It made him the final arbiter."

But this was not the whole man. There was also the Himmler who was obsessed with the Nordic ideal, with dreams of racial purification for all SS men. Himmler had moved far from the traditional Catholicism of his parents. Nevertheless, he maintained admiration for the discipline of the Catholic monastic orders and was keen to establish a centre which would owe much to them. Thus many of the doctrinal trappings of the SS were modelled on the principles of the Order of Jesuits. The service statutes and spiritual exercises presented by the founder of the Jesuits, Ignatius Loyola, formed a pattern which Himmler expected his SS men to copy conscientiously. However, the Jesuitical idea was not in itself sufficient; Himmler was also drawn to the religiously fanatical Teutonic knights founded at the close of the 12th century. It was the example of these knights which inspired him to found what he hoped would be a similar SS Order of Knights. Himmler became obsessed with the prospect of a modern Teutonic order dedicated to eradicating from Nordic German society any degenerate infiltration of Slav or Jewish blood. Himmler, in the service of this ideal, founded the new Teutonic castle of Wewelsburg in the forests near Paderborn, an ancient Westphalian town which had historic associations going back to the days of Charlemagne. The magnificently appointed castle, built at the cost of 11 million marks, was intended as tribute to Germany's greatness. Each room was named after an historic figure such as Frederick the Great; on display was a collection of sacred relics. Himmler's own room was named after Heinrich I, Henry the Fowler (875-936), the king who a thousand years before had been the founder of the German Reich.

Himmler introduces the new German police uniform to Hitler. Berlin, 1934.

Right: *In service of his Nordic ideal, Himmler built the neo-Teutonic castle of Wewelsburg, near Paderborn. Each room was named after an historic figure. Himmler's own roon was named after Heinrich I.*

Above: Heinrich I, Henry the Fowler (875-936), the King who, a thousand years before, had been the founder of the German Reich.

Opposite: Standing, as ever, at the side of the Führer, "faithful Heini" proudly watches his elite SS troops take Hitler's salute.

Himmler, according to some of his SS colleagues, actually persuaded himself that he was in fact the reincarnation of the Saxon king and even began discussions by saying, "In this case, King Heinrich I would have acted as follows." Members of the SS with a healthy sense of self-preservation, would submit to this charade in order to remain in favour with their Reichsführer who, with the gathering of power, indulged himself even more ardently with his racial preoccupations.

He was able to do so, morever, in the secure knowledge that he had gained Hitler's approval with his measures for police organization and had the regard and admiration of his Führer. Reinhard Heydrich had his shrine also, but it was not like Wewelsburg, concerned with picking over the bones of dead heroes or conducting spiritual exercises. At his leadership school at Bad-Tolz in Bavaria, Heydrich made sure that sports, gymnastics, and similar activities that imposed discipline on students formed an essential part of SS education. It seemed infinitely more practical than the bizzare activities favoured by Himmler. But then Heydrich had already been entrusted with intensely practical duties. With the Gestapo now in Himmler's control and with Heydrich as deputy and head of the SD, the foundations of the police state were solidly laid.

13

Heydrich and the SD

On 27 May 1942, a Czech agent in Prague threw a bomb at a passing Mercedes and mortally injured Reinhard Tristan Eugen Heydrich, the executive head of the Gestapo, and the man responsible for organizing the *Einsatzgruppen* (the SS Special Action Groups or extermination squads) as the engines of genocide.

Heydrich was born on 7 March 1904 in Halle an der Saale, near Leipzig. The boy grew up in a family with its traditions rooted firmly in music. His father, Richard Bruno Heydrich, had achieved the status of a founder and director of a conservatoire which had been opened in Halle in 1899 as a private school of music and dramatic arts. There was, however, little solid wealth and Bruno had secured acceptance in the high society of Halle through hard work and what was generally recognized as a "good" marriage. Bruno had originally dreamed of becoming a classical singer but he did not achieve the necessary standard and instead concentrated on composition where he achieved critical rather than popular acclaim. In addition, he had social ambitions; they were satisfied by marriage to Elisabeth Anna Amalia Kranz, a solidly prosperous and devoutly Catholic member of the upper middle class who had been born in Dresden in 1871, the daughter of a music teacher whose conservatoire had achieved royal distinction. Thus Reinhard Heydrich grew up in a cultured and educated environment, the influences of which never left him. Such an environment was even reflected in the names that his parents gave him. Reinhard meant "wise in counsel " and had been chosen after a heroic figure in one of his father's operas. The "Tristan," of course, had been inspired by Wagner, while "Eugen" – "the high born" – had been bestowed in tribute to his maternal grandfather who had been Professor, Royal Saxon Councillor, and founder of the Dresden Conservatoire.

Bruno Heydrich had seemingly achieved both the professional and social status for which he had craved. But there was a drawback. Members of the narrow, provincial society of Halle never quite accepted Bruno Heydrich as one of themselves. They saw him as a social climber: a gifted man, no doubt, but a main-chancer who had achieved recognition through an advantageous marriage. Local patricians were suspicious of what they saw as the man's calculated joviality, his constant striving to please.

What after all was known about him? It was thought that he regularly sent

money to a certain Frau Ernestine Süss who turned out to be his mother. "Süss" was a suspiciously Jewish name; soon it was being alleged that "Heydrich" had been adopted as a mere pseudonym.

Elisabeth Heydrich staunchly defended her husband against such slanderous accusations. Was he not second to none in professing his loyalty to German nationalism, to the Kaiser? The rumour-mongers were, for the moment at least, silenced. The young Heydrich was sent to the Reform Gymnasium (High School) in Halle. In Easter 1922 he entered the Navy which, of all the services, seemed to offer the best prospect of adventure. The choice seemed wise: the future appeared promising for a young man who was to become a Fähnrich zur See (Midshipman) a few years later, a Leutnant zur See (Sub-Lieutenant) in 1929, and subsequently Oberleutnant (First Lieutenant).

Heydrich, eighteen years of age on entering the service, was something of a misfit. At over six feet tall, he was awkward and gangling. The hair was very light blond, the close-set eyes a striking light blue, while the beak nose dominated the long equine face. He had a high voice with a bleating laugh – and the

Reinhard Heydrich at the wheel of his Mercedes with: left, Himmler and, sitting beside him, Himmler's Chief of Personal Staff, Karl Wolff.

47

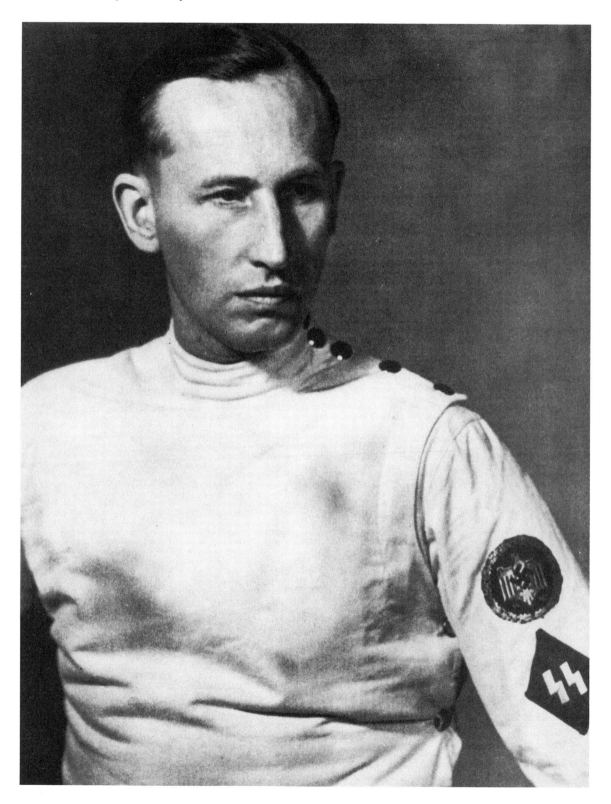

nickname Zieg (Nanny goat). At that time, he neither smoked nor drank although later he was to do both to excess. His most precious possession appeared to be his violin, a gift from his father. Although he was hard-working, capable, and highly disciplined, Heydrich remained aloof from his shipmates who found him arrøgant. Besides music, the other passion of his life appeared to be revolutionary politics.

The world war of 1914 and its aftermath had proved shattering experiences for the Heydrich family; the elegant cultured world striven for by Bruno and Elisabeth withered under the cold blast of political change and, more profoundly, of economic recession. When in 1918, the people of Halle heard that Wilhelm II had abdicated and that the Imperial Chancellor, Prince Max of Baden, had resigned and turned over power to the Social Democrats, the young Heydrich heard the same accusation repeated again and again: "Treason!"

Anarchy and the spectre of revolution stalked the streets: the proclamation of the republic, the appearance of the left radical group of the Spartacists squared up for open conflict with the bands of the Freikorps. Much nearer home was the reality of inflation; it threatened to wipe out the Heydrichs' wealth. The effect of all this on Reinhard Heydrich had been profound. He had gathered together parts of cast-off uniforms, including a steel helmet, teamed up with a Freikorps unit, and prepared to do battle fighting Communists and Socialists. He also had given allegiance to a Pan-Germanic nationalist youth association, the Deutschnationaler Jugendbund in Halle and, by 1920, had joined the Deutschvölkischer Schutz und Treubend, progressing to being what later he grandly described as "a volunteer liaison agent" with the Lucius division of the Freikorps. Street politics, however, had been an indulgence which the ungainly teenager could not afford: hence the Navy.

Heydrich drove himself tirelessly, aiming for the highest achievements in sport, especially in fencing, swimming, and sailing. In 1928, after promotion, he took up a posting in a naval station in the Baltic as a Funker (Wireless Officer). There was no reason to suppose that he had anything but an honourable career ahead of him. But Heydrich had displayed a fatal weakness: he was incapable of keeping his hands off women. And now whispers of his intrigues were to send his naval future crashing about his ears. Heydrich, so went the gossip, had been having an affair with the daughter of an officer in the Hamburg naval dockyards. It had been taken for granted that the couple would become engaged but Heydrich had informed the girl by letter that he had already promised marriage to eighteen year old Lina von Osten, daughter of a village schoolmaster from the Baltic island of Fehmarn.

Speculation buzzed in naval circles. Heydrich, it was said, had callously jilted the girl. In consequence, so went the story, he was dismissed the Navy, following a Court of Enquiry, for unbecoming conduct. That the Navy would go to the trouble to set up an official enquiry all because of a promising officer's tangled amours seems highly unlikely, but this has not stopped such a reason being advanced over the years for Heydrich leaving the service. But no real evidence has ever been produced to support it.

All we know is that in 1931 Heydrich quit the service. What really happened? One suggested explanation is that the whole affair was engineered by

Reinhard Tristan Eugen Heydrich, Head of the Reich Security Service (which embodied the Gestapo), Deputy Reich Protector of Bohemia and Moravia, Chairman of the notorious Wannsee Conference, and tipped by many to be Hitler's eventual successor. Heydrich, who devoted much of his time to chamber music was tall and athletic, one of the finest fencers in the Third Reich. After his assassination, Hitler described him as 'the Man with the Iron Heart.'

Heydrich, the devoted family man. On 24 December 1931 Heydrich married Lina von Osten. Lina, a member of the Nazi Party, persuaded her fiancée to join. The Heydrichs are seen here at home with their son in Munich.

pro-Nazi sympathizers within the Navy. The Navy's Commander-in-Chief, Admiral Erich Räder, was believed to be a keen adherent of the Nazis with some like-minded acolytes. Heydrich could have been talent-spotted by the Nazis and his release contrived.

Whatever the truth, the unemployed Heydrich cooled his heels around Hamburg, Lübeck, and Kiel, where it so happened the ardent disciples of the SA and the Nazis were using the streets for their orgies of violence. And it was the Nazis – or more precisely Lina Heydrich – who came to the rescue of the ex-sailor. When still a school girl in Kiel in 1929, Lina had been attracted to the Nazis and become Party member 1,201,380, later joining the National Socialist women's group. She persuaded her fiancé to join the Party, convincing him that there was a future there.

A meeting with Himmler at the Waldtrudering smallholding was arranged. The Reichsführer was at his most precise and schoolmasterish: "I want to establish an Intelligence Service for the SS and I am looking for a suitable man to take charge. If you are confident at being able to undertake the task, take twenty minutes and write down how you would organize the exercise." Heydrich did so, adding some of his own ideas. This was the genesis of what was to become the SD (Sicherheitsdienst – the Security Service of the Nazi Party).

Himmler expressed himself impressed and Party headquarters in Munich duly received a message: "Party member Reinhard Heydrich, Hamburg, Membership No. 544916, will, with effect from October of this year, be carried on the strength of Party Headquarters as a member of the staff of the Reichsführer-SS." Heydrich was given the rank of Sturmführer and put to work.

One hot summer day in 1931, Heydrich strode into a meeting of SS leaders in the Munich Brown House as the future head of the Secret Service. He had just two battered folders which Himmler had pressed on him. In lurid terms, he painted a picture of a Party riddled with spies and traitors. Hot on this delineation of disaster, Heydrich issued an order to all SS units: "With immediate effect every Abschnitt (District) will set up an IC desk to deal with all Intelligence activities within the Abschnitt. Subsequently an IC desk is also envisaged for every SS-Standarte" (Regiment). Heydrich soon realized that his new baby could not be nurtured and weaned within the Brown House; the staff there were much too inquisitive. With three officers he moved out and installed his indexes and files in a private apartment where security was likely to be less of a problem.

The SD in the early days was a ramshackle organization operating out of an apartment at 23 Türkenstrasse, Munich, rented from Viktoria Edrich, a widow and Party member. When a typewriter was needed it had to be borrowed and returned; most of the "files" consisted of cigar boxes. The growth in efficiency of the SD was accompanied by the upward progression of the career of Reinhard Heydrich who on 24 December 1931, married Lina von Osten. The promotions followed: 10 August 1931, Sturmbannführer; 31 December 1931 Hauptsturmführer; 19 July 1932, formal appointment as head of the SD; 29 July 1932, Standartenführer; 21 March 1933, Oberführer.

Like Himmler, however, Heydrich experienced disillusion when Hitler became Chancellor of the Reich. While the SS and the Gestapo appeared to be going from strength to strength in Prussia under Göring, both Himmler and Heydrich felt like unwanted neighbours in whose faces a front door had been slammed when they came to call.

While there appeared to be a lack of welcome in Berlin, there was no lack of achievement by the SD in Bavaria. In its earliest days it was simply

Heydrich was described by Himmler as "truly a good SS man." He is seen here in SS uniform.

Heydrich at work in his Munich police office. The year is 1934, shortly before his transfer to Berlin.

required to ferret out informers – euphemistically called Information Officers – inside the ranks of the SS and add specialized information to Himmler's already bulging files. Such information was identified by colour codes and cross-indexed under a variety of headings. Very soon the SD had become an internal espionage and investigative organization which did not baulk at any means for achieving its purposes. Heydrich, the organizer and commander, was always to contend, "One must know as much as possible about people." That came to mean minutiae about members of the Party and its opponents – their strengths, weaknesses, hobbies, habits, and scandals. All this was patiently and thoroughly recorded by, in the SD's later years, about 100,000 regularly employed agents, detectives, and informers.

Heydrich, fully taken up with his new responsibilities, received an unforeseen blow. On 8 June 1932, Gregor Strasser, at that time the Reichsorganisationsleiter of the Nazi Party, received a letter from Rudolf Jordan, the Gauleiter of Halle-Merseburg, stating that the father of "a Party member called Heydrich" who was in "the Reich leadership" was living in Halle, in Jordan's area of responsibility. There was "reason to believe," the Gauleiter's report continued, "that the Bruno Heydrich in Halle, indicated as his father, is a Jew."

The source for the rumour had been the second marriage of Heydrich's paternal grandmother, Ernestine Wilhelmine Heydrich, née Lindner, to a journeyman locksmith named Gustav Robert Süss. As the mother of a large family

Reinhard Heydrich with Kurt Daluege, far left.

by her first husband, Reinhold Heydrich, she had often chosen to call herself Süss-Heydrich. The name Süss was generally held to be Jewish, but there was no direct line of descent from Süss to Reinhard Heydrich and the Reich's investigator into racial matters pronounced himself satisfied that the locksmith Süss "was in any case. . .not of Jewish origin."

Even so, Heydrich did not relax. Until his death in 1942, he retained a fear of being thought Jewish or partly Jewish. Many commentators have ascribed Heydrich's savage conduct in dealing with Jewish victims to be a kind of perverse racial compensation. This was reflected in morbid self-hatred. One story that circulated about Heydrich at this time was that, on coming home drunk one evening, he suddenly saw his own image reflected in a large wall mirror. In swift cold rage, he whipped out his pistol and fired two shots. Himmler, the born manipulator, did nothing to discourage all this anxiety; it was a possible hold over Heydrich. Even so, the Reichsführer-SS was dazzled by the achievements of his energetic subordinate. In any event, the two men pressed on towards their ultimate goal: to become Germany's supreme policemen.

With Hitler's appointment as Chancellor, police and security matters were accelerated. As well as Himmler being appointed Police President of Munich, Heydrich, Head of the Sicherheitsdienst, became head of the existing political desk in Abteilung VI (Department VI) of the Munich Criminal Police. Heydrich was able to man it with existing personnel from his SD with the ultimate object of making the desk entirely independent of the Bavarian administration.

What was he like, this man with the hectic past and what promised to be a brilliant future? Some of his associates, notably Heinrich Müller, who was later to head the Gestapo directly under Heydrich, regarded the latter as a gangster intellectual, a flashy arriviste with a love of power for its own sake.

A meeting at the Burgerbrau Bierkeller in November 1939. From left: Frank Joseph Hüber (Vienna Gestapo Chief); Arthur Nebe (Chief of Criminal Police); Heinrich Himmler; Reinhard Heydrich; Heinrich Müller (Chief of Gestapo).

Promoted to Obergruppenführer, Reinhard Heydrich arrives in Prague on 27 September 1941. Here, with Karl Frank, he takes the salute in front of Hradcany Castle, the historical seat of the Moravian Kings, which Heydrich made his headquarters.

Others maintained that he was driven, not by personal ambition, but by conviction of the cause of National Socialism. Heydrich himself kept his own counsel and, if they were wise, so did those who worked closely with him. However, Walter Schellenberg, the able acolyte, has left us with a vivid pen portrait.

"He was a tall impressive figure with a broad, unusually high forehead, small restless eyes as crafty as an animal's and of uncanny power, a long predatory nose and a wide-lipped mouth. His hands were slender. His splendid figure was marred by the breadth of his hips, a disturbingly feminine effect which made him appear even more sinister. His voice was much too high for so large a man and his speech was nervous and staccato."

Others spoke of Heydrich's hands; Carl J Burckhardt, Swiss former League of Nations High Commissioner of Danzig, sitting next to Heydrich at a dinner party, described them as "pre-Raphaelite, lily-white hands, formed for slow strangling." They were also, however, the carefully tended instruments of a violinist and those who knew Heydrich away from the office testified that you forgot about the womanly voice because it came from the body of an athlete – a fencer, one of the finest in the Third Reich.

Göring's surrender to the urgings of Himmler and Heydrich, who had also enlisted the support of Reich Minister of the Interior Wilhelm Frick, meant that the Reichsführer-SS assumed the office of Inspector of the Secret State Police but, on 22 April 1934, it was Reinhard Heydrich who took over the leadership of the Gestapo.

He had at his disposal now the Political Police force of the entire Third Reich and he had hardly gained a foothold in Berlin before he embarked on a programme of drastic reorganization. In this work, he had the total backing of Adolf Hitler who declared:

"I forbid all the services of the Party, its branches and affiliated associations, to undertake enquiries or interrogations on matters which are the concern of the Gestapo. All incidents of a political nature, irrespective of reports made through the Party channels, have to be brought immediately to the knowledge of the competent services of the Gestapo now as before. . ..

"I particularly stress the fact that all attempts at conspiracy and high treason against the State which may come to the knowledge of the party, have to be made known to the Secret State Police. It is not the business of the Party to undertake on its own initiative searches and enquiries into these matters, whatever their nature."

For all his new responsibilities, Heydrich was certainly not deaf to the sound of the thudding footfalls of the Sturm Abteilung of Ernst Röhm. The Gestapo was soon to be assigned a killing rôle.

The Crown Jewels of Czechoslovakia. Legend has is that any person not the true heir who puts the crown on his head is sure to die. Heydrich was shown the crown by President Hacha and told this legend. It is said that Heydrich laughed and tried on the crown.

14

The Slaughter of the Brownshirts

Röhm's Brownshirts on the march. Many of the SA were little more than street thugs; their unchecked aggressions became a problem for a Nazi Party eager to win respectability.

The powder keg which Ernst Röhm had straddled for so long and so arrogantly was destined to explode beneath him during the bloody weekend of 30/31 June 1934.

Until then, the Storm Troopers remained a dangerous, formidable force, outnumbering the standing Army by at least fifteen to one. Especially worrying to Hitler was Röhm's openly expressed contempt for the existing military establishment – the very people upon whom Hitler depended for his hold on power. Röhm considered that the traditional military caste, ossified and socially irrelevant, must be replaced by true revolutionaries imbued with the fervour to sweep away the old order; above all, National Socialism had to be about Socialism.

Hitler's old comrade had gone even further in his public pronouncements, publicly accusing Hitler of betraying the revolution. Röhm was apt to express his views at the top of his voice while dining with cronies at his favourite hotel, the Fasanenhof in the Charlottenburg district of the capital. Hitler, despite everything, retained a perverse affection for his streetfighting comrade and was loathe to have done with him. There had been the sweetener of office for Röhm: Minister without Portfolio. It had failed to satisfy him and Röhm had pointed out with some pique that the same title had gone to another disciple from the early days, Rudolf Hess. Hitler had then resorted to mild threats, even to the extent of sending coded messages in the guise of news stories in the Nazi regulated press. One, carried by the *National Zeitung*, read: "From now on, the repression will be more severe. The term 'enemy of the state' is not confined solely to Bolshevik agents and agitators. It also includes all those who, by word or deed, whatever their intentions, compromise the existence of the Reich."

The warning seemed clear enough for anyone willing to listen, but it had little effect on the arrogant Röhm. His SA cohorts continued their drunken progress through the streets. Hitler was conscious of the danger lurking in every day of delay. It was true that President Hindenburg tottered on the edge of senility and was probably incapable of grasping Röhm's excesses. But a word in the President's ear from the right quarter could well prompt the obvious question: if Hitler as Chancellor was incapable of controlling his own supporters, how fit was he to run the country? Indeed, there were those who were already advocating that Hitler, or at the very least some of his closest supporters, should quit the scene. One of Hitler's most vocal critics was not a member of the SA, but General Kurt von Schleicher, the Führer's immediate predecessor as Chancellor, who, emerging from retirement and with an irresponsible disregard for discretion and his own safety, indulged in trenchant criticism of the government.

Schleicher, a sly political tactician, had professed sympathy with Röhm; indeed had reached accommodation with him. In return Schleicher let it be known that he wanted the taste of power again. He accepted that the post of Chancellor was no longer open; very well, he would agree to serve under Hitler as Vice-Chancellor with Röhm as Minister of Defence. Schleicher let his imagination soar. There would be an amalgamation of the SA and the Army. Papen, Göring, and Foreign Minister Neurath would be removed from the government. Schleicher then went on to draw up his "Shadow Cabinet:" Heinrich Bruning, the former Catholic Centre Party Chancellor, would receive the Foreign Affairs portfolio with Gregor Strasser taking that of National Economy.

The British historian, John Wheeler-Bennett, was in Berlin at the time and was later to recall, "typewritten lists of the new Cabinet were passed from hand-to-hand with a lack of discretion which was terrifying." Wheeler-Bennett went on to state that he "was shown one of the lists of the Shadow Cabinet in the course of conversation in a certain famous bar, where it was a well known fact that the barman and waiters were in the employment of the Gestapo."

As we have seen, even the super-energetic Göring had found time to cast nervous glances over his shoulder at Ernst Röhm. Göring lost no time in seeking out the Reichsführer. The latter would dearly have loved to see the subjection of the Army to the SS, but, as always, was content to wait. The problem of Röhm needed to be solved first. When Göring relinquished control of the Gestapo to Himmler he had been crafty enough to make sure that he had his own personal secret police apparatus and that it was in good order. This was the Forschungsamt (literally, Research Office). Its main task was the interception – coyly termed "research results" – of telephone conversations and signals which might effect the security of the Reich.

Göring, with Hitler's blessing, had from the very beginning an absolute monopoly of wire-tapping throughout the Reich. All that was required by a would-be tapper was the appropriate form on which Göring inscribed an enormous "G." With the Röhm purge in prospect, Göring proceeded to employ his powers to the uttermost: the service of the Forschungsamt was put at the disposal of Himmler.

Heydrich's SD agents and, at Prinz Albrechtstrasse, those of the Gestapo inherited from Göring, worked around the clock. Anything that might remotely tell against Röhm – a phrase, a word, dubious contacts, half-truths, insinuations – were recorded and filed. Heydrich's task was to supply Himmler with as much poison about Röhm as possible and feed it to Hitler. It soon became obvious to Heydrich that nothing less than the announcement of a full-scale conspiracy, of an imminent *coup d'état* would arouse Hitler from his indecision and tiresome sense of loyalty to Röhm. News of an intended putsch and

Nuremburg, September 1933. The last Nazi Party Day at which Hitler would share the spotlight with Röhm.

Ernst Röhm with members of his SA. Hitler's old street-fighting comrade went too far when he publicly accused Hitler of betraying the revolution.

An early parade of the SA (the Sturm Abteilung). First established in August 1920 as a "Gymnastic and Sports" detachment, the SA became a vast pool of manpower for the infant Nazi Party.

Anti-facists arrested by Storm Troopers. Such street arrests were called "wild concentration camps" and respectable citizens were often subjected to violence.

its total repression must, it was felt, come as such a shock that everyone, from the man in the street to the senile Hindenburg himself, would be convinced that Hitler had acted out of necessity.

In Berlin, the month of June in 1934 was sticky and humid. There was a mood of crisis. The first rumblings of the Röhm affair were discernible on 17 June when Vice-Chancellor Papen spoke to a group of students in the ancient university town of Marburg. The speech contained much that to the Nazis was irreproachable, including an exemplary attack on Ernst Röhm and the crude behaviour of the SA. But it carried something else: a clear warning to Hitler that he must take care not to alienate those conservative forces which had aided him to power. Papen also implied that the more repellent aspects of SA conduct – the persecution of respectable citizens and patriots, the ridiculing of established intellectual and spiritual institutions – were endemic in Nazism itself.

Such treason could not go unpunished, but for Hitler at this time to strike at his Vice-Chancellor, respected confidant of President Hindenburg, was out of the question. A second-best solution, Himmler reasoned, would be to attack the author of the speech. It did not take Heydrich's agents long to discover that the speech had been the work of a bright young writer and lawyer, Dr Edgar Jung, a believer in the concept of a "conservative revolution" and, as such, anathema to diehard Nazis.

On 21 June, four days after Marburg, Dr Jung was alone in his Munich home. On her return, his wife found that he had disappeared. On the bathroom wall she saw scrawled one word – "Gestapo." Edgar Jung's body, marked by appalling tortures, was later found in a ditch on the road to Oranienburg. Himmler and Heydrich had, however, earlier made it their special business to interest themselves in the activities of the Vice-Chancellor. Heydrich set out blandly to seek co-operation with Papen's supporters. In fact he intended to infiltrate an agent into the enemy camp in the guise of a friend. Heydrich's choice had fallen upon Otto Betz, a counter-espionage agent who had already worked for the SD chief in the Saar. Betz was instructed to keep Papen and Jung under constant surveillance and also to report the activities of Herbert von Bose, the Vice-Chancellor's chief private secretary. On 4 May 1934, the dutiful Betz took up his duties in Berlin. His two rooms were conveniently near Prinz Albrechtstrasse.

It was, Betz realized, no easy mission. Men from the SD and the Gestapo, however seemingly ingratiating, were scarcely the most favoured creatures at the office of the Vice-Chancellery. Betz was treated by Bose with suspicion but he persisted, presuming on his acquaintance with Jung and gaining the confidence of Papen's staff. He even went to the extent of warning them that their telephones were being tapped by the SD.

At the same time, it need scarcely be said that Betz was dutifully filing reports for Himmler and Heydrich. These achieved their intended effect. Hitler's worst fears were confirmed. There *was* to be a putsch and this was the time to act. President Hindenburg was clearly ailing. With his death, tradition-alists might well call for the return of the monarchy; the leading candidate for the throne was the Kaiser's son August Wilhelm and he was a member of the SA. Franz von Papen, Hindenburg's favourite, was known to have the ear of the old man. Papen's Marburg speech had denounced the methods of the Nazis, their violation of human rights, and their anti-Christianity. Such talk must plainly be silenced. Equally, a scapegoat had to be found: a purge of the SA could well provide the answer. Röhm and his band could be held responsible for all the ills of the past.

Then came a serious setback to the plans of Himmler and Heydrich. Ironically enough, Hitler himself could still not bring himself to denounce Röhm once and for all. Hitler himself was later to relate, "At the beginning of June, I made a final effort with Röhm. I asked him to come to my office and we talked together for nearly five hours." Just exactly what happened behind the doors of the Reich Chancellery is not known, but the outcome was that the SA would take a month's leave with the intention of thrashing out the matter afresh at the end of that time.

The news was greeted by the SS chiefs with consternation. How was Röhm to be eliminated if the SA was allowed to go on leave? In such circumstances, how could allegations that the Storm Troopers were planning an uprising appear credible? Plainly the Gestapo had to move immediately.

The strain became intolerable for Hitler. Not only was he being nagged into action by Göring, Himmler, and Heydrich, but he was incurring mounting displeasure from the Army whose members were urging him to close with Röhm. On 25 June, the Army Commander-in-Chief, General Werner von Fritsch, put his entire forces on a state of alert, cancelling all leave, and confining the troops to barracks. Three days later, Ernst Röhm was expelled from the German Officers' League. The Army had no intention of soiling its hands with the blood of Röhm and his followers. That task it would leave to Hitler. If, on the other hand, Hitler were to fail, the consequences for him would be dire.

The Führer, in fact, was to entrust the blood-letting to the denizens of Prinz Albrechtstrasse whose resources were now mobilized. On 28 June, Hitler left Berlin for Essen, ostensibly to attend the wedding of Josef Terboven, the local Gauleiter and veteran of the Bierkeller putsch of 1923. There was no particular reason why Hitler should have taken the trouble to make a journey for the nuptials of a comparatively junior official, particularly when his own position was supposed to be under threat. It was possible that he wanted to distance himself from the preparations that Himmler and Heydrich were even then making. On the other hand, the additional presence of Göring, Goebbels, and Diels at Terboven's marriage later led to the suspicion that the SD and Gestapo had wanted the Führer out of the capital so that his most senior colleagues could keep an eye on him and ensure that there would be no last minute sentimental change of mind about eliminating Röhm.

Heydrich had been given offices by Himmler adjacent to that of the Reichsführer's adjutant, Karl Wolff. Officials who had been Diels' appointees were given short shrift and unceremoniously replaced at Prinz Albrechtstrasse by men of the SS or Bavarian police, including the bizarre addition of black-garbed women with hair swept sternly back in tight coils. On the evening of Terboven's wedding, Hitler telephoned Röhm who was relaxing with some of his more personable SA youths at the Pension Hanselbauer in Bad Wiessee situated south of Munich, and instructed him to call a meeting of all SA leaders on 30 June. On the 29th, Hitler went on to inspect a labour camp at Westphalia, progressing from there to Bad Godesberg on the Rhine to spend the weekend at the Hotel Dreesen, whose proprietor he knew. The slaughter of the Brownshirts began on 30 June and ended on about 2 July 1934. At least eighty-two, and probably closer to 200, "enemies" were arrested in all parts of Germany and summarily shot. The victims were seized by Heydrich's Gestapo agents either at home or on the way to the conference which Hitler had ordered Röhm to schedule.

Lurid testaments abound. According to some accounts, Hitler, with riding whip and pistol in hand and flanked by Goebbels, turncoat SA-Obergruppenführer Viktor Lutze, and armed contingents of the Munich-based Kripo, went from room to room, beginning with Röhm's, awakening the SA slumberers and placing them under arrest. In little more than an hour, the detainees were packed off in two buses to Stadelheim prison, just outside Munich, to be shot.

The shootings of SA officials arrested elsewhere in Germany began the same day at the SS barracks at Berlin Lichterfelde. Franz von Papen was later to declare that the man responsible for preparing the death lists was a certain Hermann Behrens, one of Heydrich's SD officials. Gestapo headquarters itself was a hive of activity during those frenzied days.

The Gruppenführer of the SS high command had been ordered to bring all units throughout the Reich up to emergency strength. A link was established with opposite numbers in the Army: the support of regular Army troops and weapons could be depended upon. For the sake of secrecy, all those whose names featured on the SD and Gestapo death lists were designated by a serial number. On the telephone, in telegrams, and in messages the language was oblique and terse: "No. 8 has arrived; Nos. 17, 35, 37, 68, and 84 have been arrested; Nos. 32, 43, 47 and 59 have been shot; No. 5 is still missing."

An important witness to these events was Hans Bernd Gisevius, who served with the Gestapo in the early months of Hitler's regime but, as one of nature's born survivors, later contrived a transfer to the police department of the Ministry of the Interior. In his memoirs, *To the Bitter End*, Gisevius, who at this time was often in the company of Arthur Nebe, head of the Kripo, the detective department closely allied to the Gestapo, recounted:

"Loud shouting reached us from the adjoining room. This room was Göring's study, and here the execution committee was meeting. Now and then couriers from the Gestapo rushed into and out of this room, slips of white paper in their hands. Through the door we could see Göring, Himmler, Heydrich and little Pilli Korner, State Secretary of Göring in his capacity as Minister-President. We could see them conferring, but naturally we could not hear what was being said. Occasionally, however, we could catch a muffled sound: 'Away!' or 'Aha!' or 'Shoot him!' For the most part we heard nothing but raucous laughter. The whole crew of them seemed to be in the best humour.

"Göring radiated cheerful complacency. It was easy to see that he was in his element. He swaggered about the room, his long hair waving, in a white military tunic and blue-grey military trousers, with high black boots that reached over his fat knees. . ..

"We suddenly heard loud shouting. A police major, his face flaming, rushed out of the room, and behind him came Göring's hoarse, booming voice: 'Shoot them. . .shoot them at once!' The written word cannot reproduce the

An early photograph of Hitler on a trip to the Bavarian Alps. Beside him are Gregor Strasser, Ernst Röhm, and Hermann Göring (sitting). Hitler and Göring were directly responsible for the murders of Röhm and Strasser.

undisguised blood lust, fury, vicious vengefulness, and, at the same time, the fear, the pure funk, that the scene revealed."

Some 150 SA leaders were rounded up and stood against a wall at the Lichterfelde barracks – despatched by firing squads of Himmler's SS and Göring's own police, the Landespolizeigruppe.

Gruppenführer Karl Ernst, in control of 80,000 men of the Berlin-Brandenburg SA, had, before the round-up, set off on his honeymoon. He was arrested as his car neared Bremen. His bride and his chauffeur were wounded; Ernst himself was flown back to Berlin for the firing squad. His main crime was that he had talked too much, particularly about events surrounding the Reichstag fire. He had also spoken disparagingly of Himmler whom he had dubbed "the black Jesuit."

As much as anything else, the Röhm purge was a time to pay off old scores. On the morning of 30 June, Göring despatched his Landespolizei to deal with General von Schleicher whom he deemed a traitor. Accounts of who exactly carried out one of the most revolting double murders of the alleged putsch are confusing. Göring was later to claim that a tearaway group of Landespolizei, not authorized by him, got to Schleicher's Neu-Babelsberg villa before the "official" killers. What is known is that the hit men slaughtered the general and his wife in a hail of bullets.

As for Röhm, he was given a little longer. Right until the end, Hitler had scruples about ordering his death. Even after Röhm's arrest, Hitler ordered that a pistol should be left on the table in his cell. Röhm refused to pick it up and is reported to have said, "If I am to be killed let Adolf do it himself." Thereupon two SS officers, according to the testimony of a police lieutenant during the postwar Munich trial in May 1957, entered the cell and fired their revolvers point blank. Röhm had wanted to say something, the trial witness had testified, but the SS officer had motioned for the prisoner to be silent. Then Röhm had stood to attention stripped to the waist, his expression contemptuous. The order for the execution had been passed to Himmler who in turn had contacted Theodore Eicke, commander of the Totenkopf guards at Dachau, and told him to proceed. Assisted by his adjutant, Michael Lippert, Eicke had done just that.

Theodore Eicke was killed in Russia in February 1943 while commanding the SS-Totenkopf Division, but Lippert survived to stand trial in Munich in 1957. Another victim – and one who, by common consent, had fallen to slake Göring's thirst for vengeance and malicious spite – was seventy-one year old Gustav von Kahr, who had frustrated the ill-fated Bierkeller putsch of 1923. Kahr had long retired from politics but it made no difference. He was hacked to pieces with a pickaxe and his body flung into a swamp near Dachau.

Because of his inconvenient Marburg speech, even Papen would have been murdered had it not been for his close friendship with President Hindenburg. Two of his closest associates – his Private Secretary Herbert von Bose and, as we have seen, Dr Edgar Jung, the author of the offending speech – were both killed.

It was scarcely surprising that Gregor Strasser, Röhm's ally, was marked out for the firing squad. Kurt Ludecke, a veteran Nazi who had fallen under Hitler's spell during the early days in Munich and, as a confidant of Röhm, had been lucky to escape execution, was to recall: "At one-thirty o'clock on the afternoon of 30 June, five Gestapo officials called at Gregor Strasser's home. Strasser was at lunch with his family. They told him to come along; when he asked why, he was informed that he was suspected of treasonable activities and that his office at Schering-Kahlbaum was to be searched. When they arrived at the building, however, he was handed over to a waiting SS detachment."

Gisevius took up the story: "Daluege and I met with Nebe. He informed me that Gregor Strasser was dead. Allegedly he had committed suicide. We were outraged, and would have been more so had we known of the cowardly and treacherous manner in which he was murdered. An eye-witness told me about it some days later. Strasser had been taken to the Gestapo prison at about noon.

The wedding of Karl Ernst (1904-1934), Commander of the Berlin-Brandenburg Storm Trooper contingent. Standing behind the bride and groom in this photograph are Röhm and Göring. Ernst was shot on 30 June 1934 during the Röhm Purge.

An early meeting of the NSDAP at Nuremburg with Hitler centre, and, to his left, Strasser and Himmler.

Some hours passed and there was a great deal of coming and going. Then an SS man came to the door and called out 'Strasser.' The man who had formerly been next in importance to Adolf Hitler in the Nazi Party was to be moved to an individual cell. No one thought anything of it as Strasser walked slowly out of the room. But scarcely a minute later they heard the crack of a pistol.

"The SS man had shot the unsuspecting Strasser from behind and hit his main artery. A great stream of blood had spurted against the wall of the tiny cell. Apparently Strasser did not die at once. A prisoner in the adjoining cell heard him thrashing about on the cot for nearly an hour. No one paid any attention to him. At last the prisoner heard loud footsteps in the corridor and orders being shouted. The guards clicked their heels. And the prisoner recognized Heydrich's voice saying, 'Isn't he dead yet? Let the swine bleed to death.'

"The bloodstain on the wall of the cell remained for weeks. It was the pride of the SS squadron, a kind of museum piece. These cut-throats showed it to all the terrified inmates and boasted that it was the blood of a famous man, Gregor Strasser. Only later did Heydrich order the bloodstains to be cleaned."

Gisevius testified at the Nuremberg trial that all Gestapo documents relating to the Röhm purge were destroyed. It is therefore impossible to distinguish exactly which murders could be ascribed to Göring and his personal police apparatus and which to Heydrich and his SD and Gestapo. There is, however, one crime which can be said with confidence to carry the stamp of Reinhard Heydrich – the murder of Dr Erich Klausener, leader of the Catholic Action organization, who had carried on a personal campaign against the Nazis.

At a religious service on 1 May 1934, Klausener appealed for "a special awareness of the social teaching of the Church." The Nazis considered that the only awareness acceptable on May Day was of themselves; they set great store by the workers' traditional holiday. Klausener's actions were construed as a calculated sabotage. At the end of June, Klausener voiced further opinions said to be "against the interests of the state" while giving a heated speech at the Katholikentag (a biennial meeting of Catholics.)

As the liquidation lists for the Röhm purge flooded across Heydrich's desk, on his own initiative the Gestapo chief added Klausener's name. Heydrich did not himself carry out assassinations: for the intended murder of Dr Erich Klausener, however, there was a willing and able lieutenant to hand.

Gregor and Otto Strasser. Gregor Strasser was one of the most powerful men in the Nazi Party, so powerful that he was a threat to Hitler. During the Night of the Long Knives, Strasser was shot on the express orders of Hitler and Göring. His brother Otto, above, also a Party member, managed to survive the war.

Heydrich recalled that as early as February 1932 an organization known as the SS-Begleitkommando (Escort Commando), had been formed. It was a predecessor of the elite SS-Leibstandarte which, in the following year, became the sole personal bodyguard of the Führer. The SS-Begleitkommando was then restricted to guard and security duties. One of its number – now a Leibstandarte man – had been Hauptsturmführer Kurt Gildisch, whom Heydrich recalled as being a highly disciplined individual who did not question orders.

On the day of the purge, Heydrich gave Gildisch a direct order. "You will be responsible for the Klausener case; you will shoot him personally. Go forthwith to the Reich Ministry of Transport."

At his trial for murder in 1953, Gildisch, who described himself as "an enthusiastic National Socialist," related how he had rejected the weapons he had been given and had set out on his mission. At around 1:00 p.m., Klausener, leaving his office on the way to the washroom, encountered the killer. Gildisch, seemingly in no hurry, escorted Klausener back to his office and there told him that he was under arrest. Klausener then turned his back on Gildisch, searching in a cupboard for his jacket. The SS killer drew his weapon and fired. Still Gildisch did not hurry. After making sure that Klausener was dead, he lifted the desk telephone and dialled the Prinz Albrechtstrasse number. A high-pitched voice ordered Gildisch to make the death look like suicide. Obediently, Gildisch placed his Mauser near Klausener's right hand and put a double guard on the door.

Gildisch, who later received a fifteen year sentence for his crimes, was to claim that it was only when he returned to Heydrich that he learnt that he had shot "a dangerous Catholic leader." Gildisch was given no time for reflection but was forthwith despatched on his next mission: to fly to Bremen and arrest Karl Ernst who was destined for the firing squad.

Both Heydrich and Gildisch received official recognition for their work that day. In the name of the Fatherland, the head of the SD and Gestapo was promoted SS Gruppenführer. Kurt Gildisch was promoted by Himmler to Sturmbannführer and during the war served with the Waffen-SS.

When his fellow Germans put Gildisch on trial in 1953 for the Klausener murder, he was asked, "What did you think when you carried out a murder in this fashion?" He replied with a shrug, "Nothing really."

At the very moment that bullets were crashing into SA bodies at Lichterfelde, Adolf Hitler was seeking to deaden their effect with the genteel tinkle of tea cups. Dr Joseph Goebbels had arranged a party at the Reich Chancellery for members of the Cabinet and their wives and children. Those present later recalled that Hitler had been in excellent humour, chatting and showing particular affection for small children. By the morning of 2 July, the butchery of the Röhm purge was over and Hitler pronounced himself satisfied. Traitors had been dealt such a mighty blow that no one would dare attempt such an insurrection again. How many actually fell victim has never been established precisely. In a speech in the Kroll Opera House on 13 July, Hitler announced that sixty-one persons had been shot, including nineteen "higher SA leaders," that thirteen more died "resisting arrest," and that three had "committed suicide" – a total of seventy-seven. *The White Book of the Purge*, published by emigrés in Paris, stated that 401 had been murdered, but identified only 116 of them. At the Munich trial in 1957, a figure of more than 1,000 was claimed.

Himmler with his Chief of Personal Staff, Karl Wolff, and Reinhard Heydrich.

During his speech, Hitler said, "It was no secret that this time the revolution would have to be bloody; when we spoke of it we called it 'The Night of the Long Knives' – (Die Nacht der langen Messer). Everyone must know for all future time that if he raises his hand to strike the State, then certain death is his lot."

The full resources of Himmler, Heydrich, SD, and Gestapo together with Göring's Research Office – that finely-tuned Forschungsamt with its highly sophisticated methods of interception – had been marshalled to stitch together with consummate skill a shoal of rumours, counter-rumours, and indiscreet conversations. All these had been designed to work subtly on Hitler's suspicions until the point had been reached when the Führer had decided, however reluctantly, to act.

At a Christmas party in 1934, "jolly Uncle Hermann" entertains children with a toy pistol.

Hermann Göring held a lavish party at his beloved Carinhall for Heydrich and his staff to celebrate their work during the Röhm Purge. Bombed by the Allies, only these shattered remains mark the once luxurious villa which had cost German taxpayers fifteen million Deutschmarks.

To Göring and Himmler, the end had amply justified the means. Röhm, whom Göring had particularly loathed and feared, had been removed. The streams of blood that had bespattered the walls of the courtyard of Lichterfelde barracks had not simply tamed and badly frightened the Sturm Abteilung; the entire organization now existed only as a ghost, as a footnote in history. The SA was left to vegetate under the leadership of Viktor Lutze, whose effective power was severely limited. When national conscription in the Reich was reinstated in 1935, the problem of relocating the significant SA manpower pool was resolved: its members were gradually absorbed into the Army which had stood impassively by throughout the purge. President Hindenburg died on the morning of 2 August 1934. With the midday announcement, came the news that the Reich Cabinet had already enacted a decree, effective immediately, which merged the offices of the Reich President and Chancellor. The title of Reich President was considered by Hitler to be too democratic and was allowed to lapse. Hitler preferred the title of Führer und Kanzler des Deutschen Reiches (Leader and Chancellor of the German Reich).

The Reichsmordwoche (National Murder Week) had more than achieved its object. But what of Himmler and his lieutenants controlling the SD and Gestapo? It was true that the secret police apparatus had acquitted itself well but Himmler was only too conscious that the power vested in him over control of the police, although existing *de facto*, had not been dignified by legal status.

This omission was redressed by two decrees. The first, on 10 February 1936, signed by Göring as Minister-President of Prussia, became known as the "fundamental law" of the Gestapo. It stipulated that the duty of the Gestapo was to investigate all hostile forces throughout the entire State. The decree of 17 June 1936, spelt out Himmler's position as supreme commander of all the German police forces, uniformed and civil. The police forces were withdrawn from the jurisdiction of the Länder (States) and placed under the Reich.

Eventually, the salaries – and generous expenses – of police officials came out of the Reich budget. The decree was very precise: "Having become National Socialist, the police. . .is there: firstly to carry out the will of a single

leader and secondly to defend the German people against all attempts at destruction by enemies within and outside the country. To achieve this goal, the police needs to be all powerful."

In the wake of the Röhm purge, Himmler and Heydrich lost no time in consolidating their new status. As for Göring, he pronounced himself a happy man. With Röhm out of the way, he devoted himself with renewed enthusiasm to his plans for building Carinhall, named in memory of his late first wife and planned as a luxurious country lodge to be built in the Norse style at Schorfheide, an undulating Prussian terrain of lake and forest. Göring was inordinately proud of a projected monstrous extravagence which in the end was to cost the German taxpayer fifteen million Reichsmarks. By way of reward for their rôle in the Röhm purge, Göring decided that Heydrich and his staff would be bussed out to the site for a lavish party. Once the party was over, it was back to Berlin and the conversion, planned and inevitable, of Adolf Hitler's Third Reich into a total police state.

Tannenberg, 4 August 1934. Amidst great splendour, Hitler commemorates the memory of President von Hindenburg.

|5|
The Gestapo Is Everywhere

From the very beginning agents of the Gestapo made it their business to keep a close eye on state employees who could be punished for even a trivial criticism of the regime. Civil servants were directed to spy on one another; reluctance to do so in itself constituted an offence. But the practice of mass snooping was not confined simply to bureaucrats.

Germany was divided into thirty-two Gaue or administrative regions. Each of these Gau was then divided into Kreise, or circles; each Kreis into Ortsgruppen, or local groups; each Ortsgruppe into Zellen, or cells; and each Zelle into blocks. Each of these divisions had as its leader a Gauleiter – directly appointed by Hitler – a Kreisleiter, an Ortsgruppenleiter, a Zellenleiter, a Blockleiter. The recruit most valued by the Gestapo was indisputably the Blockleiter, an informer of potent power whose authority could extend over an entire apartment block of perhaps forty or sixty homes and who was in command of a posse of Blockwärte (Wardens).

The latter, ill-paid and despised by all as the lowest form of Gestapo life, were only too willing to peddle gossip, rumour, and the small change of overheard conversations. Anything deemed in any way suspicious would be forwarded to the Ortsgruppe who in turn forwarded the intelligence to the Kreise and so on up to the highest reaches of the Gestapo. Every business, large or small, had its Blockleiter. In the case of the famous Löwenbräu brewery in Munich, Joseph Scherl proved most assiduous. On 18 July 1933, Scherl was reporting to his Zelle on Michael Hinterauer, a carpenter, Mathias Moritz, a brewer, and Adalbert Faeth, "an employee." On Hinterauer, Scherl wrote that he was "generally known in the brewery as a presently active Marxist who is also the brother of a maid who serves the Jew and distinguished businessman Dr Herman Schulein of Richard Wagner Strasse." Moritz was "known as a good Marxist," while the sister-in-law of Faeth was also "working for Dr Schulein." The Blockleiter went on to report that the trio had taken a holiday in France. How, he wanted to know, had they found money for the trip, particularly as Faeth was always complaining of a shortage of money? Scherl further recommended that a surveillance be placed on the correspondence and contacts of all three, adding the significant recommendation, "The undeniable contact with Dr Schulein surely calls for consideration."

The reach of the Gestapo tentacles did not stop there. Martin Bormann, Hitler's future aide and confidant, signed an order on 26 June 1935 stating, "in future, the heads of the Gestapo shall be invited to be present at all the important official manifestations of the Party and its organizations."

The Gestapo sought to create an atmosphere where no one, from a next-door neighbour or a schoolteacher to the youngest member of Hitler Youth, was to be trusted any more. Children were often encouraged to denounce parents who criticized the Führer or the Party, even in the privacy of their homes. The possibility of arrest, the spectre of the gloved-hand thudding on the front door, was an ever present fear to countless families throughout the Reich. In Stuttgart, in the industrial heartland of the southwest, the first year of Nazi power presaged tragedy for one particular family, the Schlotterbecks. Its head, fifty-three year Gotthilf Schlotterbeck, an unemployed Communist locksmith, was arrested and sent to Heuberg detention camp. His son, Friedrich, who survived after the death in Dachau of his parents, sisters, and fiancée, wrote in 1945:

"The Gestapo also took away my brother Hermann. . .for distributing Communist leaflets. Ill-treatment by the SS consisted of beating him up, throwing him to the ground and crushing his bones by treading on him. After a few weeks they let him go but his internal injuries were so severe that he was a hopeless cripple. He was only fourteen years old. The Gestapo intended that he should not recover and they made sure of that by never letting him alone. Every time he paid his compulsory visit to their headquarters for 'social welfare education' they beat him up all over again."

Himmler and Heydrich, however, envisaged an infinitely more sophisticated rôle for their Gestapo than merely encouraging citizens to turn informer. Their vision was shared by Hitler himself. On 17 June 1936, by decree of the Führer and Chancellor, the Party post of Reichsführer-SS was formally amalgamated with the newly created governmental office of Chief of the German Police, giving Himmler the twin titles of Reichsführer-SS und Chef der Deutschen Polizei (ponderously abbreviated to RFSSuChDtPol). Reinhard Heydrich's position as head of the Gestapo was far from being simply a police promotion. He came to embody what was virtually the Party's annexation of the State.

Heydrich had scarcely set foot in Berlin before he took steps to transform the Gestapo, insinuating his former colleagues from Bavaria into key positions. Notable among these was a certain Heinrich Müller, a thickset, bull-necked criminal police inspector who had been a sergeant pilot on the Western Front and a member of Munich police headquarters from the end of 1919. During the Weimar Republic, Müller had been in charge of the anti-Communist desk in the political section of police headquarters. At this time he had sufficient sense of self-preservation to keep his options open by refusing to join the Nazi Party formally. One of nature's main-chancers, Müller was well aware that Hitler owed him something: in September 1931, Geli Raubal, the Führer's niece and possibly his mistress, was found dead in mysterious circumstances. The hushing up of any scandal – and the elimination of inconvenient witnesses – was said to have been entrusted to Müller.

Deputy Führer, Rudolf Hess, summed up his character: "Before the rise to power [of the Nazi Party] Müller was employed in the Political Department of

Berlin Gestapo Headquarters. To break down the morale of the prisoners, hot air was blown through this pipe into cells which had practically no ventilation.

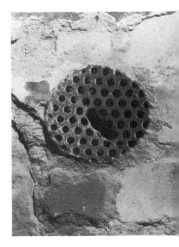

The conversations of prisoners could be overheard by the Gestapo through this crude listening grill.

One of Himmler's first acts after taking over the Gestapo was to purge all Home Office civil servants regarded as politically unsound. Here, Himmler and his new 'politically sound' appointees arrive to take over the Ministry of the Interior.

Heinrich Müller, the inspector of criminal police who would "tolerate none who might stand in his way."

Police Headquarters. He always did his duty. . .. His job was to keep on the track of Leftist movements. It must be acknowledged that he proceeded against these movements with great severity partly even in violation of legal norms. With his vast ambition and relentless drive, Müller, had it been his task to fight against the right wing, would also have done everything to win the appreciation of whoever might happen to be his superior. Politically, Müller seemed to be uncommitted. . .ideologically his place was in the National camp, and there he wavered between the German Nationalist People's Party and the Bavarian Party, but he was certainly not a National Socialist. His personal character, however, is even worse than his political attitude. He is an elbow-man. He tolerates none who might stand in his way."

Heydrich was interested above all in technocrats. Their past political beliefs were often of scant concern, provided they did not threaten his position or that of the State. It was of paramount importance that they should be "elbow-men."

Once in Berlin, Heydrich lost no time in instituting a transformation of the Gestapo that was drastic and radical. In October 1934, he drew up a plan of the division of Gestapo duties. All existing Departments were re-designated Divisions, while Offices became Departments. The chain of command was put on a military footing. For example, a function which in the time of Rudolf Diels had been called "Personal Advisor" was now called "Adjutant" – a job given to a trusted subordinate from the SD speedily promoted to the rank of SS-Obersturmbannführer. Heydrich then went on to establish three posts. Division 1 (Administration, Organization, Law) was taken over by another SD man, Dr Karl Rudolf Werner Best, a native of Darmstadt, a qualified lawyer, and a former head of the Police Division in the Hesse State Ministry. He was known, moreover, to be a gifted organizer who gave needless bureaucracy short shrift.

Heydrich's main interest, though, was in Division II which he saw as the core of the Gestapo and whose functions he would dearly have liked to retain for himself. But even so determined a workaholic as Heydrich – it was not uncommon for him to be at his desk for a twelve-hour stretch – felt obliged to delegate. In sub-Department II 1D, Müller – " Gestapo Müller" – reigned supreme.

In Munich there had been the inconvenience of the local civil police. There was no need for such obstruction to be tolerated in Berlin. Müller would be free to sort out left wing radicals and, of course, his old enemies – Marxists, Communists, and their associated organizations. Conservatives and "reactionaries" came under the microscope of another Department as did Austrian affairs. Yet another Department looked at threats posed by existing Party members. The concern of another was with the denominational religious groups which included Freemasonry. In Division III, however, Heydrich firmly held on to the reins of power: it dealt with Counter-Espionage. He saw himself primarily as an SD man – the supremo of the Sicherheitsdienst, the security right-arm of the National Socialist Party of which the Gestapo would form an essential part.

Insignia of Divisions of the Waffen-SS.
From top to bottom:
Totenkopf Division;
Polizei Division;
Skanderberg Division;
Maria Theresia Division

On paper at least, the functions of the two organizations were separate. The SD had a monopoly of political intelligence, but at this time enjoyed no executive power of the kind invested in the Gestapo. The Geheime Staats Polizei alone had the right to carry out arrests, house searches, and interrogations. It was the Gestapo which placed people in "protective custody" and which sent them to concentration camps. In theory, the division of functions seemed clear enough, but in fact the Gestapo carried out its own intelligence work – and could only do so with information fed to it by the SD.

The threat to efficiency of a top-heavy bureacracy was not lost on Heydrich. On the other hand, the very complexity of the workings of SD and Gestapo bewildered many, a considerable advantage in a police state.

Heydrich, however, had his worries. Himmler's avowed desire to unify the entire SS and police posed a real threat to the Sicherheitsdeinst. Above all, Heydrich was wary of Heinrich Müller, the professional policeman with complete contempt for the SD and its self-styled "intellectuals." Gestapo officials, encouraged by Müller, edged into the SD. The latter saw themselves being swamped by rank-parity Gestapo officials, many of whom were not even members of the Party, let alone the SS. In mid-1936 only 244 out of the 607 Gestapo officials belonged to the SS and when, at the outbreak of war, the Gestapo had grown to 20,000, a mere 3,000 were SS members. The Gestapo was undeniably privileged when it came to the allotment of funds and Heydrich was constantly begging for money, pleading the cause of SD men who

did not enjoy the same pension rights as their civil service colleagues. Whatever his personal feelings, Heydrich was a realist: the SD and security police would have to merge officially so that the SD could also become a State organization with its bills met by the Reich. But that would have to wait until after the outbreak of war.

Nothing illustrated the newly assumed muscle of the Gestapo more profoundly than its wide-ranging powers of arrest. Dr Werner Best, obliged by Heydrich to don a cloak of legality, declared that the police should be ubiquitous "in order to suppress and avert any disturbance of governmental order in the Third Reich, even though an infringement of law and order may not, or not yet, have taken place." Heydrich watched the card indexes, his files of suspects, proliferate.

The Gestapo also encroached on SD territory in the field of espionage. Gestapo operatives engaged in spying were designated as "Frontier Police," a bland term covering the pursuit of anyone suspected of treason. Anonymous, these operatives crouched behind their own desk: Referat G of Hauptabteilung III of the Gestapa (Gestapo Main Office).

The bid to turn Germany into a police state did have its opponents within the legal system. As early as 2 June 1933, the Public Prosecutor of State Court II, Munich, was aware of numerous unexplained cases of death in the concentration camp at Dachau. A memorandum to the Bavarian Minister of Justice stated that "the proceedings regarding the events in Dachau Concentration Camp are to be pursued with all determination." In the second week of May 1933, there was an enquiry into the deaths of four Dachau prisoners. It found that they had been tortured to death by the camp guards.

At numerous postwar trials, apologists for the Gestapo claimed that, dating from the time Himmler set up the Totenkopf (Death's Head) Regiments charged exclusively with duties as camp guards, the camps had solely been his responsibility. For the years before 1936, this is difficult to disprove because the cost of running the camps was charged to the Länder and not to the general Reich budget. After 1936, however, there is abundant documentation to confirm direct Gestapo involvement. Stateless individuals earmarked for deportation were consigned as an interim measure to concentration camps. In ponderous legalistic terms, Dr Best, responsible for such measures, declared, "The acceptance of the stateless person will take place through the Land Police Authority, under the provisions of Gestapa Form No. 240, together with the index card Gestapa No. 98 carrying a photograph of the deportee."

Only when some other country had shown its willingness to accept the deportee was he allowed to quit the concentration camp. Even then the threat of the Gestapo remained. Best laid down, "Before passing him across the frontier, the Frontier Police authority will obtain from the stateless person a statement in duplicate recognizing, that should he return, he runs the risk of detention in a concentration camp."

The gradual extension of police powers in the hands of Himmler and Heydrich led to many scrambles for the available spoils. Among those on the look out for any possible advantage was Kurt Daluege, who had held the position of SS-Gruppenführer Berlin but, on the dismissal of Diels, had hoped for higher

The Gestapo dog training school. A frightened Bora Pavlovic was to encounter dogs like these while hiding in the Obed Marshes (see pages 220-221).

things. Himmler realized that it would pay to placate Daluege. The opportunity came with the division of available Gestapo resources into two branches: Heydrich was given the Sipo (the Central Security Department of the SS), the Gestapo under Heinrich Müller, the Kripo (Criminal police) under Arthur Nebe, the Frontier police, and the Counter-Espionage police. What was left was given to Daluege whose branch was designated Orpo (Ordnungspoliziei), approximating to the civil police.

For all his steady accumulation of offices, Heydrich remained frustrated by Himmler in one department. The Reichsführer-SS had viewed with alarm Heydrich's incursion into the concentration camps but, characteristically, he lacked the resolution to oppose the latter directly on this. Instead, Himmler circulated on 20 December 1934 a document announcing the creation of a new position. According to a decree dated ten days previously, "the service department Inspector of Concentration Camps will have its head office in the service building of the Gestapo in Berlin, Prinz Albrechtstrasse 8. . .to which it will be directly subordinated. The matter regarding the organization, administration and conduct of the economics of the concentration camps, which has up until now been conducted by the Departments II I D of the Gestapa will be dropped and will be transferred to the new department."

Himmler then went on to state that the office of Inspector of Concentration Camps would be filled by SS Brigadeführer Theodore Eicke, the same unsavoury Alsatian who had been a leading figure in the Röhm purge. Himmler's overall authority, however, was in no doubt, for the same document carried the instruction that all relevant papers were to be sent out under the heading "Prussian Secret State Police" to which was added "Inspector of Concentration Camps."

Although, because of this decree, Heydrich lacked control of these camps, he still had say over those "enemies of the State" who even on bare suspicion of hostility or defiance could be consigned there by the Gestapo. Victims had no legal recourse whatever. Once caught they were lost to the outside world until the Secret State Police decreed otherwise.

As SD chief, headquartered at the Hohenzollern Palace, 102 Wilhelmstrasse, backing on to the Prinz Albrechtstrasse Gestapo building where he had constant access and where Himmler also had offices, Heydrich concentrated on those whom he considered to be the worst potential enemies – those within the Party and the police. For all his insistence on bureaucracy and correct procedure, Heydrich did not hesitate to bend the rules when he chose – shamelessly poaching members of other departments into his SD, and incurring hatred and fear in the process. Besides internal surveillance, in which SD Amt 11 (Inland) worked closely with corresponding departments in the Gestapo, the SD deployed a net of foreign and counter-espionage agents from Office III (Ausland).

Here Heydrich forged a working partnership with an old acquaintance, Admiral Wilhelm Canaris, head of the Abwehr (Military Intelligence). Canaris was a shadowy, enigmatic personality whom Heydrich had first encountered during his naval service. The Abwehr was part of the military which could only mean to Heydrich that it contained its fair share of "reactionaries", men with old ideas and attitudes who would need watching if the Nazi revolution

Kurt Daluege, appointed head of Orpo (the civil police) by Himmler, was to succeed Heydrich in Prague after the latter's assassination in 1942.

Forced labour of political and Jewish prisoners at Sachsenhausen Concentration Camp.

Admiral Wilhelm Canaris (1887-1945) head of the Abwehr (Military Intelligence) from 1935-44. Canaris first encountered Reinhard Heydrich in his Naval service days.

was to succeed. Moreover, the SD and the Abwehr were in the same business and it had to be recognized that the Abwehr was a considerable force within Intelligence. A good working relationship was clearly desirable.

Canaris, although a professed National Socialist, was known to dislike the cruder excesses of the Nazis and certainly had little in common with some of Heydrich's recent recruits. The short and dapper Hessian, SS-Obersturmbann-führer Dr Werner Best, was in a rather different mould. A meeting between he and Canaris was arranged; the latter was agreeably impressed by the lawyer's reasonable and conciliatory manner. At what he deemed the appropriate moment, Best produced what became known as "The Ten Commandments", a seemingly clear division of responsibility between the SD and the Abwehr in matters of espionage.

In essence, the document drew a line between the rival intelligence services of the Wehrmacht and the SS, shielded the Abwehr from interference by the SS, and – most important for Canaris – appeared to establish the Abwehr's predominant rôle in espionage and counter-espionage.

But there were deliberately vague clauses in "The Ten Commandments" that were to become apparent in the years leading up to the outbreak of war. For example, the provisions stated that the Gestapo would be concerned primarily with acts of treason, while the Abwehr would have as its responsibility military espionage in foreign countries. Heydrich and his men would survey foreign diplomats, representatives of the press, businessmen, and suspicious foreigners, but gradually the struggle against *all* enemies of the state, both inside and outside Germany, came, willy-nilly, into Heydrich's purview. Soon Heydrich was carrying out his own surveillance of the Abwehr, tapping its sources of information with the plea that it was his job to keep in the picture both militarily and politically.

At the same time, there were other equally pressing matters requiring Heydrich's attention. Harder to deal with, because they were less tangible than the brown threat of the Army, were the ideological demons of National Socialism – Jews, Freemasons, Jesuits, Bolsheviks. A subordinate with particular interest in these matters was the young Rhinelander Adolf Eichmann, who began his career in the SD before eventual transfer to the Gestapo. Eichmann's hatred of Jews had been fuelled by schoolday experiences. Because of a dark complexion, he had been dubbed "der kleine Jude" (the little Jew) by his classmates.

The Eichmann family had moved to Austria on the death of Adolf's mother. In early April 1932, he had joined the Austrian National Socialist Party and had been sworn in as an SS member. The Austrian police, however, had an eye on him and he thought it expedient to make for Germany where he was soon noticed by Heydrich. Eichmann's first job was virtual drudgery; he was required as a filing clerk to type data on suspects under Nazi surveillance. On his own initiative, he began reading all the material he could find on Freemasons whom, he soon convinced himself, were engaged in a gigantic conspiracy with the Jews to dominate the world.

It was scarcely surprising that so assiduous a student of racial matters – moreover one who was as colourless as he was pedantic and punctilious – should receive the approval of Himmler. Eichmann extended his researches to the appropriate SD offices, working in conjunction with Gestapo Department IIB which had the task of carrying out actual surveillance. When Himmler created a Scientific Museum of Jewish Affairs as an agency of the SD, he appointed the enthusiastic Eichmann to head the project. Whenever he could, Eichmann attended Jewish gatherings, visited the Jewish quarters of many towns and cities, making copious notes and setting up systematic files. With growing confidence, he began to see himself, not simply as an archivist, but as an intelligence agent. One of his proudest endeavours revealed that Hitler's diet cook was one thirty-second Jewish. Eichmann was obsessed with the Jews as violators of pure Aryan womanhood, a preoccupation shared by Heydrich. A law was already in existence forbidding sexual relations between Germans and Jews. The Gestapo had the power to move in and decide whether, in addition, culprits could be taken into Schutzhaft (protective custody).

Adolf Eichmann began his career in the SD before transferring to the Gestapo where he was put in charge of the 'Jewish question.'

An example was served by a report from the Gestapo office at Neustadt of serious violations of the law in Jewish sanatoria, hotels, and relations between guests and German employees. Heydrich directed that each case be examined after the court judgment to determine whether Schutzhaft was appropriate. His directive pronounced: "I request immediately after the conclusion of a case of racial violation in which a man of German blood is sentenced, the Jewess concerned is to be taken into Schutzhaft and this to be reported here [Sicherheitspolizei, Berlin] immediately."

There were other departments of SD Inland to deal in a similar way with Communists, Social Democrats, "reactionaries," and the Church. Indeed, so active did the SD intelligence machine become that its agents inevitably breathed down the neck of Gestapo officials doing similar work but who also possessed the executive powers of arrest and Schutzhaft. The SD, for its part, developed under Himmler and Heydrich into an all-seeing information service which had the standing directive to instruct the Reichsführer-SS, the state leadership, and the leadership of the Party "on the political situation in the Reich and the mood of the population."

The Führer, meanwhile, was looking searchingly at his new Army of seventeen corps and thirty-six divisions. To his taste it was far from being "new" enough. The former messenger-runner and gassed Gefreiter of the trenches of the First World War had never ceased to nurse a deep contempt for those he witheringly labelled die Oberschicht (the upper crust).These were the reactionaries whom he knew remained deeply monarchist and who despised him. A shadowy, mysterious rôle was to be played by the Gestapo Grand Masters in dealing the *coup de grâce* to this last remaining symbol of the old order.

Die Oberschicht since the spring of 1933 had been represented by the three men in command of the German armies: Generalfeldmarschall Werner von Blomberg, Minister of War; Generaloberst Freiherr Werner von Fritsch, Commander-in-Chief of the Army; and Generaloberst Ludwig Beck, Chief of the General Staff. The first two were targeted for removal in an exercise of crude character assassination engineered by Göring and Himmler. Göring in particular loathed Blomberg who was, in military terms, his superior – a fact which Blomberg delighted in rubbing in on every conceivable occasion. Göring was anxious that the Army should form closer links with the Party, the very idea of which was anathema to the military establishment. Göring's distrust and dislike of Blomberg crystallized during 1937 into a desire to become War Minister in Blomberg's place.

All German citizens had to carry identification and could be stopped at any time by either civilian or military police. This photograph shows civilian police checking the identification of a passer-by.

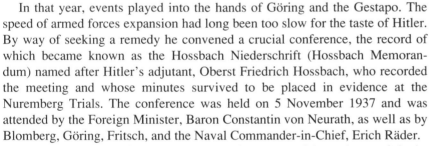

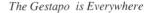

Generalfeldmarschall von Blomberg, Generaloberst von Fritsch, and Naval Commander-in-Chief Erich Räder, at the conference of 5 November 1937.

Ludwig Beck, Chief of the General Staff.

In that year, events played into the hands of Göring and the Gestapo. The speed of armed forces expansion had long been too slow for the taste of Hitler. By way of seeking a remedy he convened a crucial conference, the record of which became known as the Hossbach Niederschrift (Hossbach Memorandum) named after Hitler's adjutant, Oberst Friedrich Hossbach, who recorded the meeting and whose minutes survived to be placed in evidence at the Nuremberg Trials. The conference was held on 5 November 1937 and was attended by the Foreign Minister, Baron Constantin von Neurath, as well as by Blomberg, Göring, Fritsch, and the Naval Commander-in-Chief, Erich Räder.

Hitler expounded his ideas on aggressive war and how these might be achieved. With the exception of an enthusiastic Göring, the ideas were not well received on the grounds that Germany was totally unprepared for war. Blomberg stated a belief that France and Britain would attack at the first sign of German expansion. He was supported by Fritsch who weighed in with an added grumble about the Army being dragged increasingly into Nazi power politics. If Hitler was intending to go to war, it seemed unlikely that he could count on the loyalty of two of his most senior service chiefs. The days of Blomberg and Fritsch were, professionally speaking, numbered from then on. Whatever Blomberg's virtues may have been as a soldier, when it came to power politics of the Nazi stripe he proved to be devastatingly stupid. Certainly he was no match for Göring's ruthlessness and played straight into his hands. In October 1937, Blomberg's fatal lack of judgment led to him approaching Göring for "reassurance on a delicate personal matter." He had embarked on an affair with a lady of the lower orders and not of the military caste, and was anxious for a guarantee that this would not effect his personal position. Göring readily gave such a guarantee – at the same time using the resources of the Gestapo and police contacts to unearth as much as possible about the past of Blomberg's mistress. There were other complications. The lady had a previous lover but Göring "persuaded" him to emigrate to Argentina. Blomberg considered that he had a valuable ally in Göring whose researches were proving extremely fruitful.

The next stage in the drama unfolded on 12 January 1938 with an announcement in the press that Generalfeldmarschall von Blomberg had married Fräulein Erna Gruhn in Berlin. The witnesses to the marriage, which took place in private, were Adolf Hitler and Hermann Göring. It was known that the good-looking Blomberg was a widower and the father of grown-up children, so perhaps it was not surprising that the wedding reports were unaccompanied by comment or photograph. The bridegroom, so salon gossip had it, was known to be vain and to delight in his reputation as a lady's man. As for the bride, beyond the fact that she was of humble origin, little at this stage was known about her. Less than a week after the ceremony, however, Berlin began buzzing with rumours about the young Frau Generalfeldmarschall. Questions were posed and insinuations whispered. Why had the ceremony taken place in "indecent" haste and excessive privacy? Was it true that the bride had not produced the innumerable official documents which the law required, particularly police records or any documents relating to the status of grandparents?

Within two weeks, Göring, armed with what he claimed was serious documentary evidence about Blomberg, had sought an interview with Hitler. The evidence came from the files of Arthur Nebe, head of the Kripo and Heydrich's subordinate. It consisted of an erotic picture of a woman stark naked save for a string of pearls. Scrawled on the back was a name and address – that of Generalfeldmarschall Werner von Blomberg. Göring showed Hitler this "evidence," suggesting to the Führer that it had come as a complete surprise. Hitler, prim on sexual matters, was outraged. With suspiciously convenient timing, Göring also had in his possession a complete police file on Frau Blomberg which stated that other lewd photographs of her existed and had been pedalled by a pimp.

Göring was not slow to press his advantage, asking to be allowed to tell Blomberg personally that the marriage should be annulled. Göring, of course, had another motive for confronting the luckless Blomberg; a request that the latter should resign his office on the grounds of honour. Göring, as we have seen, considered that he was the most deserving candidate for Blomberg's job but was a sufficient realist to know that the War Minister's job was likely to go to Fritsch – a man with whom Göring had clashed bitterly at the earlier conference. Fritsch was a tiresome incubus. What could be done about him?

With a coincidence that seems breathtaking, a fresh scandal proceeded to break within the highest echelons of the Wehrmacht. Its central figure turned out to be Generaloberst Werner Freiherr von Fritsch. Accusations of promiscuous homosexuality against Fritsch emanated from a source that was, to say the least, dubious. A certain Hans Schmidt, a homosexual pimp and blackmailer, had been arrested by the Gestapo. According to the account given by Hans-

Generalfeldmarschall Werner von Blomberg, Minister of War.

Bernd Gisevius, Schmidt was given suitable inducements to unburden himself to the examining officer and "talked about someone called 'von Frisch' or 'von Fritsch.' Who else could that be but that notorious arch-reactionary, the Commander-in-Chief of the Army, whom the SS had been trying vainly to discredit? The Gestapo official wrote down everything the blackmailer told him about this excellent customer, from whom he had extorted thousands of marks."

Schmidt was shown a photograph of the Commander-in-Chief and was asked if this was the same man he claimed he had seen committing a homosexual act at the Wannsee railway station outside Berlin. Schmidt said that Fritsch had paid hush money after taking him to a house in Ferdinandstrasse, Lichterfelde. According to Gisevius, the file of statements was taken by Heydrich to Himmler who in turn took it to Hitler at the Reich Chancellery. The Führer, however, gave the file a mere cursory glance, shuddered at the presence of such "muck," and ordered Himmler to burn it. As it turned out, the Blomberg crisis prevented that happening. The Fritsch file was turned over to Heydrich who obeyed Hitler's instruction to destroy it – after making copies. Nevertheless, Göring intended to keep the Fritsch scandal on the boil. As soon as possible after Göring had told Hitler about Blomberg's wife, the Führer summoned Fritsch and, in the presence of Göring, confronted him with the now terrified Hans Schmidt. Fritsch gave his word of honour that he had never seen Schmidt before, but Hitler seemed unconvinced.

The following day Blomberg resigned as Commander-in-Chief of the Army but to the intense annoyance of Hitler, Himmler, and Heydrich, Fritsch refused to let the matter rest. He insisted upon an official hearing which Hitler could scarcely prevent. On 18 March, the enquiry, held under the presidency of a furious Göring, found Fritsch not guilty. It had been a simple matter for the accused's defence counsel to visit the address in Ferdinandstrasse given in Schmidt's earlier statement. There a cavalry Hauptmann (retired), Achim von Frisch, admitted to both the homosexual act and the payment of the blackmail. Furthermore, Frisch stated, the Gestapo had known all about the matter and had interrogated him nearly two months before.

Fritsch had proved his innocence. And, to his intense embarrassment, Hitler was obliged to write a letter of apology to the exonerated man. No evidence ever came to light suggesting that Hitler knew of the attempts to blacken Blomberg and Fritsch. All the indications are that Göring and Himmler had apparently engineered a crude frame-up. All the same, proving his innocence availed Fritsch nothing. He was not reinstated as Chief of the Army. Hitler was allowed to go ahead with the clear-out of those who opposed him. Fritsch was replaced as Commander-in-Chief by General Walter von Brauchitsch, a First World War artillery officer with a reputation for slavish loyalty to the established power. Hitler went far further. He founded a new organization to crown all the services of the general staff, the Oberkommando der Wehrmacht, (the OKW or High Command of the Armed Forces), and placed at its head the colourless and docile General Wilhelm Keitel.

Thirteen other generals were relieved of their commands, forty-four transferred or retired, and a number of senior officers met with the same fate. Dismissals and replacements extended to the politicians, including Baron

Generaloberst Werner von Fritsch, Commander-in-Chief of the Army.

Constantin von Neurath, the Foreign Minister, who was axed and replaced by a confirmed Nazi, Joachim von Ribbentrop. The coveted War Ministry slipped through Göring's fingers but the rank of Generalfeldmarschall was some consolation since it made him Germany's senior officer.

Fritsch, permitted eventually to return to the army, went to Poland in 1939 and made it his business to get himself killed as soon as possible. His Führer ordered a State military funeral with full honours. In the rain-swept square of the Berlin Lustgarten, Hermann Göring, Hitler's representative, raised his baton in a last salute. Blomberg, retired thankfully into obscurity, was destined to die in 1946 as a prisoner of the Americans. In 1974, veteran journalist Dr Edouard Calic, in a biography of Heydrich, interviewed Blomberg's widow

Where men became beasts of burden. This photograph from SS archives shows prisoners being marched from Mauthausen concentration camp carrying stones on their backs to a new road being built over a mile away.

who claimed that Heydrich had arranged long before the wedding for a set of indecent photographs to be faked and that her husband had known the identity of the retoucher who had done the job. Frau Blomberg went on to allege to Calic that the retoucher, whom Calic identified only by the initials "K M", was an amateur painter who had become an expert at falsification in the workshop organized by Heydrich. Frau Blomberg assumed that he added her head to the body of a woman photographed in pornographic poses.

The fate of two other figures in this squalid drama remain to be recorded. The genuine homosexual Frisch was whisked away in Gestapo custody and vanished into history. The blackmailer, Schmidt, admitted at the enquiry that he had lied to the Gestapo about seeing Fritsch in Wannsee station, but stated he had done so under the threat of death. Göring had assured him, "If you tell the truth now, you have my word that no harm will come to you." By way of keeping his word, Schmidt was turned over to Himmler immediately after the trial and incarcerated in Sachsenhausen concentration camp.

The humiliations inflicted on the generals in February 1938 were never forgotten or forgiven by the Army chiefs. But their views were as leaves in what was soon to be a swirling storm. The course that Hitler had set himself was now immutable. Nazi Germany was on the road to war and the secret police apparatus of Himmler and Heydrich would travel with it.

Hitler takes the salute at his 49th birthday parade on 20 April 1938. The unit passing before him is the SA Standarte Feldherrnhalle, elements of which had recently taken part in the Austrian Anschluss, 13 March 1938.

16
The Gestapo's
Road to
War

One brisk March day in 1938, Colonel Noel Mason-MacFarlane, British military attaché in Berlin, stopped for petrol on the Linz-Melk road, near where it turned off for Vienna. Suddenly a convoy of important looking cars swept past. As Mason-MacFarlane recalled, two Mercedes "filled with SS bristling with tommy-guns and other lethal weapons, came by; they were closely followed by half a dozen super-cars containing Hitler and his immediate entourage and bodyguard."

It was the Führer on his way to Vienna to confirm the details of *Anschluss* – the unification of Germany and Austria. He arrived in the Austrian capital on 13 March, putting up at the Hotel Imperial where he received an hysterical ovation. After that, it was time to get down to business with associates – Himmler, Heydrich, and Daluege. Another arrival from Berlin for *Anschluss* was Walter Schellenberg who arrived in Vienna in the early morning with a company of armed SS men and members of various paramilitary units.

Hitler had long nursed a virulent hatred for his native Austria which he considered had spurned him in his vagabond youth. The task of expressing that hatred in tangible form was given to technicians of dictatorship such as Schellenberg, acting for Himmler, and more immediately Heydrich, whose SD subordinates had long been building up a clandestine network of undercover agents within the German minorities and the Fascist and Nazi groups in Austria and Czechoslovakia.

When German troops entered Austria at dawn on 12 March, it was no spontaneous gesture. Plans had been laid by the SS and Heydrich as long as two years before. Heydrich had envisaged measures that involved a murder and a putsch, the latter to be activated in Vienna. The head of the SD had enlisted the aid of a Munich-based Austrian SS officer, Albert Rodenbücher, who would draw on the talent and resources of SD Ausland to evolve his special sabotage and murder squad.

On 25 July 1934, the Austrian SS, wearing Austrian military uniform, had occupied the government building in Vienna's Ballhausplatz and murdered the diminutive Chancellor, Englebert Dollfuss. This was to be but a prelude to the horrors that followed. After the *Anschluss*, Austrian Nazis were free to roam Vienna. Many of them – barely out of their teens and sporting cartridge belts,

carbines, and Swastikas – directed their activities to baiting Jews including such refinements as forcing them to strap on their wrists the sacred Teflin (prayer bands with the Ten Commandments) and then making them scrub floors.

Such activities had been sanctioned by Dr Ernst Kaltenbrunner, the new head of the Austrian SS and Minister of Police, whose brutality was already notorious and who, furthermore, was rumoured to draw sober breath for precisely four hours each day. Heydrich had effected fastidious distaste for Kaltenbrunner's excesses. He had preferred that the Gestapo behave rather more traditionally – arresting political opponents and decreeing which of those should be sent to concentration camps. This the Gestapo had proceeded to do enthusiastically up to and beyond Hitler's incursion into Austria. The Tagesrapport No. 8 (Day Report No. 8) of 7-8 November 1938 from the Geheime Staats Polizei of the Staatspolizeileitstelle, Vienna, reported: "According to an assessment made at 6.00 pm on 16 November 1938, 6,547 Jews were imprisoned during the Judenaktion in Vienna. Of those 3,700 Jews were sent to Konzentrationslager Dachau. 1,865 were temporarily deferred and 982 were released. Two thousand Jews who were left behind after the inspection of those sent to Dachau were considered by a doctor to be too ill to be of use in a camp."

Heydrich had a most virulent hatred for the Church; persecution of priests who dared to speak out against the Nazis received special attention. Thirty-six

Day of triumph, 17 March 1938. Adolf Hitler stands as conqueror of Austria. A few days earlier, the Führer's Army had poured into Austria, bringing with it agents of the Gestapo and SD. Left to right: Adolf Hitler; Reichsführer-SS Himmler; Army Commander-in-Chief (OKW) Walther von Brauchitsch; General Erhard Milch of the Luftwaffe and (on the extreme right) Arthur Seyss-Inquart, designated Reichsstatthalter (Reich Governor) of Austria.

year-old Graz-born Jesuit priest, Father Johann Lenz, who lived in Kalksburg near Vienna, had publicly attacked "the Führer and the conduct of the state." Assidious Gestapo officials took down the priest's remarks verbatim. These included: "When war comes, Germany will be isolated. Nobody will help her, not even Italy. Hitler is Satan let loose and all excesses take place with his blessing. . .. Crucifixes are thrown out of schools and hospitals. All we can preach is hot air. Austria has been robbed and humiliated and it is a disgrace that all this has happened with so little resistance." This section of the Tages-rapport concluded, "Investigations against Lenz are continuing. We suspect him of spreading these horror stories abroad."

One of the victims of arrest was Kurt von Schuschnigg, the successor to the slaughtered Dollfuss, who was taken to Gestapo headquarters at Vienna's Hotel Metropole. The humiliation heaped on him was closely calculated: first, he was given a broom and ordered to clean both his own cell and the rooms and toilets of his guards. His meals were placed on trays close to the exposed toilet bowl which the guards had previously fouled. An added humiliation was to treat him as if he were a lodger paying for board and food. Since Schuschnigg had little money, he was deliberately kept short of food.

Schuschnigg survived the war in Nazi captivity. So did British-born Oloff de Wett, a future resistant and agent for the French who was to experience characteristically sadistic Gestapo interrogation methods. De Wett had been unlucky enough to be in Austria at the time of the *Anschluss*. He had been picked up for questioning at the Hotel Metropole on suspicion of having con-tacts with anti-Nazis. His Gestapo interrogator, Federmann, impatient for results, would "give a little nod to one of his henchmen standing behind my chair; then thud comes the little rubber mallet in the nape of my neck, applied very dexterously at precisely the same spot just below the base of the skull – making a dull thump in my ears, a quiver behind my knees, and inside the cra-nium an evil hurt that expands and contracts in time with the thuds."

Federmann, a heavy smoker, then played the next phase of his charade, yelling, "Ash-tray!" he "blows assiduously on the burning end of his cigarette till it has a nice pointed red ember, poises the tip over my hand for a second, pulls his lips down at the corners, and pushes the cigarette end slowly onto my skin. . .. When he removes the extinguished stub he brushes away the ash and there is a neat little round leprous white patch, which in half an hour swells into a tiny shiny hemisphere. When Mr Federmann has three of these in a row they look not unlike three pinkish-yellow peas, till he hits them with a ruler, when they burst and the back of my hand is smeared with wetness from the fluid inside them."

Under *Anschluss*, Austria became a "province of the German Reich." Vienna became just another provincial administrative centre stripped of its heritage and its wealth. Those Jews not given the task of scrubbing the pave-ments or cleaning out the gutters, managed, by the time war broke out, to buy their freedom to emigrate by handing over all they owned to the Nazis.

Adolf Hitler, who had added seven million subjects to the Reich by his annexation of Austria had also gained a strategic position of immense value and was ready for further adventures. In Vienna he possessed a gateway to southeast Europe; the ease with which he had achieved *Anschluss* encouraged

him to proceed with his plans against Czechoslovakia, a country created in 1918-1919 out of former Austrian territories but plagued from its formation by problems with its minorities, one of the most clamorous of whom were the Sudeten Germans in the area of Bohemia adjoining Germany.

Hitler had laid his plans as early as 1934, following the creation of the Deutsche Heimat Front, (German Home front), by a pro-Nazi German-Czech gymnastic instructor named Konrad Henlein who had demanded autonomy for the Sudeten Germans within the framework of the Czech state. The Führer was determined to play on Sudeten feelings to eliminate the Czechoslovak state, announcing to the Reichstag in February 1938 that the Sudeten Germans could depend on the Third Reich to defend them against their Czech "oppressors."

Two western democracies, France and Britain, became concerned. The British Prime Minister, Neville Chamberlain, made three visits to Germany to plead with Hitler not to resort to armed aggression. On the third visit, in the ancient Baroque city of Munich, he went literally to beg for peace and put an end to all talk of war. Chamberlain, along with Edouard Daladier of France, and Hitler's fellow dictator Benito Mussolini, met Hitler in Munich on 29 September. Representatives of Czechoslovakia and the Soviet Union were excluded from the ensuing conference and the signing of the fateful Munich agreement which directed that Czechoslovakia was to begin the surrender of the Sudetenland.

Himmler and Kaltenbrunner visit Mauthausen concentration camp, summer 1942. The SS officer, centre, is Franz Ziereis, the camp commandant, later shot by a US Army patrol while resisting capture.

The democracies of the west were shown to be helpless. Chamberlain and Daladier, aware that their countries lagged far behind Germany in military readiness, believed they had no alternative but to accept Hitler's terms. Chamberlain, soon to go down in history as the arch-appeaser, held that he had achieved a statesmanlike settlement for world peace. Indeed, there were appeasers in England who believed that a reasonable deal had been struck.

For the Czechs, any hint of reasonable treatment was brief. With the ink barely dry on the signatures to the Munich agreement, the Deutsche Heimat Front was placed under the orders of Heinrich Himmler. It was renamed Sudetendeutsche Partei (Sudeten German Party) and "assigned police tasks, like the rest of the police, with the agreement of the Reichsführer-SS."

The campaign switched to Bohemia and Moravia. Here, the Nazi student organization of the Sudeten Germans, controlled by the SS and Gestapo, had much to do. They were in place to suppress any unseemly opposition when, at dawn on 15 March 1939, German troops poured into what remained of Czechoslovakia. The stage management was impressive. Hitler with his entourage and SS guards, bypassing the advancing Wehrmacht columns, raced through the night over icy roads to be the first to arrive as conquerors at Hradcany Castle, ancient seat of the kings of Bohemia.

For the people of Prague, life, on the surface at least, seemed normal. Shops opened at eight in the morning and the cafés carried on with their brisk early trade. Even the newspaper booths went on selling foreign newspapers. But everywhere there was the sight of black-uniformed SS and high-powered cars stuffed with officers and painted Swastika flags. Soon the Swastika standards and field-grey troops proliferated. From the castle of Hradcany, Hitler pro-

15 March 1939, Hitler's troops march into Czechoslovakia. In this photograph the Swastika is carried over the Charles Bridge in Prague. Hradcany Castle is on the hill in the background.

claimed the creation of the Protectorate of Bohemia and Moravia, incorporated within the German Reich. Constantin von Neurath, considered to be in Nazi terms a "moderate", was named Protector. Konrad Henlein received the post of Head of the Civil Administration.

Real power, however, was vested in SS-Gruppenführer Karl Hermann Frank who, within a few years, was to involve the Gestapo in one of the most notorious atrocities of the Second World War. Reinhard Heydrich, too, had been busy. Behind the columns had come the *Einsatzgruppen,* the newly formed SS Special Action Groups, which were the creation of Heydrich and Himmler and which had SD and Gestapo operatives as components. An *Einsatzgruppe*, with its individual detachments called *Einsatzkommandos*, developed into a killer squad with the function of rounding up Jews and other dissidents. A draft document prepared for the SD at the time of the Czech incursion referred to SD and Gestapo rôles within an *Einsatzgruppe*: "The SD follows, wherever possible, directly behind the advancing troops and fulfils duties similar to those in the Reich, which are the security of political life and at the same time the security as far as possible of all enterprises necessary to the national economy and so, also, of the war economy."

"Enemies of the State."
Children from the
Ghetto.

The document went on to outline how the occupied territory was to be divided up "so that members of the SD intended for employment in Czechoslovakia can be immediately assigned to their tasks. The groups intended for Einsatz from the Reich will be collected in a sub-sector corresponding to their intended sphere of activity. . .. Measures in the occupied regions are carried out under the guidance and under the leadership of the senior officer of the SD. Gestapo officials are assigned to certain operations staffs. It is important that, as far as possible, similar preparations, training, and use of materials, should be conducted in the Gestapo as in the SD."

The dismemberment of Czechoslovakia had proved by no means the only preoccupation. At home in Germany, the Jews remained a stubborn problem. One manifestation of this exploded quite literally out of a gun barrel. The individual with his finger on the trigger was an obscure seventeen year old German Jewish refugee teenager whose name was Herschel Grynszpan.

Towards the end of the previous October, Heydrich had ordered the arrest of 17,000 Polish Jews of whom the Reich had wanted to be rid. Some 60,000 Jews had originally migrated to Germany from Poland at the end of the First World War and had generally prospered. When the Nazis announced their intention to deport these Jews back to Poland that country deprived them of their citizenship and closed the border to them. Thousands of Jews became stranded without shelter and without food in the border area between the two countries.

Heydrich reacted by herding them into railway wagons for shipment across the frontier. It was the first mass deportation of Jews from the Third Reich; the victims were soon staring into the machine guns of Polish troops. Among those left wandering between the German and Polish no man's land was Zindel Grynszpan, a Polish tailor from Hanover, whose possessions had been confiscated. He and his fellow refugees were penniless, starving, soaked to the skin, and freezing.

News of his father's plight reached Zindel's teenage son in Paris. On 7 November 1938, the young Grynszpan, armed with a revolver, called at the

German Embassy, apparently intent to wreak his revenge on the Ambassador, Count Johannes von Welczeck. Grynszpan's enquiry for the Ambassador was answered by a Third Secretary, Ernst vom Rath. Grynszpan shot him five times. There was, it so happened, a sad irony in this because vom Rath was a minor official known to be an avowed anti-Nazi under surveillance by the Gestapo.

The full implications of Grynszpan's crime were not at first apparent to those who heard it announced over the radio. Certainly, its significance did not strike Joe Rose, a Jewish commercial artist living in Sudenburg near Magdeburg. In any case, Rose was preoccupied in preparing for his imminent wedding.

He later recalled, "When a good friend, Nosseck, who owned a menswear shop, offered me the job of painting his name on the front of his shop I certainly didn't connect it with the murder of vom Rath. It seemed that the local Gestapo was anxious to mark all Jewish property and had hit on this particular method. The Gestapo's orders had been precise: all Jewish shopkeepers were not to be identified as Jews as such, but were to have their names painted on their properties at eye level in identical lettering twelve centimetres high by one centimetre wide.

"I was known to be the only artist in the Jewish community who could do this particular form of shop front painting. I charged Nosseck a nominal sum because it tickled me that the fee should come indirectly through the Gestapo. Actually, it turned out to be remarkably lucrative. Other shopkeepers who had received the same orders from the local Gestapo came to me and I was overwhelmed with work."

The instructions did not strike Rose and his fellow Jews as particularly ominous. They considered that the painting instructions simply represented a convenient way for the Nazis to identify Jewish property. The real motive was in fact far more sinister. Plans were already in place for the most vicious anti-Jewish pogrom yet experienced in Nazi Germany.

Reich Minister of Propaganda Joseph Goebbels who, of course, had access to a progressively compliant Press, had, on 8 November, travelled to Munich for the annual commemoration of the 1923 Bierkeller putsch. The Party veterans were at their evening meal when a telegram announced that vom Rath had died of his wounds that afternoon. Goebbels, the born publicist, seized his opportunity, launching into an anti-Jewish diatribe, and claiming that the murder of vom Rath was obviously a planned conspiracy. The German people, he fulminated, would rise in bloody vengeance.

Violence there certainly was but it was committed by the Nazis. Germany burst into flames with a barbarism which has gone down in history as Kristallnacht (Night of the Broken Glass). Throughout the Reich, armed SA and SS men broke into Jewish homes, smashing furniture, throwing belongings into the street, looting money and valuables, and raping women and girls as young as thirteen before the eyes of their families. The slightest sign of resistance was suppressed brutally. Jews were plunged into ice-cold rivers and, when they tried to claw their way out, were bombarded with bricks and stones. Synagogues were put to the torch at the same time as the assault was sustained against Jewish stores. To Joe Rose, his sign painting commissions suddenly made sense. Some 7,500 by now easily identified Jewish shops throughout the Reich were destroyed and department stores demolished.

After the war, surviving members of the Gestapo claimed that they had known nothing of the excesses of Kristallnacht until they were well advanced. Heydrich, for example, is said to have assured his wife that he was taken completely by surprise when a synagogue went up in flames close by the Hotel Vier Jahreszeiten (Four Seasons Hotel) in Munich where he was staying. He and Werner Best were still puzzling over the cause of the synagogue blaze when they were brought news that one of Goebbels' propaganda agencies had informed the Gestapo that "pogroms against the Jews had been ordered in which the Gestapo was not allowed to interfere." What is certain is that the Gestapo did undertake a rôle in Kristallnacht and that the uprising against the Jews was in no way spontaneous. One of the key messages despatched that night came from Heinrich Müller at the Gestapa, Berlin, and had been transmitted at midnight on 9 November marked "IMMEDIATE and by the quickest route – SECRET!" It read in part:

"1) Actions against Jews, especially against their synagogues, will take place throughout the Reich shortly. They are not to be interfered with; however, liaison is to be effected with the Ordnungspolizei to ensure that looting and other excesses are suppressed.

"2) So far as important archive material exists in synagogues this is to be secured by immediate measures.

"3) Preparations are to be made for the arrest of about 20,000 to 30,000 Jews in the Reich. Above all, well-to-do Jews are to be selected. Detailed instructions will follow in the course of the night."

Reich Minister for Propaganda Joseph Goebbels used the death of vom Rath to incite the German people to "rise in bloody vengeance" against the Jews

Kristallnacht, 10 November 1938. Throughout the Reich, armed SS and SA raided Jewish shops and homes. Synagogues, pictured here, were vandalized or put to the torch.

Those detailed instructions were flashed to, among other places, Magdeburg. Joe Rose recalls, "At 6:00 a.m. the next morning – the day after I was married, as it happened – two men whom I knew from past meetings to be Gestapo came for me. They were perfectly polite and beyond asking, 'Who is this woman?' showed no interest whatever in my wife, Regina. Clearly, they had been told only to arrest the men."

There was, however, a way by which the release could be secured for the male Jews who had been seized by the Gestapo: this was legalized theft by the Nazis of literally everything the Jewish community possessed. Jewish businesses were sold "to Aryan hands" and silver and jewellery appropriated. In a further bid to swell the coffers of the State, the Jews were subjected, collectively, to a fine of one billion marks, together with the cost of the destruction of their own property. Insurance monies due were confiscated. Such brutally acquired wealth was heaven-sent for the badly overstretched Reich economy. Just about the only terror the Jews did not suffer at this point were deportations and annihilation in concentration camps. All that lay in the future, but Jewish communities had received what amounted to a final warning. From now on, there could be no security of tenure.

Hitler, fulminating against those who condemned the excesses of Kristallnacht, claimed that this proved the power and scope of "the Jewish world conspiracy." Morover, he was thinking in far broader terms than issuing a sharp warning to Jews. He was intent on continuing his programme of conquest, by diplomatic means if that were possible, but by force if it were not. In the wake of the acquisition of Czechoslovakia, the British Prime Minister Neville Chamberlain, recognized that the Führer's assurances that the Sudetenland had been his last territorial demand in Europe and that he "wanted no Czechs" were plain lies. In London, Chamberlain posed the question, "Is this the last attack upon a small State or is it to be followed by others?" A glance at the map which revealed the new positions of the Wehrmacht in Slovakia or an assessment of the bloodless incursions into Austria and Czechoslovakia left little doubt as to whom would be the next object of German attentions.

When it came to Poland, many aspects of the scenario were painfully familiar. There was the appeal to nationalist sentiments. There was great stress on "the bleeding frontiers of the east," a melodramatic reference to the detested Versailles treaty which, after the First World War, had attempted to re-create the old Kingdom of Poland. Danzig (Gdansk), the ancient seaport on the Baltic at the mouth of the Vistula, was the major point of contention. Historically, it was a Germanic Port, but the Versailles diktat attempted to solve its anomalous position by making it a de-militarized Free City. A strip of land with a coast line was given to Poland to assure access to the sea, the so-called "Polish Corridor." Needless to say, Hitler was soon demanding the return of Danzig. Nazi bellicosity was accompanied by references in propaganda to sub-human Slavic racial degenerates, a chorus of abuse in which Himmler was not slow to join.

The Führer greets German students in Prague. Escorting him are Himmler and Heydrich.

Post Card: „The thorn in the flesh."
Carte Postale: „L'écharde dans la chair."
Postkarte: „Pfahl im Fleisch."

The Polish Corridor is the thorn in the flesh of Germany.

Le Corridor Polonais est l'écharde dans la chair de l'Allemagne.

Der Polnische Korridor ist der Pfahl im Fleische Deutschlands.

What would they say? — Was würden sie sagen?

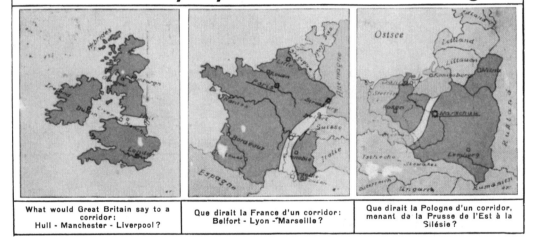

| What would Great Britain say to a corridor: Hull - Manchester - Liverpool? | Que dirait la France d'un corridor: Belfort - Lyon -'Marseille? | Que dirait la Pologne d'un corridor, menant da la Prusse de l'Est à la Silésie? |

Nazi propaganda. The Polish Corridor, a legacy from the hated Versailles Treaty.

Hitler opted for invasion but, before this could be carried out some pretext was necessary. The ostensible justification for raping Poland – a faking of frontier incidents – was conceived in the crudest melodramatic terms and was the work of Himmler and Heydrich for the SD and Müller for the Gestapo – the first major excursion by the Gestapo into the international field.

Operation Himmler was launched by Heydrich summoning to Prinz Albrechtstrasse one of his highly trusted associates, a veteran street brawler from Kiel named Alfred Helmuth Naujocks. Naujocks had joined the SD in 1934 and held the rank of Sturmbannführer. Five years later, Naujocks had become the head of a sub-section of Section III of SD Ausland, concerned, under the control of SS Oberführer Heinz Jost, with the fabrication of documents for agents working abroad.

The events leading to the invasion of Poland were outlined by Naujocks at the Nuremberg trials after the war. His task, he was told by Heydrich, was to

make a staged attack on the German radio station at Gleiwitz in upper Silesia, near the Polish border. The incident had to appear to be an act of aggression committed against the station by a force of Poles. Documentary "proof" of Polish aggression would be made available, along with German convicts decked out in Polish uniforms. The latter were to capture the transmitter and hold it until a Polish-speaking German was able to broadcast a violent denunciation which Heydrich had prepared.

Uniforms, weapons, identity cards, and even Polish cigarettes were provided by the SD and the Abwehr of Admiral Canaris. The rôle of the Gestapo emerged when Naujocks was ordered to Oppeln, a small Silesian town forty miles north of Gleiwitz. There, Heinrich Müller and SS-Oberführer Herbert Mehlhorn explained that the Gestapo had been ordered by Heydrich to provide a commodity referred to as "Konserven" (Canned Goods) The commodity in question turned out to be a dozen men who were under sentence of death in

The Polish border, 1939.

concentration camps but had been prized out by Müller. At Nuremberg, Naujocks testified: "Müller declared that he had twelve or thirteen condemned criminals who would be dressed in Polish uniforms and left for dead on the spot to show that they had been killed in the course of the attack. To this end they had to be given fatal injections by a doctor in Heydrich's service. Later they would also be given genuine wounds inflicted by firearms. After the incident members of the foreign Press and other persons were to be taken to the spot. A police report would then be made. Müller told me that he had an order from Heydrich telling him to put one of these criminals at my disposal for the Gleiwitz action."

The criminal in question, a Pole, was anaesthetized and brought to the radio station where he was then shot. The body was photographed on the spot for the benefit of the Press. The attack on the station then went ahead. A Polish-speaking member of Naujocks' team broke into a broadcast in accented German: "This is the Polish rebel force. Radio station Gleiwitz is in our hands. The hour of freedom has struck!"

Müller had pretended to his Polish-uniformed prisoners in "Canned Goods" that they were taking part in a film and that, in exchange for their patriotic participation in the action, they would be pardoned and set free. The radio station secured, Naujocks and his men promptly retired. The dead bodies of the conscript "actors" were left on the scene. They were not the only witnesses to be disposed of, which goes some way to explaining why details of the affair did not leak out. All participating members of the SD who had been involved, with the exception of the fortunate Naujocks, were liquidated.

On the day following the Gleiwitz action, 1 September 1939, when German troops had already been advancing since dawn into Polish territory, Hitler, speaking in the Kroll Opera House, mentioned an attack "by regular Polish troops." The Army parroted that it had been forced to take action because of Polish behaviour. The entire affair was a source of immense satisfaction to Himmler, Heydrich, and Müller. It had demonstrated above all what a superbly organized machine was represented by the various police offshoots of the SS. There was highly successful co-operation between the SD and the Gestapo, as well as Canaris' Abwehr, which came under Wehrmacht control.

Operation Himmler far from slaked the thirst of the Gestapo. It sharpened its operatives for even more audacious acts to come.

The Gestapo
— Campaign in the —
East

Within three days of the outbreak of war, German troops sliced into Poland; by 8 September tanks rumbled through the suburbs of Warsaw. Hitler transferred his headquarters to a point nearer the front. Three special trains crossed the Polish frontier near Katowice, in the area of Gleiwitz, carrying the entourage of Hitler, Göring, and Himmler – the latter in his special train, Sonderzug Heinrich.

Defeated Poland was divided into four main administrative districts, each controlled by a Party-appointed Kommissa. The whole southeast was designated General Gouvernement of the Occupied Territories, under the authority of a Governor General, Hans Frank.

Police power, it was made clear very early on, would be assigned to the representatives of Himmler and Heydrich. The *Einsatzgruppen,* who had already proved such a baleful presence behind the advancing Nazi columns in Czechoslovakia, were on that occasion withdrawn to make way for the Sipo. But in Poland things were to be different. Here, detachments of the Sipo, composed of the Gestapo and the SD, were formed into five *Einsatzgruppen* with their subsidiary *Einsatzkommandos.*

They went about their work with relish; they rounded up Jews, aristocrats, priests, and the professional classes in every community they entered. Atrocities became commonplace. On 27 October, Father Pawlowski, the 70-year-old parish priest of Chocz, in the Warthegau District of Western Poland, was arrested by the Gestapo and charged with illegal possession of arms. In fact, the only weapons he possessed were sporting guns for partridge shooting. After his face had been beaten so badly as to be unrecognizable, the priest was taken to the nearby town of Kalisz where an execution post was erected in the main square. There, the Gestapo forced local Jews to bind him to the post, to unbind him after he had been shot, and then to kiss his feet before burying him in the Jewish cemetery.

The SS did most but not all of the brutal work: on hand were fanatical ethnic civilian Germans, formerly a minority in the Polish state, who, formed into "self-protection" formations, were persuaded that they had long-standing scores to settle with the Poles. Heydrich made scant attempt to conceal his aims. On 21 September, he addressed SD and Security Police departmental

Opposite: Einsatzgruppe *execution in Poland, 1939.*

chiefs and *Einsatzgruppen* commanders, proclaiming that the Polish nation was to be wiped off the map and, through liquidation, deprived of its leaders and educated classes.

In a document headed "The Tasks of the Secret State Police in War," Heydrich declared that these tasks were an extension of the peacetime rôle – "to investigate and fight against all activities which might endanger the total security of the State." This applied particularly to the "kommandos of the State Police" who "with the advance of the German army, have the responsibility to restore and uphold security and order in the rear lines. The tasks of the kommando in the occupied areas of the enemy are the same as that of the State Police at home."

For Himmler and Heydrich, the inclusion of members of the Gestapo in the *Einsatzgruppen* strengths was an especially gratifying extension of power. But it created its own problems. The Nazi sphere of influence was now well out-

Right: *Himmler and Hitler at the front.*

100

side the borders of the Reich. It had become necessary to regroup the entire security machine of State and Party under one commodious umbrella.

This was brought about in two stages. A decree of 23 June 1938, had laid down that all Security Police (Gestapo and Kripo) personnel must be enrolled in the SS. The Gestapo, a State organization, was brought under the control of the SD, a Party organization, but for all practical purposes the two were merged. The final stage of the regrouping was reached by a further decree of 29 September 1939, after Warsaw had fallen. All the existing police forces – including the Gestapo, Kripo and the SD – were to come under a single umbrella organization designated the Reichssicherheitshauptamt (RSHA: Reich Central Security Office), under Heydrich. The RSHA would serve as a central office for both the Reich leadership of the SS and the Reich Ministry of the Interior. Himmler's decree sanctioning the RSHA brought into being a monstrous bureaucracy of terror. The RSHA, with its seat at No 8 Prinz Albrechtstrasse, in the premises occupied by the Gestapo, comprised six (later seven) main divisions or offices or services (Amt, plural Ämter) (see diagram, page 228). Heydrich revelled in Himmler's nickname for him of Triebfeder (Spring); power was a commodity not simply to be exercised and enjoyed but to be demonstrated on all possible occasions. A circular, issued by Heydrich on 18 May 1940, outlined a rigid syllabus for promising entrants to the RSHA. The entrant, product of the SS school or university with a law degree, was required to spend four months with the Kripo learning the scientific elements of police work. This would be followed by three months each with the SD and Gestapo with eventual transfer, based on potential and merit, to one of the seven Ämter.

The Gestapo was designated Amt IV of the RSHA, under Heinrich Müller who was promoted SS-Brigadeführer. Amt IV was to undergo many internal transformations, but its organization and specific powers were to remain broadly the same until the collapse of the Third Reich. Amt IV was in turn to be divided into eight sub-divisions, dealing with such enemies as Marxists, "reactionaries," and liberals. Section IVB, for example. dealt with the political activity of religious sects, but more notorious was its sub-group, IVB4, which was entrusted eventually with the "final solution" of the Jewish problem under the direction of Adolf Eichmann.

Heydrich (left) *with Daluege.*

Executive unity for SD and Security Police offices might well have been the dream of Heydrich, but inevitably Himmler, forever concealing his own ambitions behind bespectacled impassivity, was loathe to relinquish his empire in its entirety. The Reichsführer-SS, so often pictured as the eternal bureaucrat with veins of ice, was nevertheless prone to fears in the small hours: fears that somehow a single authority would, of itself, gain enough power to threaten his supremacy. Himmler's way of neutralizing his fears was to block Heydrich from control of the Ordnungspolizei, which remained firmly under Kurt Daluege whom Heydrich loathed and for whose gifts he had scant respect. Indeed, the RSHA chief saddled Daluege with the scathing nickname of "Dummi-Dummi." Neither did Heydrich gain control of the ethnic German formations or the Totenkopf police reinforcement units, which were to play such a major rôle in the further enslavement of the Poles.

As the Reich expanded, the intricate net of competing authorities became, if anything, even more complex. The servants of the elephantine Gestapo hacked their way through a monstrous bureaucratic maze, installing themselves as the agents of repression and terror, wherever Hitler was master. Europe had become a vassal state; only England remained unsubdued. By the end of September 1940, the special Jewish section of the Gestapo within the RSHA was in place under Eichmann's ultimate control from Berlin. But already Hitler's thoughts were turning east, towards the Soviet Union.

On 18 December 1940, acting on the instructions of the Führer, Generalleutnant Alfred Jodl, Chief of Operations, ordered his deputy, Generalmajor Walther Warlimont, to prepare a general plan for operations against Soviet Russia by way of a Blitzkrieg campaign to be commenced on 15 May 1941. The object of the operation was, initially, the destruction of the Soviet Army in western Russia by a series of envelopments, to be followed by the establishment of a defence line from Archangel to the Volga River.

In fact, *Fall Barbarossa* (Operation Barbarossa) was launched at 4:11a.m. on 22 June. Nineteen panzer and fourteen motorized divisions spearheaded the German attack. Hitler's rhetoric was once again to the fore, ("The world will hold its breath!"), but the truth was that the strength of German armour totalled no more than 3,550 tanks against (if the Soviet figures are to be believed) a total of 24,000 Russian tanks, of which half were in western Russia. Nevertheless, early German successes were as chilling as they were impressive. Within hours, German troops were in control of every bridge across the border rivers from the Baltic Sea to the Carpathian mountains. German armour raced east with the Luftwaffe destroying many Russian aircraft on the ground.

Barbarossa, however, was no mere military adventure. to be thought of in terms of logistics, strategy, and tactics. Himmler, in an address to Waffen-SS early in the struggle, outlined the real nature of the campaign by proclaiming, "Here in this struggle, stands National Socialism: an ideology based on the value of our Germanic Nordic blood." In a later speech, the rhetoric was replaced by Himmler with the brutal declaration, "We must make sure that in the clearing of territories in the Ukraine no human, no animal, not an acre of agricultural land, not a line of railway remains, that no house is left standing, that no mining installation can be used, that there are no wells that are not poisoned. The opposition must find a totally destroyed and burnt out land."

In this work, the *Einsatzgruppen* were to be his willing servants. For their work in the Soviet Union, four *Einsatzgruppen*, each with a strength of between 1,000 and 1,200 were created. Their spheres of operation were: Group A, the Baltic States; Group B, Smolensk and Moscow; Group C, the Kiev region; Group D, southern Ukraine. Each *Einsatzgruppe* was, as in Poland, divided into a number of *Einsatzkommandos*, the staff of which were a composite of various skills. Out of around 1,000 men, there might well be some 350 Waffen-SS members, 150 drivers and mechanics, 100 members of the Gestapo, eighty auxiliary policemen, 130 of the Ordnungspolizei, forty or fifty from the Kripo, and thirty to thirty-five from the SD. Nor was this the entire strength. Each *Einsatzgruppe* had its own Executive, an office on the move, with interpreters, radio operators, teletypists, office clerks, and female staff. Headquarters personnel were drawn from the Gestapo, the Kripo, and the SD.

Their tasks were outlined by Heydrich to the Chiefs of the Sipo (comprising Gestapo and Kripo) and SD in a circular from Berlin dated 2 July 1941. This

Arthur Nebe, Head of the Criminal Police (Kripo), had previously commanded one of the Einsatzgruppen *in Russia. Nebe fell under suspicion following the July Bomb Plot in 1944 and was among those arrested and executed.*

Himmler caught in a rare off-guard moment as he is driven around the Ghetto at Terezin, a few miles outside Prague.

document, after stating that "the immediate goal is the security-police pacification of the newly occupied areas" and that "all those search and execution measures that contribute to the political pacification of the occupied areas are to be undertaken," went on to be a great deal more specific in the document's Clause 4: "Executions. To be executed are all functionaries of the Comintern (as are the Communist professional politicians in general); the senior, middle-ranking and radical low-ranking functionaries of the Party, the Central Committees, the District and Area Committees; other radical elements, (saboteurs, propagandists, snipers, assassins, agitators, etc.); Jews in Party and state posts."

Confirmation that Heydrich's orders were effectively carried out was provided by a former *Einsatzgruppe* member, Andreas vom Amburger, who, in Allied captivity after the war, revealed, "On 18 July 1941, I was assigned to the staff of *Einsatzgruppe B* of the Security Police and the SD. I had signed up for service in Russia because I could speak Russian, without knowing very much about the assignments of the *Einsatzkommandos*. In Minsk, I reported to the head of the *Einsatzgruppe*, SS-Brigadeführer und Generalmajor der Polizei Arthur Nebe. . ... The annihilation of the Jews was, as was repeatedly emphasized, an order of the Führer. One could not refuse to take part. The Reichsführer-SS threatened punishment and brought anyone who tried to get out of fulfilling this duty before an SS and police court."

Amburger added that the psychological effect on those who had to carry out the executions was so great that Nebe wanted to devise a way of getting rid of the Jews that would not be so hard on his men. "He began experimenting with killing peopie (in one case, eighty inhabitants of a lunatic asylum) with exhaust gas from his car, an eight cylinder Horch." Nebe went about the task with an enthusiasm that he was incapable of keeping to himself. He was a keen amateur film maker: after the war, footage showing a gas chamber worked by the exhaust gas of a lorry were found in his Berlin apartment.

Minsk, the capital of Belorussia, became a notorious dumping ground and killing centre for German Jews; the city was said to have a Jewish population of more than 50,000 and, as such, commanded Himmler's keen personal interest. On a visit, Himmler told Nebe that he wished to witness a liquidation; the latter obligingly supplied 100 alleged partisans from the city jail; all but two were men.

According to one account, Himmler ordered Nebe to seduce the two women before shooting them: a useful way of obtaining information about the activities of partisans. *Einsatzkommando* 8 and Police Battalion 9 of *Einsatzgruppe* B led the victims towards a previously prepared ditch. They were forced to climb in and to lie face down. The next step was for the police unit to fire a salvo from above. After the completion of each killing round, the bodies were covered with earth and the next group brought forward for the process to be repeated. The spectacle discomforted Himmler who had no stomach for facing the results of his own orders. SS-Gruppenführer Erich von dem Bach-Zelewski, who had been designated the specific task of subduing partisans, pressed Himmler to reserve any momentary sympathy, not for the victims, but for the executioners who had to carry out such work.

The so-called "Incident Reports" on the activities of the *Einsatzgruppen* consisted of daily radio reports; written ones were despatched by courier back to RSHA headquarters. Instructions to the killing units were also sent by Himmler and Heydrich. Activities in the Soviet Union and the Baltic states represent an appalling catalogue of mass murder, all of it recorded with chilling detachment.

One of the earliest actions happened along the Soviet frontier in the days following the initial invasion. At the village of Virbalis, the *Einsatzgruppen* forced Jews to lie down along five kilometres of an anti-tank trench and killed them with machine-gun fire. The process was repeated seven times. "Only the children were not shot. They were caught by the legs, their heads hit against stones, and they were thereupon buried alive."

A report on 19 December 1941 from *Einsatzgruppe* B states: "In checks on the exit roads from Ogilev carried out with the assistance of the regular police a total of 135 people, most of them Jews, were seized. 127 people were shot." Another report, from Lithuania, stated that "about 500 Jews, among other saboteurs, are currently being liquidated every day." The licence given to the *Einsatzgruppen* for their programme of slaughter appeared to have no limits. Thus SS Oberführer Dr Otto Rasch, Commander of *Einsatzgruppe* C from Kiev, reported more than 51,000 executions: "The executions carried out by the squads are directed against the following: political functionaries, plunderers and saboteurs; active Communists and political ideology-mongers; Jews who have wormed their way out of prison camps by giving false statements; agents and informers of the NKVD; persons who have given false information and influenced witnesses in order to have ethnic Germans deported; Jewish sadism and lust for revenge; undesirable elements, anti-social persons, partisans. . .the danger of infection and contagion; members of Russian guerrilla gangs, irregular volunteers, the suppliers of Russian gangs with provisions, insurgents and agitators, degenerate youth."

Gruppenführer Otto Ohlendorf, Chief of an Einsatzgruppe, *pleads not guilty during his trial at Nuremberg in 1947.*

Dr Otto Ohlendorf, the Chief of SD Inland and of *Einsatzgruppe* D, was another enthusiastic killer whose *Einsatzkommando* 12 despatched around 8,000 Jews in Nikolayev, a city of about 100,000. According to some accounts, Himmler was so satisfied with this one achievement, that he promoted Ohlendorf to the rank of Oberführer on the spot.

During his trial at Nuremberg, Ohlendorf admitted readily that he had received reports of executions by his subordinates, but pleaded justification on ethical grounds, citing historical precedents such as the killing of gypsies in the Thirty Years' War. Such human feelings as he did exhibit were reserved strictly for his own side. "I never permitted the shooting of individuals, but ordered that several of the men should shoot at the same time in order avoid direct personal responsibility. Other group leaders demanded that the victims lie down flat on the ground to be shot through the nape of the neck. I did not approve of these methods because both for the victims and for those who carried out the executions, it was, psychologically, an immense burden to bear."

Ohlendorf went on to say that later victims were despatched in gas vans, but he complained that only fifteen to twenty could be put to death at one time until ovens were brought into use. He also claimed that some of the figures of deaths had been inflated deliberately by their compilers in order to curry favour with the chiefs of the RSHA. Even allowing for this, though, it was calculated that not less than 300,000 Jews were murdered in the first year of the German invasion into Russia alone, although more recent research in Russian archives has led some to believe that previous estimates of the overall figure have been too low.

With the collapse of the Soviet Union in 1991, some twenty miles of shelves containing the files of the Soviet Extraordinary Commission for German Fascist Crimes, locked away in the time of Stalin, are being made available. Shmuel Krakowski of the Yad Vashem Memorial in Israel, speaking at a conference on the Holocaust held in London said, "Indications are that previous figures for deaths may have to be increased by a quarter of a million – an extra 25,000 Jews from the Ukraine and Belorussia alone may have been murdered." Certain historians have made much of the fact that there were no written orders by Hitler to establish the genocide policy and that therefore he cannot be held responsible for it. Indeed, Adolf Eichmann at his trial said that he had never seen such an order. But Eichmann, who concealed nothing and had no reason to lie, told the court that he had no doubt that he was acting on Hitler's personal authority. "All I know is that Heydrich told me, 'The Führer ordered the physical extermination of the Jews.' "

With or without the sanction of the supreme authority, the SD went ahead to assume still more awesome powers, even encroaching on the preserves of the Army on the treatment of prisoners of war. Shortly after the beginning of the Russian campaign an agreement was reached between the OKW (Oberkommando der Wehrmacht) and the SD for the latter to "screen Russian prisoners." A document was drawn up to serve as "Guidelines for the selection of civilians and suspect prisoners of war of the Eastern campaign who are in the occupied territories." The Army was told it "must divest itself forthwith of all those elements who could be viewed as having Bolshevik motives. . .. At the present time, instructions relating to the treatment of prisoners of war are

Opposite page: Within weeks of the German entry into Poland, Einsatzgruppen *were rounding up Jews, aristocrats, priests, and the professional classes. Men and women were stripped naked and kicked through the streets as the Nazis entered the towns and villages. Thousands were sent to concentration camps such as Mauthausen or were executed out of hand.*

Adolf Eichmann seen here relaxing with his small son. His loathing of Jews began as a schoolboy when he was nicknamed the "little Jew." He joined the Austrian NSDAP in 1932, and was moved to Berlin in 1934 where he was put in charge of "Jewish Affairs." In 1938 he built up a "Central Office for Jewish Emigration," where he was charged with finding a "Final Solution" to the "Jewish problem."

founded on *military* considerations. From now on such orders must have a *political* aim so as to protect the German Volk from Bolshevik rabble-rousing propaganda and in order to ensure a firm hold on the occupied territories."

The document was the result of a meeting at Prinz Albrechtstrasse where Heydrich, in the presence of Adolf Eichmann, had explained to the Commander of the *Einsatzkommandos* the nature of their mission – the extermination of all Jews. Predictably, Adolf Eichmann took the closest interest in these proceedings. His credentials were impressive. During the *Anschluss*, he had come into his own; with considerable energy he had set about ridding Austria of the Jews, making him the automatic candidate for directing similar operations in Nazi-occupied Czechoslovakia. By January 1940, the dapper Eichmann was installed at the Berlin headquarters of the newly created RSHA in charge of the Gestapo's Jewish Affairs Office, officially designated sub-section IVB4 of the RSHA. He was responsible for the execution of Nazi policy towards the Jews in Germany and all German occupied territories.

It was this Eichmann bureau which became the headquarters for implementing the master plan for the extermination of Jewry. Once again, the obscene delicacy of the language employed was in evidence; in officialese, Eichmann was deemed responsible for "the Jewish Problem." His task required the facilities of a four-storey building – 116 Kurfürstenstrasse, Berlin.

This photograph of victims of Eichmann's "Final Solution" was used as evidence at his trial in 1961.

From there, Eichmann was at the centre of a gigantic web which was to trap the Jews of sixteen countries over four years. Their lot was to be deportation and massacre. The Jewish Problem became the Final Solution (Endlösung). Endlösung was to be implemented by gassing – termed Sonderbehandlung (special treatment) – or by on-the-spot massacres which were tagged simply Aktionen (actions).

To achieve these things, Eichmann had only to throw a switch to activate the machinery of slaughter within the RSHA. His authority knew no boundaries. Just over two months before the attack on the Soviet Union, the Luftwaffe had launched, on 6 April 1941, *Operation Castigo* (punishment), Hitler's blow against Yugoslavia. The move had been the tangible expression of the Führer's fury and spite. He and Ribbentrop had forced Yugoslavia's signature to the Tripartite Pact, the original agreement between Germany, Italy, and Japan. Hitler's cynical calculation had been that the addition of Yugoslavia to the pact would permit the free passage of German troops through Yugoslavia to Greece. But the Yugoslav government and the country's Regent, Prince Paul, had been overthrown on the night of March 26-27, by a popular uprising backed by the Air Force and Army. The young Peter had been declared king and, although the new regime of General Dusan Simovic, offered forthwith to complete a non-aggression pact with Germany, it became obvious to Berlin that the Tripartite Pact, as far as the Yugoslavs were concerned, was dead. Hitler's northern route to Greece had been lost.

Certainly, the pact went unmourned in Belgrade where a crowd had spat on the German minister's car amid delirious celebrations. Not for the first time when crossed, Hitler in a fury presented a terrible spectacle. His military commanders were left in no doubt of his determination "to smash Yugoslavia militarily and as a State." It had to be beaten down "with merciless harshness." In the meantime, internal tensions between Croats and Serbs would be fuelled and encouraged: political assurances would be held out to the Croats, for example. Then "the ground installations of the Yugoslav Air Force and the city of Belgrade will be destroyed from the air by continual night and day attack."

The first bombs fell on Belgrade at 5:00 a.m. on 6 April 1941. The aim was to terrorize a virtually defenceless civilian population. The result bore out Hitler's success: 17,000 civilians perished, representing the largest number of civilian deaths by bombing in a single day in twenty months of war. The Yugoslavs were soon overwhelmed. By 13 April, German troops and those of the Reich's satellite, Hungary, had crushed Yugoslav resistance. Four days later, twenty-eight divisions of the Yugoslav Army surrendered at Sarajevo. The Yugoslav government signed the act of surrender. The Croat nationalist leader Ante Pavelic had already declared Croatia a separate state. Hitler also got his way in Greece; on 23 April the Greeks surrendered to the Germans and the Italians. Four days later, the Swastika flew over the Acropolis.

All was now set for the extermination process in Serbia. It followed a predictable pattern. Incident Report 108, issued in Berlin by the Chief of the Sipo and the SD on 9 October 1941 and subheaded "Serbia" stated: "The mopping up action of the German Army in the area around Sabac has led so far to the taking of 22,000 male prisoners. . .. As a punishment measure for twenty-one soldiers who were shot at Topola a few days ago, 2,100 Jews and Gypsies will be executed. . .. 805 Jews and Gypsies will be taken from the camp in Sabac, the rest from the Jewish transit camp in Belgrade."

A camp in Savebogen in the region of Mitroviea was to have a capacity of 50,000 and would be expanded to 500,000. Incident Report 108 concluded: "The camp will be built on the model of the German concentration camp, its supervision being in the hands of the *Einsatzgruppen* of the Sipo and SD."

Nine months later, in Berlin, Heydrich convened a conference at the former Interpol Headquarters at Am Grossen Wannsee, a comfortably appointed villa in a pleasant lakeside suburb of southwest Berlin. The purpose of the conference was to review progress to date and to give pointers for the future. To all outward appearances, the proceedings, with the SS in the chair, resembled an inter-departmental meeting of the kind held as routine in any civil service. The event, however, was of particular value to Heydrich personally for it provided him with a useful stage to underline his authority afresh.

Leading personalities from the Ministry for the Occupied Eastern Territories, under the authority of the Nazi's racial theorist Alfred Rosenberg, were among those attending. Present also were officials from the departments of the Interior, Justice, Foreign Affairs, and Economics. Perhaps the most ideally qualified of those present was Dr Rudolf Lange, even though he was of the lowest rank. His *Einsatzkommando* had killed more than 35,000 Jews and countless other victims during the six months of the Nazi occupation of Latvia. There were also prominent Nazi Party members, the staff of the Chancellery, Himmler's Race and Settlement Office (Rasse und Siedlungshauptamt, RuSHA), and Heydrich and Eichmann as representatives of the RSHA.

The bulk of the transcript of the Wannsee Conference has survived. Heydrich's address began by referring to the instruction which he had received from Göring on 31 July 1941 and which had read in part: "I hereby charge you with making all the necessary preparations in regard to organizational and financial matters for bringing about the total solution of the Jewish question in the German sphere of influence in Europe. I further charge you to submit to me as soon as possible a draft showing the measures already taken for the execution of the intended Final Solution of the Jewish question." According to Staatssekretär Martin Luther, head of Abteilung Deutschland (German Section) of the Foreign Office and an expert on Jewish policy who was present at Wannsee, Heydrich also said that he had been entrusted with this task by Hitler.

Heydrich then went on to review the battle against the Jews and how it had been waged so far. First, there had been the forcible removal of the Jews out of various sectors of German life, followed by physical removal from German territory. The Reich Central Office for Emigration had speeded up the emigration process; between the Nazi takeover in 1933 and the end of October 1941, Heydrich was able to claim some 537,000 Jews had been removed by emigration. Wartime conditions had now put paid to the policy of emigration; besides, Heydrich added, "there were other possibilities in the East."

The next step had been the authorization of evacuation of Jews to the East. "Evacuation" was subsequently to be revealed as a euphemism for deportation, ghettoization, and mass killing of the type indulged in by the *Einsatzgruppen*, but the minutes of the conference suggested that Heydrich was also in favour

Convened by Heydrich, the Wannsee Conference was held in this room of the former Interpol headquarters at Am Grossen, a suburb of Berlin. Under discussion was the deportation, ghettoization, and mass killings of Jews. At Wannsee it was stated that "Europe would be combed of Jews from East to West."

of the Jews forming a vast slave labour pool. A large part of them would, of course, die or "fall away" through natural reduction. Those who survived would have to be dealt with "appropriately;" "Europe would be combed of Jews from east to west."

The Gestapo enjoyed a high profile at Wannsee. Only one of thirty copies of the minutes, (deodorized personally by Heydrich to remove such infelicities as "death" or "extermination"), has survived. On trial for his life in Israel in 1961, Adolf Eichmann attempted to play down his rôle at the conference. He was, he implied to the court, merely a humble bureaucrat: "My orders from my superior, SS-Gruppenführer Müller, were to ensure that the proceedings of the meeting were properly recorded and I spent most of the time sharpening the stenographer's pencils."

When the conference, which Heydrich had ordered to be as short as possible, was over, the RSHA chief allowed himself to relax, knocking back cognac with Eichmann. As he took his leave, Heydrich expressed himself pleased with the way that the conference had gone.

At the same time as the German Army descended upon Yugoslavia, plans had been launched forthwith to annex a portion of Slovenia to the Reich. To prepare for what was termed the "resolving of national problems in accordance with the Führer's decision," plans were made, under the direction of Eichmann, to uproot the non-Jewish Slovenian population and evacuate them to Serbia and Croatia.

A vivid instance of this enthusiasm was provided by the plight of Serbian Jews who were a source of vexation to Gesandter Felix Benzler, the Foreign Office (Äuswartiges Amt) representative in Serbia. The camps in which the Jews were confined were becoming increasingly vulnerable to attacks by partisans. To free the Jews was out of the question: they would join "rebel bands. . . their presence in the country contributes greatly to unrest and disturbance." Benzler proposed therefore that the Jews be deported to Poland or Russia and wrote as much to Franz Rademacher of the Foreign Ministry, but when the latter contacted Eichmann he learnt that there were no trains available. In the margin of the letter he wrote, "According to information received from the RSHA Department IVB4, deportation to the Government General [Poland] or to Russia or to the Reich itself is not possible. Eichmann suggests death by shooting ("Eichmann schlägt erschiessen vor").

After the war, at Nuremberg, Rademacher was questioned on the incident and added that he sought confirmation from his chief: "I telephoned the RSHA. I was speaking to Eichmann. . .Eichmann said that the police were responsible for order in Serbia, and should shoot rebellious Jews. When I asked him again, he simply repeated the word 'Shoot' and hung up the telephone." It was later claimed at his trial that some 10,000 Serbian Jews were liquidated as a result. Of the 75,000 Jews in Yugoslavia at the start of the war, some estimates suggest that only 15,000 survived.

Eichmann's activities in Yugoslavia were helped considerably by Heydrich's choice of a suitably co-operative police chief for Belgrade. Appointed in January 1942, SS-Standartenführer Emmanuel Schafer, a man of upper middle-class origins from the German border area of Upper Silesia, had long proved his loyalty. He had, for example, served as head of *Einsatzgruppe* II for

the Polish campaign; its *Einsatzkommando* could claim a high number of executions.

As in Poland, the Yugoslav *Einsatzgruppe* was dissolved after the Nazi occupation. Schafer set about reorganizing its remnants on the lines of the RSHA in Berlin. His Amt IV comprised the Gestapo under Sturmbannführer Bruno Sattler, who had served a bruised apprenticeship in Weimar Germany, including involvement in the Potsdam Freikorps and the abortive Kapp Putsch.

For the two men, key responsibility within the Belgrade Gestapo was for the Judenreferat, (the Jewish desk). One of the main preoccupations of the Judenreferat was the concentration camp at Semlin, situated across the Sava River from Belgrade. At Semlin, the prisoners were mostly women and children, who had survived earlier *Einsatzgruppen* massacres. During the spring of 1942, it became the scene of grim episodes in the overall plan of Heydrich and Eichmann for Serbia. Events there were revealed at subsequent war crimes trials, notably Schafer's own arraignment in the summer of 1953 in Cologne.

After the fall of Belgrade, Yugoslav partisans waged constant guerrilla warfare against the invading army.

113

Heinrich Müller, as head of the Gestapo, had despatched a telegram to Schafer – "Subject: Jewish Operations in Serbia" – which made mention of the impending arrival of a *Sonderkommando* (Special Detachment). In SS terms, this could have meant one of two things. A *Sonderkommando* might consist of special SS units which were employed "for police and political work tasks" in the occupied territories of the east or, more frequently, be detachments of male Jews earmarked for special work in the extermination camps. Whether such actions were to be carried out by SS or Jews, however, made little difference to the ultimate fate of the victims. In the case of the 76,000 Jews of Yugoslavia, most notably those in Serbia, such fate was likely to be dire indeed.

There is nothing more monotonous than a catalogue of mass killing; for the purpose of this narrative, the focus will be on one internment camp – at Semlin, outside Belgrade, which was to prove notorious. Conditions in this *Judenlager* were particularly cruel. Witnesses of life there were later to recall that cells were unheated, sleeping space consisted of wooden scaffolding. The beating of children who begged for food became routine. At that time, the extermination camps were only in the course of preparation and death of those interned tended to be by mass shooting. It was decided that this was too slow.

Müller's telegram to Schafer sealed the fate of the Jews around Belgrade. The latter informed SS-Hauptsturmführer Bruno Sattler, in his capacity as head of the Gestapo for Jewish affairs and the Semlin camp, that a Saurer truck designed to hold fifty people was en route for what was termed a "special assignment." In the obfuscating language of bureaucrats everywhere, the camp commandant, Herbert Andorfer, was informed that those in his charge would be "put to sleep" *(eingeschläfert)*. Preparations for the fate of the Jews in Semlin were made with an exactitude which was chilling, even by the standards of the SS and Gestapo. There was an elaborate subterfuge. The prisoners were led to believe that they were bound for Rumania via a Yugoslav transit camp. The Germans even went to the trouble of drawing up a false itinerary. Jewish doctors and nurses were interviewed and reassured that they would look after the prisoners on what might prove to be an arduous journey. The provision of sweets for the children was another way of lessening suspicion, although the presence of a separate open truck ("to carry the baggage") might well have caused doubts.

The two Sipo-SD drivers, Goetz and Meyer, drove the prisoners through the centre of Belgrade, making for the Avala shooting range some ten kilometres to the southeast of the city. At some point in the journey, the vehicle's exhaust was connected to the sealed passenger compartment and those inside asphyxiated. Waiting at the Avala was a guard detachment of Ordnungspolizei. The guard detachment appeared to have two tasks – to finish off prisoners in the unlikely event that any of them survived the gassing and to supervise a waiting group of Serbian prisoners. These had the gruesome task of carrying out the mass burials – not once but for a two full months up to May 1942, pausing only at weekends. The cast of killers and conspirators remained constant: Andorfer, a colleague named Edgar Enge, the Ordnungspolizei, and the unfortunate Serbian captives who, in the end, were shot and buried with the rest.

By the War's end, it has been estimated that some 47,000 people had been done to death at Semlin. The successful implementation in Serbia of this facet of the Final Solution, the responsibility of Adolf Eichmann within Gestapo sub-section Amt IVB4, was not lost on the higher authorities in Berlin and the Balkans.

Franz Rademacher, the Jewish expert of the Foreign Office, could not conceal his satisfaction at the tidiness of it all when he noted on 29 May 1942, "The Jewish question in Serbia is no longer acute. Now it is only a matter of settling the legal questions concerning property." Emmanuel Schafer was also a well satisfied man. As far as he was concerned, the inconvenience in Serbia had ceased to exist.

While the high tide of conquest in the east rolled on, its victims were not just the so-called "untermenschen" of the vassal states of the Soviet Union and the Balkans. As yet, of course, retribution for the crimes of the leading Nazis was a dream for the future. But there was one notable exception. At the same time as German troops launched a wholesale assault on partisans in the rear areas and set about strengthening their front line at Kharkov, plans were underway in England for *Operation Anthropoid*.

Its intention was the assassination of Reinhard Heydrich.

28 September 1941. Reinhard Heydrich and the President of Bohemia and Moravia, Emil Hacha, on the day of Heydrich's arrival in Prague.

18

The
— Assassination of —
Heydrich

As Wehrmacht forces raced towards Moscow in the summer of 1941, Adolf Hitler was faced with other worries. Chief among these was Bohemia-Moravia, the designated Czech Protectorate. It was vital for Hitler to safeguard his hold on this country; apart from Germany itself, it was Bohemia which constituted the core of the German armament industry. Up to now, resistance in the Protectorate – notably from the Communist party – had remained subdued so long as the Soviet Union was left alone.

But once Hitler invaded Russia, the tactics of the resistance hardened, even to the extent of creating a boycott of the Czech press which, of course, was German-controlled. The Communists in particular became steadily more militant, encouraged by Eduard Benes, the President of the London-based Czech government-in-exile. There was an alarming increase within the Protectorate of mass demonstrations, sabotage, and strikes.

One man who closely watched this situation developing was Reinhard Heydrich. Above all, he watched the man who held the position of Reich Protector – Freiherr Konstantin von Neurath. It was well known that Hitler regarded Neurath as too soft. Heydrich, driven as always by the engine of ambition, began to covet the job of Protector which he saw as an extension of his already formidable powers.

To institute a programme of intrigue against Neurath was not difficult. The man was actually on record as condemning the methods of the Gestapo. The scruples he had shown were insupportable. For instance, in the face of Gestapo demands for wholesale arrest and indiscriminate punishment, Neurath had opted for such old fashioned constraints as "evidence" and some semblance of a trial before conviction. He had been consistent in such an attitude throughout his career and as such was anathema to Hitler who a year before the war had sacked him from Cabinet office for what the Führer saw as lack of commitment. Many of the sabotage incidents now developing in Bohemia-Moravia may have represented genuine resistance initiatives or, as has been suggested by at least one historian, may have been fabricated by the SD and Gestapo, acting in league with SS-Gruppenführer Karl Hermann Frank, Secretary of State for the Protectorate. This cannot be established for certain. What is indisputable, though, is that the bloodthirsty and brutal Frank, a man detested even by those who worked for him, had stated that acts of sabotage provided ample justification for the harshest measures possible. One of the reasons for Frank's vehemence was a bid for attention; he himself coveted Neurath's post. Heydrich, meanwhile, watched the situation develop but as yet made no overt move. There was no need for unseemly haste. There was already an SD file on Karl Hermann Frank which contained useful details of the Secretary of State's corrupt financial dealings.

A meeting was summoned at Hitler's headquarters, the Führerhauptquartier at Rastenburg, deep in the forests of East Prussia. An industrious subordinate, Karl Böhme, who was the commander of the Sipo and SD in Prague, produced extensive documentation on the successes of the resistance to Nazi rule in the Protectorate and Neurath's failure to combat them. The evidence was irrefutable and Neurath was told bluntly by Hitler that he must give up the post. It was a dubious consolation to him that the new holder of the post, Reinhard Heydrich, would be designated as only the "Acting Reich Protector" since it would be given out that Neurath was ill and had gone on holiday. There was to be no consolation prize either for Karl Hermann Frank. Frank had tended to take his succession to Neurath for granted, believing that he knew the local situation in the Protectorate better than anyone and he had knowledge of the Czech language as well. But, as it turned out, Frank got nothing. It was indisputably Heydrich's day.

Heydrich was at first euphoric, dazzled by the prestige of his new office as, indeed, was Lina Heydrich. Heydrich, however, was far too much of a realist not to appreciate the dangers attendant on his new position. His numerous offices had been fashioned into a complex maze with himself at the centre and in control, but that could also mean that anyone with a comparable lack of scruples could take advantage of his absences in Prague, penetrate his empire, and displace him. Before journeying to the Czech capital, Heydrich made sure that his links with the RSHA remained firm and that transport to Berlin was ready to hand.

On 27 September 1941, a bright Sunday, the tall, slim Saxon in the smart uniform of an SS-Obergruppenführer arrived in Prague. He did so with considerable ceremony, the Reich news cameramen following the armed contingents as they marched into the courtyard of the ancient Hradcany Castle which Heydrich had made his headquarters.

The Czechs would soon learn that the arrival of Heydrich was no mere change of personnel, although the Acting Reich Protector was careful to make this appear to be the case at his first meeting in the Hradcany. His remarks there were recorded and locked away in a safe, only to be released twenty years later by the Czechs. Heydrich began blandly enough, "Party comrades, gentlemen, three days ago, by order of the Führer, I assumed control of affairs incumbent upon the Protector in place of Reichsminister and Reich Protector von Neurath who is ill." Such blandness did not last long. His listeners were soon left in no doubt as to how he intended to conduct affairs. From now on matters in the Protectorate were firmly in Heydrich's hands.

One of his first moves was, predictably, against the Jews. On a gently sloping plain among the meadows and low hills of Bohemia, stood the former fortress town of Terezin (to become known as Theresienstadt). Heydrich

established a ghetto there. To lull the suspicions of the incarcerated, it was designated "a model ghetto" serving the elderly. At first the Jews took the place at face value. In reality it served Heydrich's actual purpose: that of a transit station on the way to the extermination camps.

Heydrich then turned his attention to the Czech people. His policy toward them threw the resistance, both in London and in Czechoslovakia, into consternation. Although Heydrich made sure no mercy was granted to anyone caught in acts of sabotage, it was not long before a seemingly inexplicable volte face in SS policy became apparent. Life was made easier for the workers and Heydrich set out to woo them even receiving a labour delegation at the Hradcany. Workers were told that provided they were loyal to the Reich they could expect rewards. Factory workers who produced the required output of armaments would receive an increased food allowance. To show that his promises were genuine, Heydrich announced that rations of fat to armaments workers would be raised to 400 grammes. The overall motive, of course, was not humanitarian; the Protectorate needed to be mobilized behind the German war machine.

Against resistance activities, however, the noose was tightened. The hunting out of members of the underground, carried out by the same men who had previously served Neurath, was efficient and successful. "Safe houses" in Prague were penetrated either by traitors or the Gestapo. The Gestapo was also given the power of protective custody – the right to detain anyone they pleased indefinitely. In the meantime, the executions continued relentlessly alongside the "carrot and stick" measures. Black marketeers were arrested and shot alongside resistants. The newspapers of the puppet press splashed such headlines as: FOURTEEN BLACK MARKETEERS HANGED. GERMANS AND CZECHS. Heydrich went to the extent of encouraging the Gestapo to investigate members of the occupying power suspected of lining their pockets with gains from undercover deals.

There was, however, a world for Reinhard Heydrich beyond Prague; other duties and further promotion awaited him. On 27 May 1942, he was due to fly to Berlin to report personally on the progress of *Endlösung,* on arms production in the Protectorate, and on the state of employment in the arms industry.

At the same time, far away in England, a group of determined individuals was finalizing plans to make sure that this was one journey Heydrich would never take. The London-based Czech government-in-exile, evaluating reports from its agents in Prague, reasoned that, while the intensified measures being taken against the underground forces of the so-called "Home Army" and the resistance were bad enough, Heydrich's overtures to conciliate the workers were equally damaging. It could lead the Czechs to believe that German "protection" was not as oppressive as they had imagined. Eduard Benes in London also had to contend with the unrest of the Communist element within the resistance which was all for going on the offensive. A plan evolved whereby Czech agents in Britain, trained by the Special Operations Executive (SOE) would be flown to Prague to assassinate Reinhard Heydrich. Benes was fully aware of the almost certain outcome if the killing succeeded: there would be large scale reprisals. Even so, the risk was considered well worth taking. Czech hatred of the Germans would be rekindled.

Opposite: *Lina Heydrich attends a reception in Prague with her husband, the newly promoted Obergruppenführer Reinhard Heydrich.*

The idea was greeted by the underground in Prague with horror. There were pleas to the British government to persuade Benes to call off the assassination. The British were unmoved and on 28 and 29 December agents were flown out from two groups. The first, known as *Anthropoid,* was to carry out the assassination and consisted of Warrant Officer Josef Gabcik and Warrant Officer Jan Kubis. The pair had the assistance of Warrant Officer Josef Valcik, a member of another group, *Silver A,* which had been equipped with a strong transmitter for an intelligence rôle. Some groups landing subsequently succeeded in contacting underground organizations and using "safe houses" in Prague. Others, careless or unlucky in their choice of landing places, were picked up and executed.

Heydrich had selected as his private residence the closely guarded estate of Panenske Brezany, lying some distance from Prague, a choice which enabled Heydrich to play the rôle of country gentleman. The Protector was cautious enough to insist on heavy security at Panenske Brezany itself, but for his journeys around Prague, Heydrich was apt to be singularly cavalier, frequently making trips in an unescorted, unreinforced Mercedes, trusting in his driver, the bulky Oberscharführer Klein, and the pistols which both men carried. In his memoirs, Albert Speer, Hitler's Minister of Armaments, recalled that such rudimentary precautions caused Berlin some considerable anxiety, since assassination by members of the resistance was always a possibility. Heydrich's arrogance led him to disregard the warnings he was given. It was a mistaken attitude that was now to prove fatal.

Intelligence about Heydrich's projected visit to Berlin suggested that it was

Heydrich in the centre of Prague shortly before his assassination. His driver, Oberscharführer Klein, holds the door of Heydrich's open-topped, green Mercedes.

not simply to discuss affairs of the Protectorate but possibly a totally new assignment. He might be posted elsewhere. This news reached the assassins from a Czech agent. The need to act quickly was obvious.

On the pleasantly sunny morning of 27 May at 10:30, Heydrich's three-and-a-half litre Mercedes convertible, sporting two pennants on the mudguards – the SS flag and that of the Reich Protector – was being driven at speed through the streets of Prague. It would be obliged to slow down at the bend of a street called V Holesovice in the Liben district of the capital leading down to the Traja bridge. Here waited Heydrich's assassins. They had chosen their spot carefully. Heydrich would be at his most vulnerable, cut off from the SS garrison at the estate and at Hradcany.

Gabcik was armed with an automatic weapon, Kubis with a specially designed bomb. They waited nervously beside the road for the approach of Heydrich. At 10:32 they received a pre–arranged signal. The car was coming. Kubis was distracted by the unexpected sound of a tram which, it seemed likely, would reach the hairpin corner at the same instant as the Protector's car. Withdrawal was impossible. Gabcik had already taken out his Sten gun and as Heydrich's car drew level with him he took aim. Kubis shouted, "Now'," and Gabcik squeezed the trigger. To both men's horror, the Sten malfunctioned. Heydrich had by then spotted his would-be assassin. If he had ordered Klein to speed off he would undoubtedly have saved his life. But Heydrich made a fatal mistake. He shouted to Klein to stop. Klein jammed on the brakes and the Mercedes squealed to a halt, zigzagging past Kubis who at this point threw his bomb at the nearside front panel. The bomb fell short. There was an explosion which shattered the windows of the tram and an enormous flash. When the smoke cleared the Mercedes was immobilized.

Not so Heydrich. Although he had been badly wounded, he leapt from his car with drawn pistol and gave chase, firing at his attackers who nevertheless managed their escape. Klein, built like a barge, could not move fast enough and Gabcik managed to out-run him. As for Heydrich, he stood alone and isolated. Suddenly, he began staggering like a drunk, clutching his right hip, obviously in agony. He was rushed to the Bulkova hospital for surgery to remove splinters and fragments from his shattered body.

For a week Heydrich clung on. His injuries were serious: a broken rib, a ruptured diaphragm, and splinters from the car, the bomb, and his own uniform had been driven into his spleen and soft tissues. Infection was inevitable. The patient's temperature soared. His condition steadily worsened. Finally, on 4 June 1942, after a final meeting with Himmler, Heydrich died. According to some accounts, Kurt Daluege and Karl Hermann Frank were hovering anxiously outside his door, as much concerned about Heydrich's successor as about Heydrich himself. An anonymous clerk at the hospital wrote tersely in the register opposite the name of Reinhard Tristan Eugen Heydrich, "Cause of death: wound infection."

Heydrich's body lay in state for two days at the Hradcany. Then, draped in Swastikas, it was conveyed to Berlin under heavy guard, first to RSHA headquarters and from there to the Reich Chancellery and its ultimate destination – the Invaliden Cemetery.

Once the formalities of the funeral were out of the way, Hitler screamed for

Members of the assasination team.

Top: *Warrant Officer Jan Kubis;* Centre: *Warrant Officer Joseph Gabcik;* Bottom: *Warrant Officer Joseph Valcik.*

A photograph taken at the scene of the assassination shows the wrecked Mercedes. The tram had been coming round the corner at the very moment Kubis threw the bomb.

Inset: *details of where the assassins were waiting for Heydrich on the morning of 4 June 1942.*

revenge. The murder of Heydrich, he stormed, would be paid for in oceans of blood. 3,000 Jews were deported from the "privileged ghetto" of Theresienstadt to the death camps. There were to be many others. Panic gripped the SS in Prague. If results in the hunt for Heydrich's killers were not forthcoming, Hitler's bloodlust, it was reasoned, could now easily turn on those responsible for the failure. Arthur Nebe, on behalf of the RSHA ordered a special rush edition of the *Deutschen Kriminalpolizeiblatt*, which carried a copy of a telex also sent to regional police departments and district mayors. It directed: "Special surveillance must be carried out in stations and on trains and all means of transport. All foreign arrivals in workers' hostels must be checked. The suspects must be prevented from crossing the border." With ruthless efficiency, an escape proof net was drawn around the assassins.

Nebe also revealed that "an English-made machine pistol, a raincoat, two briefcases containing bombs (also English-made), a bicycle and a cap" had been found. There were wholesale arrests, particularly of Jews. Random shootings were carried out in sheer panic.

For Hitler, the assassination of Heydrich called for more than the death of Jews. The most spectacular act of vengeance, and one which the Czech people have never allowed the world to forget, involved the small mining village of Lidice in the district of Kladno, to the northwest of Prague. Lidice was a pleasant place within a shallow valley with attractive, colour-washed cottages clustering around the church. On the outskirts of the village were larger farms and orchards. The women did a lot of the work on the spot, while the men commuted to Kladno for industrial jobs. They all led self-contained lives. They had small interest in politics.

The first search of Lidice was on 4 June, the day Heydrich died. Eye-witnesses still recall how a column of troops from Prague peeled off from the main road, roared into the village, and lined up the inhabitants for identification. Interrogations were carried out by SS and Gestapo. There was bullying and hectoring, but in general the inhabitants of Lidice were not harmed. By way of diversion and possibly out of frustration at finding no arms or anything to incriminate the village, Wehrmacht and police contingents invaded the neat little houses, either looting the contents or tossing them into the streets. It became clear to the Gestapo that "evidence" would have to be fabricated. Eventually, the Wehrmacht trucks roared away back to Prague.

No connection between Lidice and the assassination of Heydrich has ever been discovered. One pretext for choosing the village was that two families who lived there – the Horaks and the Stribnys – had sons serving with the Czech forces in Britain. Moreover, the Germans claimed that machine guns were concealed in the village and that it was an area where parachutists had landed, facts that the few survivors from the ensuing massacre resolutely deny to this day. Members of the Horak and Stribny families were arrested but there was no trace of parachutes.

The body of Heydrich lies in state in the main courtyard of Hradcany Castle. On 9 June, Heydrich was given a full state funeral in Berlin.

1 July 1942. A telegram sent to Himmler by Wiesmann, Gestapo Chief of Kladno, confirms that the destruction of Lidice is complete.

The telegram from Himmler ordering the immediate deportation and extermination of 10,000 Czechoslovakians. Dated 27 May 1942.

The second crucial incursion came on the night of 9 June. It was on the initiative of Karl Böhme, who telephoned Himmler in Berlin on the day of Heydrich's funeral to present the "evidence" against the village and recommend retaliation. Böhme's report ran: "Subject: Lidice village, Kladno region. On 9 June 1942, at 1945 hours, SS-Gruppenführer Karl Frank telephoned from Berlin and instructed me verbally that, on the day, in accordance with the Führer's command the village of Lidice was to be treated in the following manner:

1. All adult male inhabitants are to be shot;

2. All females are to be evacuated to a concentration camp;

3. The children are to be collected together: if capable of Germanization they are to be delivered to SS-families in the Reich and the rest are to undergo other forms of education;

4. The place is to be burnt and flattened. The Fire Brigade's help is requested."

Böhme set off for Kladno to direct the operation with Dr Otto Geschke, the Gestapo chief in Prague, together with Wiesmann, Gestapo chief of Kladno. The Kladno regular police surrounded the village. Only entry by the inhabitants was allowed. Then a squad of Sipo under SS-Hauptsturmführer Max Rostock moved in. The Gestapo was later to report that 199 men were executed in the operation and 195 women arrested. The special extermination squad which had come out from Prague propped up a line of mattresses against the wall of the barn to prevent richochets. They brought out the men and boys, ten at a time, and shot them. The women, younger boys, and small children were shipped to a transport camp; the destination of the women was Ravensbruck. Of ninety-five children, nine were ultimately considered to be worthy of Germanization. The majority simply vanished and only sixteen could be traced after the war. The nine who were chosen were given over to the Lebensborn organization, a system – particularly beloved by Himmler – of maternity homes and welfare for children who, usually, had been fathered by SS men.

The village was then burned, dynamited, bulldozed flat, and the rubble carted away. Pets were shot and the graveyard disinterred. Nothing was left but a barren plain which was then grassed over so that no trace of the village remained. A statement was prepared for broadcasting the next day: "In the course of the search for the murderers of SS-Obergruppenführer Heydrich, it was ascertained that the population of this village supported and assisted the perpetrators. Apart from the help given to them, the population also committed other hostile acts, such as the keeping of munitions and arms, the maintenance of an illegal transmitter and hoarding of an extraordinarily large quantity of goods which are controlled. . ... The buildings have been razed to the ground; the name of the community has been erased."

In one sense, however, Lidice had not been erased and it was the Germans themselves who were responsible for the deficiency. Many of the details of the slaughter were captured by the cold lens of a Reich film unit. Footage of the

Lidice, a quiet mining village outside Prague. On 10 June 1942, a Sipo squad moved in and took away the women and small children. The village was then burnt down. An extermination squad shot 199 men and boys over the age of fifteen.

The children of the school at Lidice with their teacher a week before the tragedy. Only three of these children survived the War.

Labour was brought in from the nearby ghetto of Terezin to build a special railway to take away the rubble so no trace of Lidice would remain.

massacre of Lidice turned up as evidence at the Nuremberg trials, a dreadful tribute to Nazi thoroughness. Preserved forever were the last hours of the village: the Lidice homes flaming, German troops and police patrolling the streets and, of course, the pile of corpses at the Horak farm. The body of a dog is filmed chained to its kennel. The course of the operation was followed by an officer through binoculars, clearly annoyed that the church tower blew up only after the third charge. The pastor had already been shot. The film also contains footage of the destroyers themselves, laughing and joking into the camera as if for home movies.

To the frustration of the Gestapo the deliberate resort to terror in Lidice and elsewhere failed to flush out the assassins. Statements that had been taken and checked appeared to be worthless. Heinz von Pannwitz, in charge of the anti-sabotage section of the Prague Gestapo, proposed to Frank that an amnesty should be extended to anyone who, within a designated time, was prepared to talk. Frank was persuaded to accept a five day period and the amnesty notice was issued on 13 June.

As for the parachutists, they had moved from house to house under the constant shadow of betrayal. There was no way for them to escape and they had at last been given refuge in the Greek Orthodox church of Karel Boromejsky on Ressel Street not far from the city centre. The church's lay preacher, Dr Vladimir Petrek, was a willing confederate. The parachutists began arriving at the church from 30 May onwards.

As it was to turn out, *Operation Anthropoid* had a weak and traitorous link, one of those who had parachuted into Prague. He was Karel Curda, of the resistance group *Out Distance*, who as well as being badly scared had been appalled at the level of reprisals and feared that they would fall on his family as well. He decided to turn traitor. He betrayed a great deal to the Gestapo, including the resistance "safe house" of a family named Moravec – a middle-aged railwayman, his wife, and their twenty-one year old son, Ata, who had been used as a courier. All three were heavily involved in the mainstream of the Prague resistance and would represent a considerable coup for the Gestapo.

The early morning calm of Bishop's Road in the Prague suburb of Zizhov was shattered by the swoop of the Gestapo raid. Interrogation was direct and brutal; the Gestapo was not prepared to waste time on slow, subtle methods. Marie Moravec quickly realized this. She had a heart condition and did not know for how long she would be able to hold out under interrogation. On the pretext of going to the lavatory, she left the room where the family was being held. Hurriedly, she swallowed the brown cyanide pill she always carried and was dead within seconds. The guards took father and son to the Petsche Palace where they were questioned under torture. Ata held out valiantly, resisting

Outside the Karel Boromejsky Church. Curda identifies the bodies of his former comrades. Frank leans over one of the bodies. The men in trilby hats are Gestapo.

every torture including having alcohol forced down his throat. In the end, however, it was more than flesh could bear. He cracked. Ata Moravec told all he knew. From this the Gestapo was able to deduce that its quarry lay in the catacombs of the Karel Boromejsky church.

A ring of steel was hurriedly thrown around the church on the morning of 18 June. Vladimir Gavrinev, the priest in charge of the church in 1992 (it has now been renamed St Cyril and Methodius), was a teenage postulant at the time that the parachutists were hiding there. He recalls, "I was not told by my elders who was in the crypt but I remember baskets of food arriving and I assumed they were for the poor. On the morning of 18 June, I tried to get to the church but it was impossible because the SS had cordoned off the area. From then on I went into hiding."

Pannwitz had mustered a cordon of nineteen officers and 740 NCOs and men. They were detailed to deal with the assassins and five other agents who were holed up in the church. The ensuing battle, which lasted for two hours, ended at 7:00 a.m. Those inside, who had hidden in the upper nave and in the cellar, steadily refused to surrender although greatly outnumbered,. To force them out, tear gas was pumped into the cellar which was then flooded. Not one of the agents was taken alive. All fought to the last or turned their weapons on themselves. Two parachutists took poison. The bodies were unceremoniously laid out on the stone flags of the church – Gabcik and Kubis among them – and identified by Karel Curda who, brought to the scene in handcuffs, can clearly be seen in photographs pointing out his former comrades to black-hatted Gestapo men. The severed heads of Gabcik and Kubis, also photographed, were later displayed to their relatives.

All the officials of the Karel Boromejsky church, including its bishop, were put on trial and shot as were Mr Moravec and Ata. There were countless other reprisals including an horrific massacre at another village, Lezarky. The church where the resistants made their last stand is today much as the Gestapo left it half a century ago; the bullet–pocked facade has not been altered. The catacombs are a museum and memorial while the shelves upon which coffins once rested – and which were desecrated by the SS that day out of sheer spite – remain empty.

In the aftermath of Heydrich's death, Kurt Daluege, whom Heydrich had despised, became Deputy Reich Protector. Again the ambitious Karl Hermann Frank was passed over although he retained his title of Secretary of State.

Fevered attempts were made by the Nazis to keep alive in Prague the memory of the dead Heydrich. A monument was erected at the fatal street corner with a permanent SS guard of honour. (The monument was destroyed by the Czechs immediately after the war). Laudatory obituaries were prepared for the newspapers. In one of these Kurt Daluege enthused: "With his death there can only be a fresh obligation to pursue the courageous political and military fighting spirit which he personified. . .. Only his old SS comrades and colleagues knew the positive inner strength the man needed in his daily fight against the rabble of the Jewish community."

Himmler's eventual choice of a successor to Heydrich as head of the RSHA fell on Ernst Kaltenbrunner, the same towering scar-faced Austrian doctor of law and political economy who, at the time of the Austrian *Anschluss* had

The trial of the officials of the Karel Boremejsky (Orthodox) Church. Left to right: Jan Sonnevend, Vladimir Petřek, Václav Cikl, and Bishop Gorazd. All were found guilty of treason. All were shot.

Objects found where Heydrich was attacked were put on display in a shop window in the centre of Prague. A reward of 10,000,000 crowns was offered.

The Karel Boremejsky Church in Ressel Street on the morning of 18 June 1942. When the parachutists refused to surrender, tear gas followed by water was pumped into the crypt to flush them out. This photograph was taken with a hidden peephole camera.

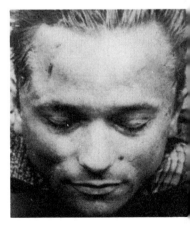

The head of Jan Kubis was displayed to his relatives.

The death mask of Reinhard Heydrich.

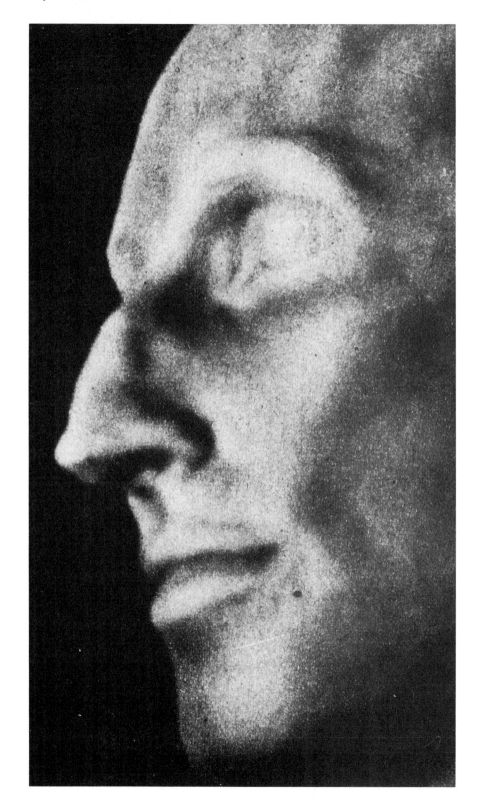

evoked in Heydrich such fastidious distaste.

It would be hard to imagine a greater contrast between two men. In accordance with SS ritual, a death mask was made of Heydrich. A police official named Wehner, summoned to Prague to investigate the circumstances of the assassination, said the mask demonstrated "deceptive features of uncanny spirituality and entirely perverted beauty, like a cardinal of the Renaissance." Nothing remotely like this could ever have been said of the heavily-built Kaltenbrunner. One colleague said, "He had remarkably broad shoulders and clawlike hands – whenever I shook hands with him I worried." He was not the only one. Hans Bernd Gisevius was unhappy about the mark of a narrow legal mind like Kaltenbrunner's on the RSHA. "Kaltenbrunner came and things got worse daily. We realized that the impulses of a murderer such as Heydrich were perhaps less terrible than the cold legal logic of a lawyer who had such an instrument as the Gestapo in his hands." When it came to loyalty, however, Hitler could scarcely have made a better choice to take over the citadel of bureaucracy that was the RSHA with its offices, its filing systems, its listening posts, its radio centre and laboratories. This leviathan had long outgrown Prinz Albrechtstrasse 8 and was now sprawled all over Berlin occupying no fewer than thirty-eight buildings.

The record of the Gestapo was at its most vile in the vassal states of the east but in western Europe, in the wake of the invasions of 1940, it also proved itself a presence to be loathed and feared.

Hitler had ordered that no trace of Lidice should remain. After the War, when rebuilding work had begun, workers uncovered this old village sign. It can still be seen in Lidice to this day.

19
Night and Fog
in the
West

The Gestapo's rôle in western Europe was intensified by the high tide of Nazi conquest. But in fact long before the field grey mass of the Wehrmacht had been ready for its sweep in 1940, the SS and the Gestapo had been been hard at work to concoct a pretext for invasion.

On 8 November 1939, Adolf Hitler, who had several times postponed his plans for attacking the west – due both to unsatisfactory weather and to deep-seated doubts about the readiness of his forces – had travelled from Berlin to Munich, to celebrate the sixteenth anniversary of the abortive 1923 Bierkeller putsch, an event permanently enshrined in Nazi myth. A bomb planted in a pillar of the hall exploded with great force after the Führer (who had held forth for just eight minutes with a diatribe against England) had departed for a top level military conference in Berlin. The roof collapsed on the audience, killing seven and injuring sixty-three, including members of the Alte Kämpfer, the old guard.

The Nazi Party newspaper, the *Völkischer Beobachter*, fulminated against "an attempted assassination" which it blamed on the British secret service and the Prime Minister Neville Chamberlain. Himmler seized on the incident to arrest some forty Bavarian monarchists and other suspected malcontents who were taken to Gestapo headquarters at the Wittlesbach Palace, near the Führer's Braunhaus. Himmler also offered a personal reward of 300,000 RM, payable in foreign currency, in addition to the official reward of 600,000 RM, for information which would lead to the arrest of anyone involved in the explosion.

The would-be assassin did not escape for long. Johann Georg Elser, a thirty-six year old skilled watchmaker and carpenter and known Communist sympathizer who had recently been discharged from Dachau, was captured the same evening by the local Gestapo at Konstanz trying to cross the German border into Switzerland. In one of his pockets was found a picture of the Bierkeller with the crucial pillar marked with a cross. He was despatched forthwith as "Hitler's special prisoner" to Sachsenhausen concentration camp.

On the following day, Hitler had still more to celebrate – a remarkable pre-planned coup by the SD and Gestapo in kidnapping two British intelligence agents in the Netherlands who had been lured over the Dutch-German border

The Bürgerbraukeller in Munich was shattered by a bomb on 8 November 1939, sixteenth anniversary of the Bierkeller putsch. Hitler had left the hall shortly before the explosion.

National Party Day Parade. 9 November 1938.

Walter Schellenberg (1910 – 1952), rose to be head of SS Foreign Intelligence. As such, he was charged with drawing up the Sonderfahndungliste-GB (Special Search List for Great Britain).

at Venlo. For this particular mission, Heydrich teamed Walter Schellenberg, of Amt IVE (responsible for Gestapo counter-espionage in Germany and eventually in the occupied countries) with a bright talent from RSHA's Amt VI (Ausland) named Helmuth Knochen, an SD adherent of three years standing. Knochen's responsibility was to create effective spy networks abroad.

Schellenberg, posing as a certain Hauptmann Schaemmel (who actually existed and who had prudently been posted elsewhere), gained the confidence of two British agents, Captain S Payne Best and Major RH Stevens, whom he met during the course of several meetings at Arnhem and The Hague. Schellenberg-Schaemmel urged on his listeners the undoubted strength of the resistance movement in Germany, of which he (Schaemmel) claimed to be spokesman and representative. All the members of the movement asked was that they should be listened to and treated fairly by London.

The British, who had indeed received some genuine peace feelers from anti-Nazis, rose to the bait. Best and Stevens were given a small radio transmitter and receiving set; further meetings with "Schaemmel" were arranged in a number of Dutch towns. Eventually the two Englishmen began pressing "Schaemmel" to be more specific: what concrete proposals were the anti-Nazis prepared to make? Matters were clearly coming to a head. Another SD specialist, a familiar figure when it came to acts of dramatic duplicity, arrived on the scene. Alfred Naujocks, who had staged for Heydrich the notorious "Polish attack" on the Gleiwitz radio station, mustered a group of SD men and prepared for a frontal attack on the café at Venlo where "Schaemmel" and the British had agreed to meet, the latter making the journey in a large Buick, accompanied by a Lieutenant Coppins.

The occupants of the Buick, which had been parked behind a café where "Schaemmel" was waiting, ran into a hail of bullets from an SS car crammed with Naujock's men. Best and Stevens were tossed into the SS car "like bundles of hay," as Schellenberg described it, along with the wounded Coppins.

Best and Stevens were driven into Germany, held prisoner for the duration of the war, and finally liberated in 1945. The most unfortunate victim of what became known as "the Venlo Incident" was "Lieutenant Coppins," who was in fact an officer of the Dutch General Staff named Klop. He died in a Düsseldorf hospital of the wounds he had received from the SS gunmen.

As for the Bierkeller affair, Himmler's explanation of a British plot, if credible to the German public, did not convince outsiders. The celebrated American broadcaster and journalist William Shirer, operating from Berlin, confided to his diary: "The thing sounds fishy to me. . .. What Himmler and his gang are up to obviously is to convince the gullible German public that the British government tried to win the war by murdering Hitler and his chief aides."

Shirer was by no means the only observer of the events surrounding the Bierkeller bombing and the Venlo incident to sense on the wind a whiff from the embers of the Reichstag fire, still smouldering after five years. Could it be that Georg Elser was a successor to poor, mad, pyromaniac Marinus van der Lubbe? At the very least, the timing of Venlo seemed highly suspicious. Naujocks' team in Holland, incidentally, had been in position from 7 November, conflicting with Schellenberg's claim in his memoirs that the decision to seize Best and Stevens was taken only *after* the bomb had gone off in Munich. It seemed an irresistible conclusion that both events had emanated from the same source. The Gestapo had been afforded a heaven-sent opportunity to enmesh the British secret service in an alleged plot against Hitler. On 21 November, came Himmler's announcement that he had found and arrested Georg Elser who had been aided and abetted by two British secret service agents, Captain S Payne Best and Major RH Stevens. The Englishmen had been arrested at the German-Dutch border. Himmler further revealed that Best and Stevens had been given "a wireless apparatus tuned to England through which the Geheime Staats Polizei have up to now maintained contact with the British government."

A top-level commission of enquiry into the bombing, headed by Arthur Nebe, only raised further questions. Had the Bierkeller been searched before the arrival of Hitler? If so, why was the bomb not found and defused? If no search was made, why were those responsible – likely to have been Heydrich's men – left undisciplined for unbelievable slackness? During his imprisonment, the wretched Elser was alleged to have told anyone who would listen that certain men, posing as Hitler's enemies and offering him freedom and money, had arranged for him to make a bomb and place it at the Bierkeller inside a pillar behind the speaker's rostrum. Whether this was true, or the pure invention of a man acting alone as a Communist and genuine hater of the Nazis, has never been established. There was talk of bringing Elser to trial but the idea was postponed several times on various pretexts.

It was only at the war's end that the fate of Georg Elser became known. An order from Heinrich Müller sealed his fate: the "special prisoner" was, at a time which would coincide with an Allied air-raid, to be taken out and "mortally wounded in a terror attack." It seemed probable that the order came originally from Himmler who, faced with the collapse of his empire, eliminated many opponents. On 16 April 1945, the announcement came that Georg Elser had been killed in a bombing attack. What is indisputable is that the Venlo and the bomb explosion incidents gave Hitler his pretext for attacking in the west, notably the Low Countries. Had not the Dutch tolerated treachery towards the Reich on their own soil?

Germany had reached the point of no return. Those genuinely desirous of eliminating Hitler were suitably cowed, at least for the time being. Dissidents and "defeatists" alike realized that Heydrich and the Gestapo could, given the pretext of the Bierkeller attack, pounce at any time.

The generals, meanwhile, had cast all previous doubts aside. Their forces, already triumphant in Denmark and Norway, now advanced into Belgium, the Netherlands, and France. The men of the XVIIIth Army of General Georg von Kuchler entered Paris on 14 June 1940, some thirty-five days after the offensive had begun on the Dutch frontier. Two formations of Kuchler's troops advanced, respectively, towards the Eiffel Tower and the Arc de Triomphe. Their progress was followed by General Bogislav von Studnitz, the first commandant of "Greater Paris" who was quartered at the Hotel Crillon.

Among the regular flow of German troops who entered or passed through Paris, there was one group which, as was intended, attracted no special attention. They were men decked out in the uniform of the Geheime Feld Polizei, (GFP), controlled by the Abwehr, whose function approximated to military

General Otto von Stülpnagel, Military Governor of France from October 1940 until January 1942, when he was retired because he was not "firm" enough with the French. He committed suicide in 1942.

police. But these were not real GFP; Heydrich's men, as a disguised *Sonderkommando* (*Special Commando*) had entered Paris in sheep's clothing. The deception had been adopted because the Wehrmacht had demanded that there be no overt secret police presence, and certainly no *Einsatzkommado*.

Installed in Paris on the evening of 14 June in the area of the Hotel du Louvre, the *Sonderkommando* had its Gestapo presence vested in Sturmbann-führer Carl Boemelberg of Amt IV of the RSHA who, like his superior, Müller, was a skilled former professional policeman. Boemelberg had lived previously in France and was fluent in the language. In overall charge of the tiny group was Helmuth Knochen, the key figure from "the Venlo Incident." The rest consisted of bright young SD men.

It was not long before the head of military command (Militärbe-fehlshaber), General Otto Stulpnagel, was complaining that the *Sonderkom-*

mando was insinuating its way into the occupation machinery and was seeking to undermine it. Above all, he detested SS-Brigadeführer Dr Max Thomas, a giant ox of a man who was Heydrich's personal representative with orders to supervise all the *Sonderkommandos* already at work. Stulpnagel had every reason for apprehension. The undercover SD men wasted little time. Indeed, on the morning following their arrival, one of Knochen's acolytes was round at the Paris Prefecture, demanding the dossiers of German *emigrés*, Jews, and known political opponents of the Nazis. This information supplemented that already known to the SD and Gestapo who, for the previous four years, had made a close study of the French police administration and, where possible, of its records.

Of particular interest to the Berlin Gestapo had been Paris, designated "Region V." It was now possible to close the Paris offices of all suspected political opponents and seize their records. Arrests of Freemasons and the rest were, however, carried out by the genuine GFP, installed in Paris at a strength of 2,500 men. This police offshoot of the Wehrmacht had little love for Knochen's ersatz miniscule force but was obliged to tolerate it. As soon as he could, Knochen began acquiring more staff; his energy was matched only by that of Boemelberg, representing at that time the Gestapo and Sipo in France, quartered in Paris at 11 Rue des Saussaies.

New offices were soon opened in Bordeaux; the eyes of the Gestapo and Sipo were felt along the entire Atlantic coast from the Spanish frontier to the Loire, and over the whole of that part of France occupied by the Germans. Knochen's period of absolute power in covert Gestapo and police operations in France lasted into 1941. His responsibilities included seeing off sundry rivals, including Dr Thomas, who had soon shown a marked taste for the fleshpots of the Place Pigalle, rather than the mundane routine of intelligence work. Not that dismissal did his career any harm: he went on to be head of the Sipo-SD in Kiev.

From the start, Knochen had attempted to organize his services on the line of the Berlin RSHA. His men were divided into sections, corresponding as far as possible to the Ämter of head office. The day would come, he was con-

The official photograph of the Paris Gestapo.

vinced, when, like it or not, the Army would be obliged to call on his services. And so it proved. The GFP of the Abwehr soon found itself grossly overworked. A division of duties was hammered out; the Gestapo and SD were designated as responsible for the security of the rear of the Army in civil and political matters. The Abwehr was to retain exclusive control over all matters of military intelligence.

The SD was still very much Heydrich's creature, still carrying the stamp of his personality and style, even though this particular section was in Paris and not in Berlin. The SD proved constitutionally incapable of minding its own business; if Knochen felt like muddying the waters for the Abwehr he did not hesitate.

As might have been expected, Adolf Eichmann's influence had by no means waned either. His fresh disciple was a finicky, anti-Semitic bureaucrat, twenty-seven year old Theodor Dannecker from Munich. Although nominally responsible to Knochen, he in fact answered to Eichmann, presiding over section IVB4 with the specific responsibility of deporting French Jews to the concentration camps and gas chambers.

Equally, in Belgium Heydrich found scant love for his SD and *Sonderkommandos*. The Army had occupied Belgium and they regarded the SS and all its works as highly suspect. This came as no surprise to Heydrich. He had earlier expressed fears that the Army "led by the retired and reserve officers in the counter-espionage offices who were not always politically reliable" might set up a rival police organization independent of the RSHA.

By way of protection, he produced a standard demand for a senior SS and Police Commander (HSSPF) to be appointed to command the local police units and to be responsible to Himmler alone. The Army's response was predictable: it rejected the demand. No *Einsatzkommandos*, with their notorious reputation, were to be permitted in Belgium. Eventually the High Command agreed reluctantly to tolerate a ten-man detachment of Sicherheitspolizei – so called "representatives" – to enter Belgium but then only after intervention by Göring and on condition that they wore Wehrmacht uniforms.

Thus it was not until 27 July 1940 that Heydrich, accompanied by his RSHA heads of section, together with SS-Brigadeführer Thomas, at that time Beauftragter (Representative) of the SS in Belgium and occupied France, came to Brussels for the official installation. Security matters came into the orbit of the Dienststelle, headquartered in Brussels and divided into six sections, of which section IV, the Gestapo, in turn segmented into sub-sections, was by far the largest. It had the predictable function of searching out and exposing the political enemies of the Reich. Among its senior functionaries was Obersturmbannführer Ernst Ehlers, Commander of the Sipo of the SD. The spider's web with the Dienststelle as its centre extended to provincial towns: with the agreement of General Alexander von Falkenhausen, the military commander in Belgium and northern France, Aussendienststellen (outstations of Sipo and SD) were established in such centres as Anvers, Lille, and Charleroi.

Himmler made it his business to see things for himself and in the company of his adjutant, Karl Wolff and four other SS officers, rode around, often incognito, on a tour of inspection. Both Himmler and Heydrich were keen to have a reliable SS Fifth Column with senior SS commanders in place as administration advisers in certain of the military districts, not only in Belgium, but in other European countries under Nazi control. In Belgium, this rôle was filled by SS-Brigadeführer Eggert Reeder, formerly the senior government official in Aachen and now head of Military Administration on the staff of the Commander-in-Chief Belgium and northern France.

Reeder, was, by the standards of Himmler and the men in Prinz Albrecht-strasse, too mild a Nazi. SS-Gruppenführer Gottlob Berger, Head of the SS Hauptamt and a reliable confidant of Himmler, fulminated that Reeder appeared "not to realize that his policy was a Belgian one; he should change it and make it a Reich policy." As time went on, Reeder was to demonstrate unacceptable scruples over the programme proposed by Himmler for the anni-hilation of the Jews. Indeed, in March 1942, Reeder rejected a proposal by Knochen to introduce the Star of David to Belgium.

Himmler had a handy mouthpiece to express impatience with such obstruc-tion. That instrument was SS-Obersturmführer Kurt Ashe, whom postwar Jewish survivors recalled as possessing the mild demeanour of a provincial bank clerk but who, despite his junior rank, proved an able disciple of Eich-mann. He had, like Eichmann, studied Jewish culture and was acquainted with Yiddish. As a ready disciple of the head of Gestapo Section IVB4, Asche was an industrious Jew-baiter. Indeed, he had been known to boast of his pre-war proficiency as a burner of Berlin synagogues.

Himmler and Heydrich.

Six months into the German occupation, anti-Jewish policies were promul-gated; Jews were defined according to German racial standards and their regis-tration ordered. When deportations began two years later, representations were made by Queen Elisabeth of the Belgians, through diplomatic channels, for the exemption of at least Belgian Jews, the majority of whom were imprisoned in the transit camp at Malines from where, in August 1942, the first convoy of deportees left for Auschwitz.

Falkenhausen agreed to the release of at least some Jews, but Ashe did everything he could to block Falkenhausen's initiative, bluntly telling a repre-sentative of the Association des Juifs en Belgique (AJB): "The liberation of the Belgian Jews is not envisaged. A new regulation concerning Belgian Jews in general is under consideration." On 29 June 1943, he declared: "In confor-mity with the order of the Reichsführer-SS, Jews must be included in the evac-uation action." Recognition of Falkenhausen's consent to the release of some Jews was made, but many, due to obstruction by Ashe, slipped through the net.

Hitler had a clear purpose in allowing military-administration regimes to be set up in Belgium and France: these occupied territories were a necessary base for a possible invasion of Britain. But Himmler saw the presence of the mili-tary as putting an unwelcome brake on his racial intentions. Where possible, Himmler was determined to remedy matters. He made it clear that he was by no means satisfied with the strength of the repressive powers that his secret police were able to exercise. But there was at least one area in which the Gestapo's writ of terror in France and the other occupied countries was soon running deep. This was with the implementation of the infamous Nacht und Nebel Erlass, the Night and Fog Decree of 7 December 1941.

This decree had arisen from Hitler's manifest irritation at a policy of taking hostages among Communist resistants. Such hostage-taking, it had been felt, would put a curb on undercover activities. In fact, the seizing of hostages had precisely the opposite effect; resistance increased all the more. The new Erlass, conceived by Adolf Hitler, endorsed by Generalfeldmarschall Keitel, and administered by the SD, Kripo, and Gestapo, was intended to implement something infinitely more drastic.

Himmler issued the provisions of Nacht und Nebel to the SD:

"The following regulations published by the Chief of the High Command of the Armed Forces, dated 12 December 1941, are being made known herewith.

"After lengthy consideration, it is the will of the Führer that the measures taken against those who are guilty of offences against the Reich or against the occupation forces in ocupied areas should be altered. The Führer is of the opinion that in such cases penal servitude or even a hard labour sentence for life will be regarded as a sign of weakness. An effective and lasting deterrent can be achieved only by the death penalty or by taking measures which will leave the family and the population uncertain as to the fate of the offender. Deportation to Germany serves this purpose.

"The attached directive for the prosecution of offences correspond with the Führer's conception. They have been examined and approved by him."

Keitel issued a covering letter dated 12 December 1941 which said: "Efficient and enduring intimidation can only be achieved either by capital punishment or by measures by which the relatives of the criminals and the population do not know the fate of the criminal. This aim is achieved when the criminal is transferred to Germany. . .. The prisoners are, in future, to be transported to Germany secretly, and further treatment of the offenders will take place here; these measures will have a deterrent effect because: (a) the prisoners will vanish without leaving a trace; (b) no information may be given as to their whereabouts or their fate."

On 12 June 1942, an order, under the authority of Heinrich Müller, authorized the use, where it was thought justified, of third degree methods of interrogation. A study of the captured files of the SD reveal abundant orders for "NN," especially those concerned with keeping the burial places of the victims secret.

The stipulations of Nacht und Nebel were applied with especial viciousness in France, at first in those northern areas occupied by the Germans but ultimately throughout the entire country when the unoccupied southern zone, administered by a French government under Marshal Philippe Pétain, eventually came under German control. Early that same year proved a disastrous low point for the French resistance, in particular for Combat, the largest of the underground groupings. A traitor, Henri Devillers, who was revealed as a double agent working for the Abwehr, turned over a list of leading names to the Gestapo. There were forty-seven arrests and the resistants were sent to Saarbrücken concentration camp where they received the designation "NN." The sentence was death for seventeen men and six women. Others among the accused received long prison sentences, although the sentences of the women were commuted to life imprisonment. The method of execution was decapitation by axe. Many prisoners, who fell victims to the "NN" decree had been acquitted by military tribunals; all the same they were still handed over to the SD, Gestapo, and Kripo, and thence to the concentration camps.

The Gestapo did not scruple at using torture methods like these. Torture, however, was found to be counterproductive. Coherent information was more readily obtainable by skilled interrogation. Above left: To these execution posts in France – their grim counterparts existed all over occupied Europe – were tied victims of the firing squads. The Gestapo was empowered to ordain death, but the executions were usually carried out by the military or the Orpo.

Carl-Albrecht Oberg, came to Paris on 5 May 1942, a personal nominée of Heydrich. Oberg oversaw the re-organization of regional branches of the SS and Gestapo throughout France.

The power of Nacht und Nebel notwithstanding, the Germans remained concerned by what they regarded as the worrying successes of the French resistance. The number of recruits to the so-called "secret army" had risen. New heart had been put into France because of the setbacks experienced by the German Army in the Soviet Union. Hitler had been impressed by Heydrich's tirelessly issued directives to the leaders of his *Einsatzgruppen* killers. Prompted by Himmler, Heydrich conceived now of similar "cleansing" methods in the west. Uneasy co-operation between the SD and the Army, Hitler had declared, was no longer sufficient; a high SS official should be given broad powers and sent to work with the military governor of occupied France with the title, as in other occupied territories, of Höhere SS und Polizeiführer (Higher SS and Police Leader, HSSPF).

The eventual choice was a nominee of Heydrich: stocky forty-six year old Gruppenführer Carl-Albrecht Oberg from Hanover, a former executive with a firm of banana importers, who, along with millions of others, had been thrown on the streets in the depression. His reasons for joining the SS had been purely practical; it had meant an end to money problems. Oberg trailed Heydrich, whom he felt held the key to his future, to Munich within months of the Nazis coming to power. His rate of promotion in the intervening nine years was impressive: a mere Untersturmführer on 1 July 1933, he was by September 1941, SD und Polizeiführer (Chief of Police) at Radom in Poland where he had been most assiduous in his pursuit of Jews.

From Radom on 7 May 1942 Carl-Albrecht Oberg went to Paris escorted in some pomp by Reinhard Heydrich. The lights from the chandeliers of the Ritz Hotel shone on an event which for sheer lavishness recalled the pre-war capital for many of those present. The proceedings seemed comfortable and reassuring not least because Oberg himself appeared, to all outward appearances, harmless enough: a fair-haired, pink-cheeked individual in early middle age.

The softening up process for the Parisians did not last long. Once Heydrich had departed for Prague, and his duties as Acting Reich Protector of Bohemia-Moravia, Oberg felt free to shape his empire. That section of the military which had kept on eye on the French police was transferred to the SD. The head office of the German police services in Paris, was modelled on the lines of the RSHA in Berlin and regional offices were established throughout occupied France. The actual Gestapo was controlled, not by Oberg, but by *Sonderkommando* IV, later IVB4, engaged in the anti-Jewish campaign under the control, as we have seen, of Theo Dannecker.

Dannecker was soon reporting to Eichmann that it was "almost impossible" to instil an ideological hatred of Jews in the French people. Might they not be tempted if they were offered a share in the plunder of 100,000 Jews due to be rounded up and deported? In the event, the bribe did not work but the Jews were rounded up nonetheless. Those who were not deported were incarcerated in concentration camps inside France, notably Drancy, Compiegne, Pithiviers, and Beaunes-la-Rolande, and from there to the death camps of the east, the most notorious of which was Auschwitz.

In these measures, Eichmann exercised his authority to the full. Occasionally, the German embassy in Paris would suggest through the Foreign Office, that, for diplomatic reasons, further deportations should be delayed. Eichmann, faced with such temerity, simply went over the head of the Foreign Office and exerted his considerable power through the RSHA, often dealing with Himmler direct. On 9 March 1942, for example, he wrote to Franz Rademacher, of the Foreign Ministry: "We intend to deport to Auschwitz 1,000 Jews who were detained in the course of punitive measures on 12 December 1941, following attempts to assassinate German soldiers. These Jews are now in detention in the Compiegne Camp and will be transported in special trains. I should be grateful for a statement that you have no reservations. Eichmann." The Foreign Ministry replied, "We have no objections. We agree to this action."

Of all the occupied countries in the west, a special fate was reserved for the Netherlands and a proportion of its 140,000 Jews. Holland was in the control of a Reichskommissar – that same Austrian Arthur Seyss-Inquart who had gone on to be Reichsstatthalter of Ostmark (Austria) after the *Anschluss* and Deputy Governor of Poland under Hans Frank. Indeed, several Austrian personalities stood at the helm of a ruthless, destructive machine; they had gained the approval of Dr Joseph Goebbels who had declared his admiration for the Austrians because their Hapsburg training had endowed them with

A cartoon by Dutch cartoonist L Jordaan for the magazine De Groene. *It shows Mussert, the Dutch Nazi leader, marching behind Treason, Terror, and Misery. Treason carries a Gestapo file in his hand. Circa 1941.*

special abilities in the treatment of subject peoples. The Austrian who was Seyss-Inquart's director of security, Klagenfurt-born Higher SS Leader Brigadeführer Hanns Albin Rauter, designated Generalkommissar fur des Sicherheitswesen (Commissioner General for Public Safety), met the Propaganda Minister's specifications exactly.

In the 1920s, Rauter had joined the Styrian Home Guard (Steierische Heimatschutz), a pan-German and fanatically anti-Semitic paramilitary corps. When links were forged between the Styrian Home Guard and the embryonic Nazi Party, it was the making of the crude street fighter, Hanns Rauter. He was soon attracted to the potential for a powerful police apparatus within Nazi Germany. Once the Reich was at war he was to be awarded with the job of supremo of the Netherlands. Under Rauter, the Gestapo, frequently harnessed operationally to the Kripo, went about its business of detecting and repressing political crimes. Always, too, there were the wider activities of the SD, devoted particularly to building up a network of Dutch informers, known as V-men (Vertrauensmänner) whose task was to infiltrate underground organizations.

At the same time, the machinery of the SS and Gestapo was concerned with the persecution and removal of Dutch Jews to the killing centres of the east. Anne Frank, the Jewish teenager destined to perish in Belsen wrote in her diary: "Jews must wear a yellow star. Jews must hand in their bicycles. Jews are banned from trams and are forbidden to drive. Jews are only allowed to do their shopping between three and five o'clock and then only in shops which bear the placard 'Jewish shop.' Jews must be indoors by eight o'clock and cannot even sit in their own gardens after that hour. Jews are forbidden to visit Christians. Jews must go to Jewish schools and many more restrictions of a similar kind."

The squeezing of Jewish businesses accompanied those personal restrictions; the next stage was firmly in the hands of Reichskommissar Seyss-Inquart and Higher SS Police Chief Rauter. Below them was the post of Befehlshaber der Sicherheitspolizei (Commander of the Sipo, BdS), with ultimate responsibility for the Gestapo.

The Dutch were, until 1943, at least spared an ideological Nazi as BdS. Dr William Harster was a professional police officer, although not above authorizing third-degree methods and torture when he considered it necessary. As for the Gestapo, it pursued Jews mercilessly. The orders came, not from Harster or his successors, but from Eichmann who was to express himself far from satisfied with the rate of progress of the anti-Jewish pogrom, notably deportations.

At the end of August 1943, Eichmann ordered his field representatives to Berlin for consultations. Minutes of the meeting, produced at Eichmann's trial, revealed that he had fixed July 1943 as the final date for the despatch of Jews.

From that time on, dangers lurked at every street corner for the Jewish community; the only recourse was a voluntary prison of attic, basement, or cellar. In an old Amsterdam house on the Prinsengracht canal, Anne Frank's immediate relations, together with another family, hid in a "Secret Annexe," con-

Reichskommissar Arthur Seyss-Inquart was in control of Holland, with (left) fellow Austrian, SS-Brigadeführer Hans Albin Rauter, as his Director of Security.

Anne Frank, who, with her family, hid from the Gestapo in a converted attic. In these photographs we see the rear of the house and the hidden door to the secret annexe. On 4 August 1944, Gestapo agents arrested Anne Frank and her family. Anne was taken to Belsen where she died in March 1945 at the age of sixteen.

cealed behind a hinged bookcase, for more than two years. Anne Frank's diary entry for 29 October 1943 read, "I wander from one room to another, downstairs and up again, feeling like a song-bird whose wings have been brutally clipped and who is beating itself in utter darkness against the bars of its cage."

The following August the Gestapo (aided by the Ordnungspolizei, the uniformed "Green Police") broke into the annexe. The Franks and the rest were rounded up, eventually to be gassed or to die of starvation in Auschwitz, Buchenwald, Belsen, Mauthausen, or Theresienstadt. Of the Frank family, only Otto, Anne's father, survived.

When it came to appointing representatives in the occupied countries, Hitler displayed conspicuous loyalty to comrades from the earliest days of the Nazi bid for power. The Reich Plenipotentiary in Denmark, for example, was that dependable SS legal adviser Dr Werner Best. He had been serving in the German foreign service; it was from there that Hitler plucked him for the Danish assignment. A Former First World War pilot, Josef Terboven, who had joined the National Socialists in the 1920s, rising through the ranks by strong-arm tactics and street-brawling in the "Red" strongholds of the Weimar Republic had, by 1927, become an important member of the Party, and by 1933 Gauleiter of Essen, a post he relinquished to become Reichskommissar of Norway.

In occupied Denmark, there were three Gestapo headquarters. In Copenhagen there was the Shellhus building which had housed the international oil company, overlooking reservoirs and Saint Jorgen's Lake. The second was in an agricultural college near Odense, while the third was in Jutland's Aarhus University buildings.

Interrogations at the Aarhus Prison were notoriously brutal. One of its most celebrated captors was fifty-year old Pastor Harald Sandbaek who in April 1940 had been in Finland as military chaplain to some 600 Danish volunteer troops who had been fighting the Russians. Early in the occupation he had sold illegally printed resistance books and in 1942 organized members of his small congregation in Hersum in north Jutland to receive British air drops and to help the escape of Allied airmen. Then came the day when he and six colleagues were ambushed in a Jutland high school and removed to the Aarhus prison.

Each day, Sandbaek and the others were taken for interrogation by Gestapo officers who proved well briefed on resistance activities. A session would begin at nine in the morning, continue all day and night, and all through the following day until midnight. In the course of a session, his interrogator, who was probably fresh to the roster, would snap triumphantly, "Come on, Sandbaek, twenty hours ago you gave us a different answer."

To assist his memory, the Gestapo beat the pastor with clubs and fists, kicking him as he sprawled handcuffed on the floor. In the end, they told him, he would be executed. He had no reason to doubt them, recalling that a close friend, the pastor and playwright Kaj Munk, one of the most respected men in Scandinavia, had been beaten to death and his body abandoned by the roadside. Sandbaek, however, survived, thanks to an Allied raid on Aarhus during the autumn of 1944.

At Shellhus from September 1943 presided yet another of Himmler's loyal disciples, SS-Obergruppenführer Karl Heinz Hoffmann. The Reichsführer-SS's high opinion of Hoffmann was not shared by an SS handwriting analyst who was required to submit a report on the man's character. It declared: "There is not much evidence of clarity, decisiveness and self-discipline. He is highly egocentric and his sense of responsibility is not very developed. His intelligence is small, but there is a certain ambition and application." Such a character assessment did not, however, bother the Reichsführer-SS. At Shellhus, Hoffmann was to share responsibilities with SS-Obergruppenführer Gunther Pancke and his chief aide, Otto Bovensiepen, a protégé of Ernst Kaltenbrunner.

Previous to the arrival of Hoffmann, Hitler had assigned a hardline Wehrmacht officer, Generalleutnant Hermann Hanneken, to take over the Wehrmacht. As for Dr Best, he received new orders that the Danes – and in particular Jews – were to be treated with even greater harshness. For three years, Denmark had been able to maintain a degree of independence in wartime Europe, remaining relatively prosperous with its self-sufficiency in food and an increase in agricultural exports to Germany. The 8,000-strong Jewish community represented no threat to the Reich but with Himmler and Eichmann this was to count for nothing. On 14 September 1943, Hoffmann arrived in Copenhagen. The next day he was joined by police battalions and security officials under the command of Dr Rudolf Mildner, whose previous post had been at Katowice in Poland, where he had served as an SS area Commander and head of the political section at Auschwitz.

Sturmbannführer Rolf Günther, one of Eichmann's deputies, was the next arrival in Denmark. The Gestapo was to be the prime mover in anti-Jewish policy, as Dr Mildner was to testify in an affidavit after the war: "By orders of Reichsführer-SS Himmler, the special Sonderkommando 'Eichmann' was sent from Berlin to Copenhagen to remove all the Jews from Denmark. It was under the direct jurisdiction of SS-Gruppenführer Müller, Chief of Bureau IV."

An outbreak of strikes and increased activity by the Danish underground was seized upon as a pretext for the round-up of Danish Jews. The date set for the operation was the night of the 1st and the day of the 2nd of October, a Friday night and Saturday – the Jewish Sabbath. On the Friday, the sweep began on Jewish houses, apartment blocks, and old people's homes. To the chagrin of the Gestapo, most of the apartments were empty. After three weeks of frustration, the net total of arrests was 472; all of those arrested were sent to Theresienstadt. The rest, some 7,200 Jews had disappeared – saved through the swift action of one of Werner Best's closest aides, George Duckwitz, who sympathized with the Danes, had many friends in Danish political circles, and little stomach for delivering individuals into the hands of the Gestapo.

The Danish underground was accordingly tipped off, although it had received an earlier warning when the Gestapo forced the librarian of the Copenhagen synagogue to hand over membership lists. Faced with this obvious threat the underground set about mustering fishing and other available vessels in which the Jews were ferried to neutral Sweden. Jews who could not get out in time were hidden in non-Jewish homes and, over the course of the three weeks of the Gestapo dragnet, smuggled at the approach of darkness to waiting boats.

In Norway, throughout the five years of war the icy, humourless Terboven was to wield an authority at times exceeding even that of Himmler's police apparatus. The country's armed forces were crushed, her king and government fled to London. Only one home-grown political party was permitted: the Nasjonal Samling of the notorious pro-Nazi, Vidkun Quisling.

The SD and Gestapo turned their attention to the threat represented by the resistance movement in Norway, Milorg, which after slow beginnings was, by the start of 1942, operating in conjunction with the SOE, a military organization created by the British to carry on the war against Germany from inside Nazi-occupied Europe. During that year, a small fleet of Norwegian fishing vessels began making regular runs between Norwegian ports and the Shetland Islands lying some 100 miles northeast of the northern tip of Scotland. The vessels were used for highly dangerous special missions from British soil, carrying agents, saboteurs, and arms to Norway, as well as bringing volunteers and refugees back to the Shetlands in a series of hazardous voyages known as the "Shetland bus."

The arrest in 1945 at the Danish Gestapo Headquarters of lawyer, Dr Krenchel, who made speeches for the Nazis on Danish radio during the occupation.

Inevitably, the two way traffic reached the ears of the Gestapo. At Alesund, in the extreme west of the country abutting the Atlantic, Henry Oliver Rinan, a Norwegian informer posing as an anti-Nazi, infiltrated an "export" group. On 23 February 1942, the Gestapo, primed by Rinan, seized a fishing vessel with twenty-three men on board as it was due to sail. Other arrests followed. Some of those who managed to escape to London testified that there was little mercy to be expected in the dungeons of the four-brick building at Victoria Terrasse in Oslo which housed the Gestapo, or at Mollergaten 19, a holding centre for prisoners due to be transferred to the Grini concentration camp.

One witness, who had shared a cell with a resistance fighter testified that his companion "found great difficulty in talking. . .. I had to feed and wash him. The policemen had broken four of his fingers and had pulled out the nails from two of them. Afterwards they had hit him with sticks wrapped in cloth until he collapsed. They then turned him on his back and jumped on his stomach. He stated that he had asked his tormentors to shoot him. I myself saw that he was bleeding through the mouth and the rectum and that four fingers had been broken and were bent backwards. I also noticed that two nails were missing."

The Gestapo had reacted with enthusiasm to Hitler's move in 1942 – that is, when the tide of war was beginning to turn against him – ordering the extermination of captured Allied commandos. The Führer's "Top Secret Commando Order" of 18 October stated:

"From now on all enemies on so-called commando missions in Europe or Africa challenged by German troops, even if they are in uniform, whether armed or unarmed, in battle or in flight, are to be slaughtered to the last man."

Shortly after this, two Halifax bombers, each towing a Horsa glider packed with heavily armed troops, took off from Wick Airfield, Scotland, on the evening of 19 November 1942. The object of the mission was to destroy the Norsk Hydroelectric Company plant at Vemork, lying deep in the mountains of southern Norway. The plant produced the substance known as heavy water, the key element in the Third Reich's secret bid to produce a German atomic bomb. One of the bombers and two of the troop-laden gliders crashed in bad weather. The captured men were interrogated and shot; in one case the Gestapo, controlled by SS-Obergruppenführer Wilhelm Rediess, brutally beat the British soldiers, taking the fullest advantage of a provision within the commando order for the interrogation of prisoners before execution. By the end of 1942, the Gestapo had ensured that its masters had every reason to be well satisfied with the situation in Norway.

Of those issuing the orders from Berlin, none by the end of the following year had greater cause for satisfaction than Heinrich Himmler. In August 1943 he was to secure the office of Minister of the Interior, giving him total say over all questions of race and Germanization, far greater influence than before over the concentration camps and, near home, absolute control over the tangled bureaucracy of the RSHA which now had a strength of 60,000 – a figure that did not include 40,000 employed in various offices within the SS.

There was scarcely a single activity in which the influence of the Reichs-führer-SS could not be detected. For example, despite Hitler's reservation over the effectiveness of taking hostages, the practice continued throughout occupied Europe, particularly in France. The creak of officialdom was audible when it came to activating the hangmen or the execution squads; Himmler, with all the old prissy exactitude, had seen to that. It was true that the decision as to which hostages were to be executed was taken by the Feldkommandantur and not by the Gestapo; nonetheless, the Gestapo as Amt IV was there to nudge elbows with a list of favoured candidates who included those "detained for reprisals and punishment." They were invariably sentenced to death.

In one corner of eastern France, postwar memories of Gestapo terror bit particularly deep; indeed, they were not to be fully exorcised after forty-two years when Lyon was obliged to face painful memories. The source of these memories dated back to 1942 when the city had been in the charge of Gestapo chief, Klaus Barbie, the village schoolmaster's son from the city of Triers in Germany's western borders who became notorious as the "Butcher of Lyon" and who, so many years later, stood in the dock accused of torture, massacre, and the deportation of Jews to the death camps.

The Netherlands had served as Barbie's training ground. On 2 May 1941, he had arrived in the Hague to assume his duties as an intelligence officer in the Bureau of Jewish Affairs. He was soon detached to work in Amsterdam's Gestapo headquarters at Euterpestraat (now Van der Veen Street) amid the town's network of canals. There he discarded his SD uniform for the trench coat and trilby hat of the Gestapo operative. His instructions were to concentrate on the Zionists, Jewish financiers, Marxists, and Freemasons who were regarded by the Nazis as presenting a special threat. Intelligence gathering, however, was regarded with impatience by Eichmann; he wanted the branches and sub-branches of RSHA Section IVB4 to start earning their living and for the deportation trains to start rolling. By May 1942, the first of these had arrived in Holland.

By November of that same year, however, Klaus Barbie, nursing the Iron Cross (Second Class) as recognition for his services to the Reich had moved to France. By November, he was in Lyon, which is located in the eastern part of the country at the confluence of the rivers Rhone and Saône. Lyon had been unoccupied by the Germans until the successful Allied landings in North Africa.

Barbie's first commander, SS-Sturmbannführer Rolf Müller, took an instant dislike to the new arrival and from the start vowed to have as little as possible to do with him. Barbie was left much to himself in Lyon, answerable, nonetheless, to Obersturmbannführer Helmut Knochen of Amt IV at Sipo-SD headquarters in Paris. Knochen's brief to Barbie was simple to the point of crudity – penetrate and smash the resistance in Lyon. As for the headquarters of Barbie's own little empire, this was the luxuriously appointed four-star Hotel Terminus near Perrache station in the city centre. The numerous spare bedrooms did duty for interview rooms and temporary cells. For his private office, Barbie requisitioned a house nearby in the Rue Lintier.

The Hotel Terminus was not the only HQ of Amt IV in the city. Across the Rhone sprawled the grim edifice of the Ecole Sante Militaire, where doctors

Klaus Barbie. Barbie's reign as the "Butcher of Lyon" dated from November 1942 when, as a mere Obersturmführer, he became Gestapo chief of Lyon, third largest city in France.

for the French Army had once been trained. The military prison of Montluc, a fortress of high walls and iron gates, was another obvious choice, not the least of its advantages being its proximity to a railhead from which the transportations to the camps could begin.

Those who had dealings with Barbie during his time in Lyon were to testify that they encountered a split personality. There was the pose of informality, even to the extent of scorning the protection of an official car so that he could wander openly through the streets, greeting passers-by as old friends. To the waiters in the gastronomic restaurants around rue Mercier and the quays of the Saône, Barbie was known to be generous and affable. But the affability could not be depended upon; without warning it could be replaced by uncontrollable rages and sporadic acts of sadism.

During Barbie's reign of terror and intimidation in Lyon the horrors were numerous, but it is likely to be remembered above all for two events. On 2 June 1943, the village of Caluire, a northern suburb of Lyon had its post-lunch slumbers shattered by a posse of black Citroens roaring into the Place Castellene, where it debouched a group of Gestapo. Barbie and his men had learnt that the local doctor, Dugougon, was using his three-storey villa for a meeting of prominent resistance members, the most notable of whom was a Monsieur Martel, claiming to be a patient needing treatment for rheumatism.

When the Gestapo broke in, they fell upon those they found, kicking and punching, knocking heads against walls, and calling on the prisoners to raise their hands. Jean Martel attempted to flourish a letter signed by the doctor which vouched for his rheumatism. Dugougon was kicked in the stomach by Barbie's men. All the captives were manhandled into the Citroens but the Gestapo appeared to be particularly interested in Jean Martel.

They had good reason. Their captive was in fact Jean Moulin (cover name, Max), who was to become one of the great heroes of the French resistance. A native of Chartres, at the age of forty the youngest Prefect in France, he had been dismissed from his position by the Germans early in the Occupation and had retired to Provence. But retirement had not meant rest. Moulin had lost little time in contacting the main resistance movements in southeast France, later to be merged under the banner of Combat. He managed to make his way to London where he offered his services to General de Gaulle. Parachuted back into France on New Year's Day 1942, he was entrusted with the task of fusing the various disputatious strands of the French resistance into a single National Council of Resistance (CLR, Conseil National de la Resistance) attracting the loyalties of politicians trade unionists, churchmen, and freelance resistants.

Jean Moulin, French resistance leader, whose tortured body was sent to Germany. He died on the journey on 8 July 1943.

Despite their political differences, all these groups had the common aim of evicting Hitler and Pétain, while some, but by no means all, wanted to bring in de Gaulle as the leader of a liberated France. The first meeting of the CLR had taken place under Moulin's leadership at 48 Rue de Four in Paris on 27 May 1943. It injected new confidence into the resistance, yet within six weeks Jean Moulin was dead.

His long slow death had begun with the ministrations of Klaus Barbie. There were few agents of the Gestapo who could have taught "the Butcher of Lyon" much about the refinements of torture. Trades unionist Christian

Pineau, who had been arrested and imprisoned in Montluc jail in Lyon, told how he had identified Moulin, stretched out on a bench and guarded by an armed soldier. Pineau stated, " He was unconscious, his eyes dug in as though they had been punched through his head. An ugly blue wound scarred his temple. A mute rattle came out of his swollen lips."

Desperately ill with a fractured skull and brain damage, Moulin was sent to Paris where he spent several days in a coma at the villa of SS-Standartenführer Boemelberg. Sometime early in July, Moulin's torn and battered body, barely conscious, was sent to Germany. On that journey, he died. Moulin's sister, Laure, received a death certificate from the registrar of the Paris Gestapo which stated that her brother had died in Metz on the border with Germany on 8 July 1943. Cause of death was given as Herzlähmung (cardiac arrest).

The identity of Moulin's betrayer has never been established, although unproven suspicions still plague resistance survivors and historians. The death of Moulin and the Caluire arrests shattered the Gaullist resistance initiative; it was not to become effective again until spring 1944. Fresh arrests and tortures were sprung in the Lyon area, but these are not remembered with the same poignancy as when, in April 1944, Klaus Barbie went hunting for young victims.

The result of his quest can be gathered from a surviving signal dashed off to Berlin by Barbie on Thursday, 6 April. It read :

IN THE EARLY HOURS OF THIS MORNING THE JEWISH CHIL-DREN'S HOME "COLONIE ENFANT" AT IZIEU-AIN WAS RAIDED. IN TOTAL 41 CHILDREN AGED FROM 3-13 WERE TAKEN. FURTHER-MORE THE ENTIRE JEWISH STAFF OF TEN, FIVE OF THEM FEMALES, WERE ARRESTED. CASH AND OTHER ASSETS WERE NOT TAKEN. TRANSPORTATION TO DRANCY FOLLOWS ON 7.4.44 – BARBIE

Left: *Taken from the children's home at Izieu on Barbie's orders, these three brothers were to die in the gas chambers of Auschwitz.*
Right: *A roadside memorial to the children of Izieu.*

TOUT HOMME EST UN MORCEAU DE CONTINENT, UNE PART DU TOUT, LA MORT DE TOUT HOMME ME DIMINUE, PARCE QUE JE FAIS PARTIE DU GENRE HUMAIN.

Julien Favet arrives at the Lyon courthouse in 1987 for Barbie's trial. For Favet it was an ordeal of horror during which he re-lived the moments when he witnessed the forcible removal of terrified children, aged between three and fourteen, from the Jewish school at Izieu.

On that Thursday, the Jewish children of the Colonie Enfant went to school as usual in the grey house standing in the hamlet of Izieu-Ain in sight of the distant Jura mountains. Forty-one Jewish youngsters from all over France had lived there for about a year, sent by parents who had realized the danger posed by the operatives of the Final Solution. Izieu, like so many other similar places in France, had been regarded as a haven from the prying eyes of the Gestapo.

But, thanks to informers, Klaus Barbie had known about Izieu; in the early hours of a spring morning a convoy of trucks and vans wound its way up the hill to the courtyard in front of the house. Members of the terrified staff were dragged out into the courtyard and held at gunpoint while the SS and Milice, the armed force of the collaborationist Vichy, combed the house and drove the children out. Julien Favet a farmworker still living in Izieu and interviewed by John Beattie, a British journalist in 1984, testified:

"I was working in a nearby field when I heard the commotion and walked over to investigate. It was horrible to watch – the Germans just flung the children, even the tiny ones, into the back of the vehicles as if they were so many sacks of rubbish. One of the SS jabbed me with his gun and forced me towards the back of the van but his chief – later I was to realize he was Barbie – saw what happened and came over and shouted at the man. Then he began yelling at me and dragged me out of the way, saying 'Get out of here and clear off!' I was only too glad to escape, but my heart went out to those poor children who were crying in their fear and pain. Long after the trucks had vanished from sight round a bend in the road I could hear them sobbing and screaming."

Barbie was later to deny vehemently that he had anything to do with the Izieu arrests and it was admitted that Favet's identification of him was suspect. When questioned in the 1970s about the telex, Barbie claimed that he had signed it "only because Eichmann's people were not around at the time." This was a transparent evasion of responsibility: the Gestapo's Jewish sub-section was under his command.

Drancy was a mean dingy suburb on the northeastern fringes of Paris near Le Bourget airport. In August 1941, it was chosen by the Pétain government as an internment camp for those destined to die in the gas chambers of Auschwitz. For three months, the bulk of the children from Izieu languished in Drancy. On Friday 30 June 1944, with the Allies already in France following the D-Day landing twenty-four days earlier, the children were loaded into railway trucks and shipped to Auschwitz and death in the gas chambers.

Throughout France, the year 1943 proved a disaster; more than 40,000 resistants and others had been rounded up and the figure kept mounting. The Gestapo held absolute sway and Knochen's agents seldom slept.

All the same, it was possible that they were experiencing nightmares about the uncertain future. Europe was no longer theirs alone; the most formidable armada the world had ever seen had landed on the coast of Normandy. The Nazi reign of cruelty still had a little while to run. But it was not only resistants in France and the occupied countries whom the Gestapo had to face. Other enemies had stirred and they came from within.

Enna Léger, a former French resistance fighter, recalls her wartime memories for a radio broadcast in Lyon prior to Barbie's trial. May 1987.

10

The Gestapo and the Enemy Within

It took the fourth year of the war for a sense of catastrophe to grip the Reich both at home and at the battlefront. The defeat at Stalingrad in January 1943 of the German Army was a blow from which that formidable machine never recovered. An uncompromising demand for "unconditional surrender" had come from the Casablanca Conference of the Western Allies held on 14-23 January 1943. All but the most blind of Germans knew that the writing was on the wall. Disillusion and resentment became the prevailing mood: corrosive symptoms that, for all its brutality and its bid to control men's minds, the SD and Gestapo, were unable to stifle.

The Allies had already sensed a decline in morale during the year before Stalingrad as was revealed by agents reporting for the *Weekly Political Intelligence Summary,* published by the British Foreign Office in May and marked SECRET. A passage from Summary No 137 read:

"The Gestapo is. . .taking all precautions to complete its stranglehold on every aspect of German life, thought and action, in addition to making more effective its policing of the occupied territories – of which the recent journeys of Himmler to the Netherlands and of Heydrich to the Netherlands and France (he is now back in Prague), are the most open manifestations. The latest SS infiltration has taken the form of the replacement of the existing postal guard service (*Postschutz*) by specially selected uniformed SS units. This will give the SS additional opportunities for supervising and interfering with postal correspondence throughout German Europe, and between soldiers at the front and their relatives at home. . ..

"Observers have noted a more marked downward tendency in ordinary civilian morale in Germany recently, and it has also been asserted that the morale of the Officer Corps is by no means what it was before before the attack upon Russia."

Any signs of defeatism were monitored closely by the SD which, following Stalingrad, received reports that many party members were no longer giving the traditional greeting of Heil Hitler! and some were even seen in public without their party badges.

Such dissidence worried Hitler who, five months after the death of Heydrich, summoned Kaltenbrunner to Berchtesgaden and gave him increased police powers. Fresh vexations soon piled up on Kaltenbrunner's doorstep. In the very month of the Berchtesgaden meeting, the Abwehr and Gestapo had finally defeated the so-called Rote Kapelle (Red Orchestra), a Communist spy network operating throughout western Europe. Now it seemed that many towns and cities throughout the Reich, and Munich in particular, were being targeted for large-scale distribution of highly inflammatory leaflets. One of these had called for resistance against fascism before all of Germany's cities were turned into rubble, before "the nation's last young man has given his blood on some battlefield for the hubris of a sub-human." In addition, Hitler's *Mein Kampf* had been described "as written in the worst German," while German intellectuals had "fled to the cellars, there, like plants struggling in the dark, away from light and sun, gradually to choke to death."

The Gestapo were baffled about the origin of the leaflet campaign which showed signs of having some effect. A report from Kaltenbrunner stated: "Some sources of our information stress the point that the population apparently no longer meets such manifestations as before, by prompt removal of the inflammatory writings or the handing over of leaflets, but instead reads the contents and passes them on." That the dissidents, above all, appeared to be operating in Munich came to be regarded by the Nazis as nothing short of blasphemy; after all, Bavaria had served as the cradle of National Socialism.

Five months after the assassination of Heydrich, Hitler summoned Kaltenbrunner to his mountain headquarters at Berchtesgaden and gave him increased powers to deal with anyone found agitating against the state. Below: *Gestapo Headquarters at Berchtesgaden.*

Hans and Sophie Scholl, students at Munich University and members of the Weisse Rose (White Rose) Group.

In fact, the leaflets were not the work of a serious, co-ordinated resistance movement at all, but of some 100 student activists, fuelled by anger at what they saw as the wholesale Nazi assault on the human spirit. The fact that such dissidence was fuelled in many cases by adolescent idealism and was often ineffectual by no means inhibited the Gestapo from clamping down, often with great cruelty.

A key figure in the Munich opposition, and one who served as an inspiration for the students, was Professor Hans Huber, the popular, middle-aged Swiss-born head of the Philosophy and Psychology Departments at Munich University. Like his students, Professor Huber hated the Nazis and in the spring of 1942, launched a one-man war from his Munich apartment. His weapon was an 800-word leaflet drawn from sermons delivered earlier by the Bishop of Münster, Count Clemens von Galen. In them, the bishop condemned the Nazi euthanasia programme that had consigned 70,000 mental patients, cripples, and victims of senility to internment between the years 1939 and 1941. The bishop had also attacked the SS for its seizure of Münster's monasteries and the expulsion of monks and nuns.

By a quirk of fortune, the bishop had not been arrested for his sermons. Three priests from Lübeck, however, had been seized and executed for distributing the texts within the Army. Huber was anxious that the work of these priests should not be wasted, so he cranked out the bishop's sermon on an ancient duplicating machine, and distributed copies by the simple, if highly dangerous, method of posting them in public letter boxes to selected addressees in a number of German cities.

One of Huber's leaflets arrived at the home of the Scholl family in Ulm and was studied avidly by twenty-four year old Hans Scholl, on leave from his studies at the university. Scholl had seen action in Russia where, as a gesture of personal protest, he had shaken hands with Jews in cattle-trucks at railway stations in eastern Poland. Later he was given special leave to continue his medical studies at the university where his sister Sophie was also a student.

Before 1936, Hans had been an enthusiastic member of the Hitler Jugend (Hitler Youth), along with no less than eight million young people between the ages of ten and eighteen. But Hans had been born a Catholic and soon found the anti-Christian policy of the Hitler Youth repellant. Sophie shared her brother's views, as did another former member of the Catholic Youth movement, Willi Graf, and two other students, Alexander Schmorell and Christoph Probst.

All began meeting in the apartment of their mentor, the nucleus of a group that became known as Die Weisse Rose (the White Rose). The choice of name was revealing of the aims and attitudes of the group. Hans chose it from a novel by Ben Traven, an American writer, whose recurring theme was the basic inhumanity of large institutions, but *The White Rose* was also a stirring adventure story set against a Mexican background of romance and mystery. Perhaps this appealed to the youth of the Scholls and their compatriots.

In February 1943, the Gauleiter for Munich and Upper Bavaria, Paul Giesler, had addressed the students of Munich and ranted at them for their low morale. If Giesler had been seeking co-operation from his audience, his entire approach turned out to be a blunder. Any male students who were physically fit would be put to appropriate useful war work, he had announced. As to the women students, they could fulfil a useful rôle by bearing a child each year for the good of the Reich. With a leer, Giesler had added: "If some of the girls lack sufficient charm to find a mate, I will assign each of them one of my adjutants. . .and I can promise her a thoroughly enjoyable experience." Even allowing for the coarse humour of the Bavarians, this was altogether too much for the students. They set upon the speaker's bodyguard and known members of the Gestapo who were there. Then the students flowed out of the auditorium and into the streets. On the same day there were public anti-Nazi demonstrations, hitherto virtually unheard of.

A fortnight after the fall of Stalingrad, on the morning of 16 February 1943, citizens of Munich walking towards the Siegestor, the arch of victory, saw inscriptions painted on walls inscribed "Freedom" and "Down with Hitler." Ukrainian women prisoners who had been put to forced labour were ordered to scrub off the slogans which appeared in a rash along Maximilianstrasse, Residenzstrasse (down whose cobbles, incidentally, Hitler had marched twenty years earlier in the abortive Bierhall putsch) and Ludwigstrasse, site of the university.

Indeed, the next campaign of leafleting was within the buildings of the university itself. Early in the morning of 18 February, Hans and Sophie Scholl went into action. They distributed the bulk of their leaflets in the lecture halls and the rest they scattered from the top floor of the main hall.

Unseen by brother and sister, Jacob Schmidt, a porter and handyman, watched Sophie at work. Schmidt was also one of the countless Blockwärte providing snippets for the local Gestapo. Schmidt now hurried away to summon one of its plain clothes functionaries, who worked in conjunction with the Streifendiest, an offshot of Hitler Youth, which monitored dissident groups. Once Schmidt had raised the alarm at the sight of the Scholls, all the university exits were sealed. Hans and Sophie were taken to the office of the Chancellor of the University, SS-Standartenführer Doktor Walter Wuest, and held there until the police arrived and took them to Gestapo headquarters at the Wittelsbach Palace. The Scholl's apartment was searched and the names of the other members of the White Rose discovered.

At first, Hans and Sophie held up well under interrogation, denying any involvement with leaflets or daubed slogans – until they were shown brushes, stencils, and duplicating equipment. With the beginnings of a confession to hand, the prisoners, worn down by the relentless questioning, were allowed to return to their cells.

There was to be no respite. Within hours they were roused from their sleep and the questioning resumed. Sophie's interrogator, a veteran policeman named Robert Möhr, tried sweet reasonableness, offering her coffee and cigarettes. He adopted the tone, not of the hectoring Gestapo official, but that of a sorrowing father with an errant daughter. Sophie heard much about the glories of National Socialism, the infallibility of the Führer, the disservice she had done to brave Germans fighting at the front. Surely, she had acted more in stupidity than malice?

If Möhr had expected repentance, he was not to be given that satisfaction. Sophie replied scornfully, "You're wrong, Herr Möhr. I would do exactly the

The balcony at Munich University from which Hans Scholl showered down Professor Huber's leaflets on the students changing classes below.

same thing all over again. It is you, not I, who has the mistaken *Weltanschaung*" (World View). Hans, who had attempted to shift the blame for everything onto his own shoulders and had told the Gestapo that he had acted alone, was returned with his sister to cells washed in the harsh glare of ceaselessly burning incandescent lights.

On the morning of Monday 22 February, the Scholls, along with Christoph Probst, who had since also been arrested, were driven to the Palace of Justice where they were arraigned before the notorious Volksgerichtshof (People's Court), where proceedings were often as not a farcical formality and judges mere rubber stamps for a verdict that was already a foregone conclusion. Under a section of the Civil Service Act, promulgated in January 1937 by Hitler, any judge who failed to "act in the interest of the National Socialist State" was removed from the bench and replaced by someone known to be amenable.

In the case of the White Rose defendants, the President of the Court was the notorious Roland Freisler who, as a prisoner of the Russians in the First World War, had become a fanatical Bolshevik and later an even more fanatical Nazi. He had remained, however, a fervent admirer of Soviet terror methods and a disciple of Andrei Vishinsky's techniques as chief prosecutor during the purge trials of the 1930s. His favourite technique involved constant badgering and haranguing of prisoners and, if necessary, witnesses.

The young defence counsel – predictably, a member of the Nazi Lawyers' Association – raised no objection to the prosecution evidence. Sophie Scholl remained impervious to Freisler's abuse. Hans and Christoph Probst made no attempt to deny the charges. The deliberations were not prolonged. All too soon, the red-robed Freisler was standing up, a black cap firmly in place. He intoned the sentences:

"Hans Fritz Scholl, Tod"
"Sophie Magdalene Scholl, Tod"
"Christoph Hermann Probst, Tod"

Proceedings had barely lasted the morning; death was to be by decapitation. The condemned young people were hustled into cars by the Gestapo and driven to Stadelheim Prison, on the southern outskirts of Munich. They were incarcerated in separate cells and told to write their last letters. The parents of Hans and Sophie were allowed to spend a few harrowing minutes with the doomed children.

Decapitation was a relatively humane form of execution when compared to other methods – including strangulation by piano wire from hooks – favoured by the Nazis. The accused was literally rushed into the execution chamber, stretched on a wooden rack with hands swiftly pinioned. It was calculated that the heavy blade was released within seven seconds of the victim's entrance. Sophie, who faced death in her school skirt and blouse, died first, escaping the additional ordeal of entering a chamber where fresh sawdust had been spread on the concrete to absorb the blood from a previous execution. The guards were to recall that Hans Scholl had cried out "Long live freedom!" The Munich newspaper *Neueste Nachrichten* carried the story of the trials and executions that same Monday afternoon; the accounts had been set in type during the trial.

The Gestapo did not let up its search for further members of the White Rose. Professor Huber, Alexander Schmorell, and Wilhelm Graf were arrested on 27 February 1943, went on trial on 19 April, and were beheaded on 12 July.

Elsewhere in Germany, Kaltenbrunner's men were to be kept fully occupied by far more deep-seated conspiracies whose overall object was nothing less than the removal of Hitler. As early as 1939, General Franz Halder, Hitler's Army Chief-of-Staff, had declared that Hitler should be shot. But Halder, like so many others, did not feel able to back words with deeds. There were those, more determined, who strove over the next few years to overcome their hesitations.

Annedore Leber, widow of Dr Julius Leber, who was tortured and executed for his involvement in the 1944 bomb plot. Annedore Leber was herself a resistance courier. Today she manages a publishing house which devotes itself to literature about the German resistance movement during the War.

Hans Oster (1887-1945). Chief Assistant to Admiral Canaris and one of the central figures of the military opposition to the Nazi regime.

Kaltenbrunner was put in control of the Special Commission for 20 July 1944 with Heinrich Müller.

Among these was Karl Heinrich Stülpnagel, Military Governor of France from February 1942, who, with Halder, had persuaded Major Helmuth Groscurth of the Abwehr and others to adopt a plan (which was to prove abortive) to occupy Berlin and raid Gestapo and SS headquarters. This and subsequent schemes involved, not just the armed forces, but individuals within the Abwehr headed by Heydrich's old mentor, Admiral Canaris.

The latter gave at the very least a nod of blessing to the activities of his chief assistant, Generalmajor Hans Oster, whose deep-seated opposition to Hitler's war aims had led him to leak the 1940 Nazi invasion plans to the heads of the various threatened governments. Oster had evolved a plan, lodged in a safe at Army Headquarters in Zossen, providing for the arrest of all the leading Nazis, including Himmler and Heydrich. This was to be followed by the installation of a provisional government headed by another leading conspirator, General Ludwig Beck, a former Chief-of-Staff who had also consistently opposed Hitler's military adventure.

The tradition of loyalty within the Army came under heavy strain as Hitler led Germany deeper into catastrophe. The need for action became even more pressing and few were more conscious of the urgency than a Franconian aristocrat, Oberst Klaus Schenk Graf von Stauffenberg, who was on the Army General Staff but was nevertheless a convinced anti-Nazi. Stauffenberg had entered the broad area of conspiracy through another opposition cell, known as the Kreisau Circle, a small group of officers and professional civilians which had been formed as early as 1933 and which derived its name from the Moltke family estate in Kreisau, Silesia, where the members met. The circle, however, was regarded with some impatience by Stauffenberg as a mere talking shop.

Stauffenberg had sustained horrific injuries while serving with the 10th Panzer Division in North Africa, losing his right arm, the third and fourth fingers of his left hand, and his left eye. It was some measure of his courage that he had refused to be invalided out of the Army; another was that he readily volunteered to place a bomb that would kill Hitler during a military conference at the Führer's headquarters at Rastenburg. Hitler, forever suspicious that his life was under threat, had put up the most elaborate security screen, even insisting that his valets carry sidearms at all times. Every morsel of food was tested for poison.

Stauffenberg was an obvious choice to pierce this daunting security screen; he was the only member of the inner circle of resistants to attend Hitler's staff conferences. And there was an added bonus: Stauffenberg's hearing had been affected by his injuries; therefore he had an excellent pretext for standing close to Hitler.

Subsequent events were pieced together by reports of the investigation of the bomb plot, carried out by the SD and Gestapo under the umbrella of a Sonderkommission (Special Commission) for 20 July 1944. This commission was ordered by Himmler and placed under the executive control of Kaltenbrunner and Müller.

Stauffenberg, accompanied by Leutnant Werner von Haerten, his ADC, flew from Berlin to Rastenburg with a time bomb in his briefcase. Stauffenberg placed the briefcase beneath the conference table near the Führer and left the room on the pretext of taking a telephone call. Though the bomb exploded, the primed briefcase had been accidentally kicked away from Hitler; a chance happening which almost certainly saved his life. Four of those at the conference were killed. Hitler's injuries were a bruised back and hands, burst eardrums, and splinters in the left leg. But the Führer's physical condition had been on the decline before the Rastenburg explosion and the injuries sustained by the assassination attempt undoubtedly worsened it.

Shortly after 1:00 p.m, Stauffenberg's aircraft took off from Rastenburg for Berlin. Since his aircraft lacked long-range radio and his thoughts were on what lay ahead in the capital, he knew nothing of what had happened, beyond witnessing the conference hut being torn apart by the explosion. But his hopes remained high. These were pinned on the success of *Operation Valkyrie* which provided for the seizure of Berlin by Wehrmacht forces under the command of General Friedrich Fromm who was a party to the conspiracy, although a vacillating one. The forces themselves were to be prepared for action and told that the measures were necessary because of a threat posed by rebellious foreign slaveworkers.

Unfortunately, the behaviour of Stauffenberg's fellow conspirators, waiting at the Bendlerstrasse in Berlin, was all fatal dither. Communications with Rastenberg had been cut so no one knew whether Hitler was alive or dead. No action was taken but the most fundamental omission was the failure to place key members of the SS under instant arrest. The delays did their worst. Stauffenberg attempted to assure leading conspirator Friedrich Olbricht, Chief-of-Staff and Deputy Commander of the Ersatzheer (Reserve Army), that Hitler was dead and demanded the instant launch of *Valkyrie*. Olbricht went straight to Fromm, whose main interest was in saving his own skin. Fromm refused to sanction any movements of troops until he was sure Hitler was indisputably dead.

As darkness fell on Berlin, so the fears crowded in on Friedrich Fromm. To establish his loyalty to Hitler was not enough; there were too many witnesses who could state otherwise. Although it was too late, Fromm did what the other conspirators had singularly failed to do: he acted. He set up an impromptu court martial for the conspirators, declaring that General Olbricht, the latter's Chief-of-Staff Oberst Mertz von Quirnheim, "the Oberst whose name I will not mention" (Stauffenberg), and Leutnant von Haeften were condemned to death. Ludwig Beck was also arrested, then bungled an attempt to shoot himself and was eventually despatched with a shot in the neck by a member of the Bendlerstrasse guard battalion. At last, just before 12:30 a.m., the conspirators were led in front of a heap of sandy earth excavated during construction work in the courtyard. Drivers were directed to position their vehicles with headlights fully on. Olbricht was shot first, followed by Stauffenberg. Then it was the turn of Mertz von Quirnheim.

If Fromm had been permitted, he would doubtless have despatched other inconvenient witnesses. Any such intentions were interrupted by the arrival at the Bendlerstrasse of a group of Gestapo officials from RSHA IVE (Counter-Intelligence) under SS-Standartenführer Walter Huppenkothen. He carried orders direct from Himmler who, by now vested with the power of Commander-in-Chief of the Reserve Army, had given orders that further executions were to cease until interrogation had yielded more about the intentions of the

Ludwig Beck, a member of the inner circle, who was arrested after the July bomb plot and executed.

Oberst Klaus von Stauffenberg, the Franconian aristocrat who was a member of the anti-Nazi Kreisau Circle. It was Stauffenberg who placed the briefcase containing a time bomb under the table at Rastenburg on 20 July 1944.

"Died for Germany."
The memorial on
Bendlerstrasse which
honours some of those
who died in the bomb
plot: Ludwig Beck,
Friedrich Olbricht, von
Stauffenberg, von
Quirnheim, and von
Haeften. The street has
now been re-named
Stauffenbergstrasse.

HIER STARBEN
FÜR
DEUTSCHLAND
AM 20. JULI 1944

GENERALOBERST LUDWIG BECK
GENERAL DER INFANTERIE FRIEDRICH OLBRICHT
OBERST CLAUS GRAF SCHENK VON STAUFFENBERG
OBERST ALBRECHT RITTER MERTZ VON QUIRNHEIM
OBERLEUTNANT WERNER VON HAEFTEN

plotters. The interrogations were carried out not only by Himmler, but by Joseph Goebbels who had been in Berlin throughout. Goebbels' official residence in the Hermann Göring Strasse took on the rôle of an inquisitorial court.

According to the postwar testimony of one of Goebbels' Press Officers, a badly scared Fromm poured out protestations of loyalty which were instantly cut short by Goebbels who snapped sharply, "You seem to have been in a hell of a hurry to get inconvenient witnesses underground." Fromm's flirtation with the conspiracy did him no good; although he survived a little longer, in March of the following year he was executed.

Shortly before 1:00 a.m. on 21 July, Hitler's recorded voice, shaky but instantly recognizable spoke on the radio to the German people. He gave no doubt as to the fate of the conspirators: "This time we shall get even with them in a way to which we National Socialists are accustomed." The wave of arrests and executions which followed were to sweep aside two field marshals and sixteen generals.

But here too there was to be a break in the ranks. Generalfeldmarschall von Kluge, commander in the west, who had promised his aid "in the event of the attempt being a success," backed down and denounced the conspirators. In Paris, where a coup was also due to be staged, matters seemed, at first, less disastrous. On the orders of Generalleutnant Hans Boineberg, Commandant of "Greater Paris," detachments of the second battalion of the 1st Guards Regiment, occupied SS buildings, including Gruppenführer Carl-Albrecht Oberg's private residence.

The latter surrendered without protest, as a little later did Helmuth Knochen. It seemed scarcely possible to conceive a more faultlessly executed coup; more than 1,200 SS and Gestapo officers were firmly behind bars in the Wehrmacht prison at Fresnes and inside the stone casemates of the old Fort de l'Est. Life was rendered somewhat more comfortable for Oberg and his senior officers at the Hotel Continental. But their future did not appear bright. Sandbags had been piled up in the courtyard of the Ecole Militaire to act as butts for the firing squads.

It was not only Oberg and Knochen who were under immediate threat. Disaster for the conspirators began to crowd in. Kluge had performed his final volte-face and informed Berlin of the activities of plotter Generaloberst Karl Stülpnagel. Such cowardice was to avail Kluge nothing, certainly not Hitler's gratitude. He was relieved of his command for not having discovered the plot in time. It was widely accepted that, anticipating the ominous swish of the red gown of Roland Freisler and the People's Court, he took poison on 9 August. However, according to an account published in 1978 by Kazimierz Moczarski, a Polish resistance fighter, Kluge had in fact been shot through the head by SS-Gruppenführer Jurgen Stroop, the Higher Police Chief for Rhineland-Westmark, acting on Himmler's instructions. Moczarski had for a time after the war been imprisoned by the Communists in the same cell with Stroop and gained from him the admission that he had been responsible for Kluge's death.

The conspirators in the takeover of buildings had, in their eagerness, overlooked at least one SD teleprinter station. A message from some SD officers who had managed to escape the dragnet reached Berlin. Nor was the support for the plotters as firm as they had imagined. Admiral Theodore Krancke, the Paris naval commandant, was livid at the very idea of a putsch; 1000 of his men were armed and formed into companies which, it was threatened, would assault the prisons and release the captives. There was also the threat of a section of a loyal armoured corps on the Normandy front peeling off to fall on Paris.

Stülpnagel was beaten and knew it. The prisoners had, regretfully for the conspirators, to be released. It was a measure of the totally unreal situation prevailing that, after Oberg had been allowed out of his hotel room and the others released, both sides agreed to sink their differences in champagne. There was a belief that plotters and victims might be able to close ranks and conceal what had happened. After all, the people of Paris had no knowledge of the bizarre happenings among the German hierarchy in a single night.

Stülpnagel, though, was tragically mistaken; with the dawn, Hitler's revenge was to be unleashed.

On his way back to face arrest and certain death before the People's Court, Stülpnagel requested to go by way of Verdun, where in 1916 he had commanded a battalion. He stopped to look at the battlefield, stepped from his car, and walked out of sight.

The driver heard a shot and found Stülpnagel floating face down in a canal. He had tried to kill himself but had succeeded only in putting out his eyes. Blind and helpless, he went to his death at Plotzensee prison on 30 August.

By then the first eight cases had already come before the People's Court. Those arraigned included Generalfeldmarschall Erwin von Witzleben, nominated to become Commander-in-Chief of the Army after the *coup d'état*; Generalleutnant Erich Hoepner, who had been intended as a replacement for Fromm as Commander of the Reserve Army should the latter refuse his support; General Helmuth Stieff, Head of the Organization Section of the General Staff based in East Prussia; General Paul von Hase, City Commandant of Berlin; and Graf Peter Yorck von Wartenburg, a prominent member of the Kreisau Circle.

Hitler had instructed the *Deutsche Wochenschau* (newsreel) chief to film the entire procedings. The red-robed Freisler seized the chance of playing up to the cameras. The accused, if they as much as opened their mouths, were shouted down and termed traitors and cowardly murderers. Finally, Freisler bellowed that all eight accused had been found guilty of the most consummate treachery to the Führer, his followers, and the German *Volk*.

Once Kaltenbrunner and his commission of Gestapo henchman had turned the conspirators over to their jailers, the torturers got to work on their broken, demoralized victims. Once the sentences had been pronounced, Hitler had decreed that the men should be executed within two hours – in his own words, "Hung like cattle." They were. The executioners fortified themselves with brandy. Sound-track cameras were mounted to record the deaths for Hitler's delectation. Each man was naked. The film was taken to the Führer's headquarters at once and shown there; photographs were still lying on Hitler's map table as late as 18 August. The prisoners were hanged with thin rope one by one from meat-hooks fastened to a girder fixed across the room just below the ceiling. The room itself was divided by a black curtain.

Previously, the prosecutor had re-read the death sentence to the condemned men in the ante-room with the added words: "Defendant, you have been sentenced by the People's Court to death by hanging. Executioner, perform your function."

One of the newsreel cameramen subsequently recorded: "The defendant went to the end of the room with his head high, although urged by the hangman to walk faster. Arrived there, he had to make an about-face. Then a hempen loop was placed around his neck. Next he was lifted by the executioners, and the upper loop of the hempen rope was attached to the hook on the ceiling. The prisoner was then dropped with great force, so that the noose tightened around his neck instantly. In my opinion death came very quickly.

"After the first sentence was carried out, a narrow black curtain was drawn in front of the hanged man, so that the next man to be executed would not be aware of the first one. . .. The executions were carried out in very rapid succes-

Left: *Ulrich von Hassell (1881-1944) was arrested and executed after the abortive coup.*

Right: *Wilhelm Leuschner (1888-1944), member of the Kreisau Circle, was hanged for his part in the plot. He was to have been Vice-Chancellor in the Goerdeler government to replace Hitler.*

Plotzensee Prison where many of those arrested for the July bomb plot were executed. Above: *The guillotine at Plotzensee Prison.*

sion. Each doomed man took his last walk erect and manly, and without a word of complaint."

The Führer's thirst for vengeance was by no means slaked. Himmler in Berlin lost no time inaugurating the regime's campaign of vengeance in person. Müller's "Special Commission" was assigned 400 investigators. The orders to the Gestapo were to root out every resistance fighter and all who had sympathized, however remotely, with the coup. Gestapo squads threw out a dragnet to every corner of the Reich, hauling in even totally innocent relatives. In most cases, their dreadful journey was the same: to Gestapo prisons, to gallows via Freisler and the People's Court, or to the concentration camps.

Many of those who mercilessly pursued the "traitors" had themselves either been conspirators, if only by association, or at least possessed knowledge of an anti-Hitler movement. For others, the attempt on Hitler's life was a heaven-sent opportunity for career enhancement. Many of those who were the most assiduous in pursuing traitors did so not because of overwhelming devotion to the Führer and Fatherland but to secure their futures.

In Walter Schellenberg's case, personal ambition was a driving force. In his scheme of things there was no room either for a Wehrmarcht intelligence service such as the Abwehr or, indeed, an autonomous military intelligence chief in the mould of Canaris. Schellenberg had envisaged an all-embracing security system, a single Greater German Intelligence Service headed by himself. It was a prospect that had already been much enhanced by the death of Heydrich.

Schellenberg knew that the concept of a unified intelligence service was favoured by Kaltenbrunner. He knew his track record to be impressive. At first there been service in the Gestapo's Counter-Espionage section, Amt IVE, under the direction of Müller, then, in June 1941, at the time of the invasion of Russia, Schellenberg had carried through the takeover and reorganization of Amt VI, the Foreign Intelligence Service. The next step appeared obvious. Ever since the RSHA had tightened its control on practically every aspect of life in Nazi Germany, it had been at drawn daggers with the Abwehr, despite the official line that both organizations worked in partnership. Staff of the Abwehr had long detested Gestapo methods and on occasion had been outspoken in saying so.

Schellenberg knew of a Gestapo file dating from the outbreak of war which Heydrich had tagged Schwarze Kapelle (Black Orchestra). It showed that the head of the Abwehr had been putting out peace feelers to the Vatican.

To have exposed Canaris then would have been to shake confidence in the Army beyond an acceptable point; Heydrich had been content to play Canaris along. There was no let up in vigilance. When it came to the July 1944 bomb plot, Canaris was nursing vain hopes that the reign of terror unleashed by Himmler and Kaltenbrunner would somehow pass him by. But the evidence was soon overwhelming. Kaltenbrunner's investigators had found the safe in the basement of the Abwehr headquarters at Zossen. They unearthed meticulous notes made by Beck and parts of a diary entry in Canaris's own hand. Here were details of the Vatican exchanges, together with a sensational revelation that Oster and others had betrayed the plans of the German High Command for the invasion of France and the Low Countries.

On 14 February 1944, a decree ordered the dissolution of the Abwehr whose Central Office had borne the full title of Amt Ausland Nachrichten und Abwehr (Foreign and Defence Intelligence Service). The residue was swallowed up in the elephantine structure of the RSHA. Hitler gave authority to Amt VI to operate outside Germany. Canaris was overthrown. Meanwhile, Himmler and Müller were busy engineering the arrest both of Canaris and Generalmajor Hans Oster. The latter was placed under house arrest.

Canaris, no mean practitioner of interrogation methods himself, at first supplied little of use to his questioners. For a time he was placed under the equivalent of house arrest and well treated by his guards who retained considerable respect for him. Once removed to Prinz Albrechtstrasse, though, his ration of food was cut to one third of the prison quota, his sleep disturbed by incessant and needless security checks. The man whose distinguished naval career stretched back to the First World War was made to scrub the prison floor and endure the taunts of the guards: "Well, sailor boy, I bet you never thought you'd have to scrub the decks again! "

Admiral Canaris, Director of the Abwehr. Although a professed National Socialist, Canaris was drawn into the resistance movement against Hitler, Canaris' personal rôle in the bomb plot remains shadowy and enigmatic, but he was arrested and hanged at Flossenburg concentration camp.

Associates of Canaris fared much worse at the hands of the Gestapo. Notable among these was Dr Hans von Dohnanyi, who had been a legal specialist working in the Abwehr central office under Oster. Kaltenbrunner's agents discovered that Dohnanyi had provided escaping Jews with papers and Abwehr funds, passing them off as agents. Such information was a gift for the Gestapo. Dohnanyi had been on its black list ever since 1938, when he had helped to uncover the extent of Gestapo intrigue at the time of the Blomberg-Fritsch affair. He was also known to be in close touch with the anti-Hitler cliques led by the conspirators Ludwig Beck, the late Army Chief-of-Staff, and Carl Goerdeler, the Mayor of Leipzig and one of the most prominent of the civilian conspirators.

Confined in a cell in Berlin's Tegel Prison, Dohnanyi had no illusions as to his fate. He reasoned that his best course was to delay interrogation as long as possible. To this end, he swallowed some diptheria bacilli which, smuggled into the prison by his wife Christine, affected his heart, loosened his bowels, and induced partial paralysis.

This drastic delaying tactic, however, had reckoned without the depths of the sadism of Walter Huppenkothen, the veteran of the Sipo and SD in Krakow, whom Canaris had once labelled "stiff, colourless and impersonal." Huppenkothen surveyed Dohnanyi in his predicament and proclaimed, "Let him croak in his own shit." Dohnanyi was transferred to Oranienburg/Sachsenhausen concentration camp along with Dietrich Bonhoeffer, a Protestant pastor who had worked with the Abwehr in an attempt to explore peace negotiations.

Post-war proceedings against Huppenkothen and Otto Thorbeck, an SS judge, before an Augsburg court in October 1955 revealed that Kaltenbrunner had informed Müller of orders issued by the Führer to the RSHA. These were that "Dohnanyi should be sentenced by a summary court to be convened at Sachsenhausen on 6 April 1945. I [Huppenkothen] was appointed to indict and prosecute." What passed for a trial had been held at Oranienburg/Sachsenhausen concentration camp presided over by three SS judges, an SS-Oberführer, and the camp commandant. Huppenkothen claimed at his own trial that he had raised objections to Müller over the proceedings. Whether this was true or not, it had made no difference.

The main Gestapo Headquarters building on Prinz Albrechtstrasse before it was bombed by the Allies. Young Paul Mayer was escorted up this staircase to his chance encounter with Heydrich (see pages 222-223).

Hans Dohnanyi, helpless, gravely ill, and not granted even a semblance of a defence, had been carried in on a stretcher by SS guards, still paralyzed. The farcical proceedings were opened by Huppenkothen reading the charges which amounted to a few brief sentences. At the approach of evening, the judges, faithful to this hideous pantomime to the last, had withdrawn to confer. The inevitable sentence was death by hanging. On or around 9 April 1945, Hans von Dohnanyi had been borne to the gallows, still on a stretcher, propped up, and hanged.

The previous February, US bombers had fired the main RSHA building, leaving cells without water, light, or heating. Müller ordered that the prisoners there be sent to areas considered still safe from Allied attack. Bonhoeffer was among those prisoners who went first to Buchenwald. Canaris, along with Oster, the former Austrian Chancellor Kurt von Schuschnigg, and others, was driven by coach to the heavily fortified Flossenburg camp, near the former German-Czech frontier. Here all the prisoners were kept shackled day and night, forbidden either to send or to receive any letters. The only consolation was that the food was infinitely better than that at Prinz Albrechtstrasse. But this was not a humane consideration: Canaris and his fellow prisoners were kept adequately nourished only so that they could undergo further interrogation.

The summary proceedings against Canaris and Oster breached even the Third Reich's own laws. The two men were members of the armed forces; no SS tribunal had jurisdiction over them. But such niceties were, by this time, academic. Canaris was charged that since 1938 he had been aware of plans for a *coup d'état*, had concealed the activities of Oster's group within the Abwehr, had incited the rebellion of military leaders, and was aware of secret negotiations with the Vatican. Both men were sentenced to death.

Canaris, dragging his fetters, was conducted back to his cell. His fate and that of Oster, Bonhoeffer – who had been redirected to Flossenburg – and two others was described at the Huppenkothen trial by physician SS-Sturmbannführer Dr Hermann Fischer who had been present at dawn on 9 April 1945. Fischer reported, "The condemned men were herded across the yard to the gallows, one by one. They were made to mount a small pair of steps. Then the noose was placed round their neck and their steps pulled away from under them." The bodies were bundled onto stretchers, taken to a pyre, and burnt.

By then Generalfeldmarschall Erwin Rommel, the ikon of the German Army and the German people alike was also dead. Whether he had assented to the assassination of Hitler is not known, but he was known to have had the ear of the conspirators. The Generalfeldmarschall was given the alternative of either taking poison – in which case his family would be protected – or submitting to the arrest and judgment of the People's Court. He chose suicide and was buried with full military honours. Hitler sent a telegram of condolence to Frau Rommel.

Fortune played strange tricks with the other conspirators. The sheer number of cases awaiting judgment by the People's Court inevitably led to delays. It was not until 3 February 1945 that Fabian von Schlabrendorff, a prominent member of the conspiracy group of Army officers who had forged close links with the Abwehr, was brought before Freisler. Business was interrupted by the ominous wailing of the Berlin air raid sirens. As the American B-17s dropped their loads, the courtroom emptied rapidly but a direct hit was scored. Freisler, struck by a falling beam and with his skull fractured, was found still clutching Schlabrendorff's file. He died later in hospital.

Schlabrendorff thus gained temporary freedom, but the Gestapo was as tireless as ever and he was re-arrested with the assurance that, as an act of extreme clemency, he would be shot at Flossenburg instead of hanged. His life was saved there by the arrival of the Americans, but not before there had been appalling tortures in the Prinz Albrechtstrasse cellars. After a bid to tear his hands apart with an elaborate mechanism that sent shafts of metal into his fingers, "I was strapped down on a frame resembling a bedstead with a blanket. Then cylinders resembling stovepipes studded with nails on the inner surface, were shoved over my bare legs. Here, too, a screw mechanism was used to contract these tubes so that nails pierced my legs from ankle to thigh." In addition to the use of a rack straight out of the middle ages, "the Police Commissioner and the police sergeant together fell on me from behind, and beat me with heavy clubs. Each blow caused me to fall forward, and because my hands were chained behind my back, I crashed with full force on my face."

Another conspirator, Josef Müller, a lawyer, who, acting under the cloak of the Abwehr, had gone to Rome to persuade Pope Pius XII to act as intermediary between the anti-Hitler faction and the British in the closing days of peace, was imprisoned at 8 Prinz Albrechtstrasse from September 1944 until the following February. He wrote of conditions there: "From my cell I frequently heard awful screams that came from some floor above me and often lasted a

Arthur Nebe was arrested in January 1945 for his involvement in the July bomb plot. He was sentenced to death by the People's Court.

Opposite: *Nordhausen concentration camp, April 1945. In the beginning, Nordhausen was administered by the Gestapo for its own purposes. American troops arrive too late to help these victims of the "Final Solution."*

long time, then turned into a whimper. . ... The screams were so awful that I could not help but think of torture. . ... My hands were continuously tied and the surface of the manacles was rough: everytime I made a rash movement, the fine hairs of my wrists were rubbed away. . ... That perpetual sensation of being hungry, being tied up all day and night, the light that was focused in such a way that it flashed through the night directly into the prisoner's face – all these factors created constant pressure which was further increased by the interrogations that lasted for hours, and by fears of physical abuse."

The higher reaches of the police establishment in Berlin nursed some of the conspiracy's most active supporters, notably SA-Gruppenführer Wolf Heinrich von Helldorf, the capital's Police President for the past decade. Among his close associates were two of the most serpentine survivors of the Third Reich, Arthur Nebe and Hans Bernd Gisevius.

Nebe, the director of the Kripo, had long led a double life, flitting in and out of the opposition camp since 1938, blowing hot and cold according to what his instinct told him was the least dangerous. Any scruples that he may have experienced in serving Himmler and his minions did not, however, inhibit him from becoming head of *Einsatzgruppe* B which had worked in the area of Army Group Centre in the Soviet Union. Gisevius, the one-time Gestapo member, had joined the resistance and, from the safety of the Consul General's office in Zurich, had, on behalf of the Abwehr, formed a useful contact with Allen Dulles of the Office of Strategic Services (OSS) in Switzerland.

In the early stages of the putsch, Nebe was the tireless policeman rooting out the guilty. But the arrest of Helldorf brought the Gestapo too close for comfort. He reckoned that he had only two allies left: his official car and the Berlin blackout. He made it his business to take advantage of both and to leave Berlin.

On 23 August 1944, SS-Standartenführer Werner of the RSHA issued a memo: "It is known that Gruppenführer Nebe has been missing for several weeks. The investigations have been delegated to Amt IVA of the Reichssicherheitshauptamt." A press release issued by the Gestapo read: "Forty nine year old Arthur Nebe. . .could be using the alias of Dr Friedrich Schwarz. He is 1.77 metres tall, thin with a clear cut face, grey wavy hair, dark shoes and was carrying a suitcase and a brown briefcase with two belts. Who saw the missing person after 24 July? Who can give any details? A reward of 50,000 Reichmarks is offered."

On 30 November, a memo was issued by SS-Reichsführer Heinrich Himmler to SS-Obergruppenführer von Herff, chief of the SS-Personalhauptamt, expelling Nebe from the SS and adding, "It is has been proved by documents found and investigations carried out by the state police that for years Nebe had maintained close relations with people directly involved in the putsch of 20 July. His betrayal had been to support the putchists, thereby breaking his allegience to the Führer." Nebe's luck ran out on 16 January 1945 and he was arrested, evidently betrayed by a girl friend. The sentence of the People's Court was death.

Gisevius had found himself in the wrong place at the wrong time – still in Berlin five months after the Rastenburg explosion. Allen Dulles, who after initial distrust, had come to regard Gisevius as a genuine Allied agent, felt

obliged to engineer his rescue. For the German, it turned out to be a period of mental agony with the ever-present fear of the Gestapo and the inability of the Americans to produce the necessary counterfeit documentation for him to get out of Germany.

His release, in January 1945, came only when his nerves were in tatters. It had all the melodrama of lurid fiction. He later wrote in his memoirs of two rings on the doorbell. "I rushed outside, only to hear a blacked-out car driving away. But there was a fat envelope in the mailbag. The first thing which fell into my hand was a thick metal badge – that well known badge of executive office of the Gestapo. Then I unfolded an official German passport with a picture of myself. I found that my name was Hoffmann and that I was a high up functionary of the Gestapo. There was a special pass and a letter from Gestapo headquarters instructing all officials of the government and the Nazi Party to assist me in my secret mission to Switzerland."

The badge and passport were masterly forgeries. Only his photograph gave Gisevius any cause for anxiety. It was a full-length portrait reduced in size; the Gestapo generally used a police photograph, showing only head and shoulders. But it was too late to do anything about that now.

Gisevius managed to quit Berlin by constant waving of his Gestapo badge. He arrived two days later at the border crossing of Kreuzlingen – a battered figure wearing the suit he had worn on the fateful 20 July. The hat was borrowed and ill-fitting. Gisevius recalled later with some poignancy that he had given his own headgear to Arthur Nebe.

As luck would have it, the tired German border officials gave his papers only a brief glance. The equally weary Gisevius replied with a limp Nazi salute. It was his farewell to Hitler's Germany. His next official rôle was as a prosecution witness at the Nuremberg Trials.

Die Schutzstaffeln

Meine Ehre heißt Treue

der NSDAP.

|11|

The Reckoning
and the
Price

Even in the war's death throes, Heinrich Himmler clung tenaciously to his power and a fast-receding dream of vassal states controlled by the terror machine of the RSHA. Protected by what must have appeared an impregnable cocoon of power, the Reichsführer-SS was the most powerful bureaucrat in Germany, master of the Police, the Secret Service, and the Ministry of the Interior. His grip on the racial policy of the regime was sanctioned by the awesome title Reich Commissar for the Strengthening of Germanism. He was also Commander-in Chief of the Reserve Army.

Even so, he feared the outcome. The Allied invasion forces had swept through France and were in sight of the Rhine. The inexorable advance of the Red Army had already meant the overrunning of some of the extermination camps with their attendant revelations.

Events forced Himmler to contemplate the unthinkable: what would be the position of Germany if all was to end in catastrophe with Hitler no longer in control? From there was but a step to pondering just who, if that catastrophe was to be prevented, would be capable of taking the Führer's place. By 1944, Himmler was well down the road to treason, putting out slow feelers among those of his informants with the ear of the resistance.

One of his principal contacts was Carl Langbehn, a Berlin lawyer, who lived in a villa next to Himmler's official residence; the daughters of the two men had once attended the same school. Langbehn had dropped hints periodically that he was no admirer of the Nazi regime and it was not difficult for Himmler to discover that the other man belonged to a resistance group. Langbehn was persuaded to contact another key resistant, Professor Johannes von Popitz, who was scheduled to become Finance Minister in an emergency government to take over when Hitler was dethroned.

Himmler had met Popitz as early as August 1943 in his new office at the Ministry of the Interior. Popitz's argument was that the war could no longer be won by Germany. The outcome would, at best, be stalemate or, at worse, total defeat. It was Popitz's belief that Great Britain and the United States, fearing the ascent of Bolshevism in a post-war world, would negotiate. Himmler had treated Popitz to the characteristic blank stare from behind those rimless spectacles, but Popitz, feeling that his ideas had not been entirely disregarded, was

During the final year of the War, Himmler clung tenaciously to power and his control of the terror machine of the RSHA.

Professor Johannes von Popitz.

optimistic in his report to Langbehn who lost no time in travelling to see his western contacts in Switzerland.

The secrecy of such moves could not be sustained. According to Walter Schellenberg, a radio message about Langbehn's negotiations with Allied representatives in Switzerland had been intercepted by the Gestapo. It implicated not only Popitz and Langbehn but Schellenberg himself; the Chief of Foreign Intelligence was also coming to see the need for peace initiatives. Schellenberg later wrote: "Göring was already more or less in disgrace. There remained only one man who had sufficient power and influence. That was Himmler." Heinrich Müller passed on his findings on Langbehn to a delighted Martin Bormann, the head of Party affairs and one of Hitler's confidants. Himmler needed desperately to cover his tracks. He began, with the aid of the Gestapo, to move in on some of the known conspirators. Langhbehn was thrown to the wolves. It was, naturally, out of the question that he should be tried by the Gestapo: the worst excesses of Müller's men would reveal Himmler's own involvement. Instead, Langhbehn was hastily put in a concentration camp out of the reach of Kaltenbrunner and Müller and executed on 12 November 1944. Popitz was kept alive until the following February in case more information could be extracted from him.

As for Himmler, he flinched from facing the full implications of betrayal, seeking to expunge reality with refuge in contemplation of the familiar SS nostrum of a magic new world order. But reality was straining the cocoon. By 1 August 1944, the Soviet Army, moving on a broad front, had reached the Vistula; its reconnaissance detachments had penetrated the Warsaw suburbs. For the Polish Home Army it was a call to arms. The Warsaw Rising was put down with savagery by the SS. On 2 October, the Polish Home Army of the resistance surrendered.

But revolt was infectious. In addition to the Warsaw Rising a new crisis threatened the rear of the eastern front. Sections of the nominally independent Slovak state rose in revolt. The SD arrested the leading resistants while Himmler marshalled the resources of his Waffen-SS. Assisted by *Einsatzgruppe H* and its Gestapo components, under SS-Obersturmbannführer Dr Josef Witiska, Commander of the SD and Sipo in Slovakia, Berger put down the revolt in four weeks. The Slovak government dwindled from a puppet regime to a mere shadow.

The Gestapo had done its work well in the suppression of those involved in the 20 July plot; still more power was the reward. The RSHA Amt Mil, formed within the RSHA to embrace the Abwehr services, was disbanded altogether. Its chief, Oberst Hansen, found to have been hand in glove with some of the Berlin conspirators, confessed and went to his death after interrogation at the hands of Müller personally .

Throughout Europe, though, the writing was on the wall for the occupiers. By mid-August 1944, the Gestapo in Paris was a mere spectre. Carl-Albrecht Oberg, who had already sped incriminating documents out of the capital, was making his final preparations for departure. Soon only he, Helmuth Knochen, and their staffs were left. Oberg reasoned that business, even under these conditions, must continue. On 18 August, he instructed that a convoy of 1,600 prisoners from Compiegne be deported to Germany. It was Oberg's swan song in Paris but not, however, in France. On the same day, Oberg, Knochen, Scheer (the head of Orpo), and the last members of the Gestapo, left Paris for Vittel, setting up, temporary headquarters in an area designated by the OKW as the stabilized frontier of eastern France.

Such conscientious attention to duty in a lost cause, however, brought them scant gratitude, least of all from Himmler. In scathing terms, their Reichs-führer reproached the pair for having let themselves be arrested on 20 July without putting up any resistance. Their courage and loyalty was called into question. Kaltenbrunner followed up his chief's strictures by recalling Knochen to Berlin where he was eventually assigned to help in the structuring of new SD groups formed by the scrapping of the Abwehr services.

Ironically, it was Oberg who was to end the war in the fighting SS. At first, he had settled in St. Die in the Vosges district but soon he and his staff were forced to move on. They were edged across the Rhine and into the arms of Himmler who, as Commander-in-Chief of the Army Group of the Upper Rhine, mustered him into the ranks of the Waffen-SS. On 8 May 1945 Carl-Albrecht Oberg made it his business to go into hiding; a certain Albrecht Heintze had a fleeting period of anonymity in Kirchberg, a Tyrolean village near Kitzbühel. But his real identity was soon established and, in August,

Popitz and Carl Langbehn on trial before the People's Court, 3 October 1944. Both men were sentenced to death.

Wilhelm Lages, head of the Amsterdam branch of the Sipo.

Oberg was handed over to the French authorities at Wildbad. He was sentenced to death but the eventual sentence, not ratified until December 1959, was twenty years forced labour. Knochen, sentenced to death, was also to have his sentence commuted to hard labour.

The Allies had, from the autumn of 1944, envisaged the sure defeat of Nazi Germany; it was reasoned that by destroying certain picked Gestapo installations the process could be hastened. The need had been particularly pressing in Denmark where the Germans were near to closing in on the resistance. Under the auspices of the British SOE and the American OSS, orders were issued for an aerial bombardment of Gestapo headquarters in Aarhus which contained files on the resistance. The intention was to destroy, not only the records, but all Gestapo staff there. The attack was assigned to the Mosquito pilots of the RAF's Second Tactical Air Force, No. 2 Group, whose Mark IVs with their high speed and manoeuvrability were particularly suited for the job. Second Tactical Air Force had proved itself previously with a successful low-level attack against Gestapo headquarters in Amiens, as well as against the central population registry in The Hague, where archives on Dutch resistance had been housed by the Gestapo.

From northern Scotland on 31 October 1944, three squadrons of low-flying Mosquitos, each consisting of six aircraft, took off for Denmark and blasted the Aarhus Gestapo and its card indexes into oblivion. Within two weeks of the attack on Aarhus, Kai Winkelhorn, an American officer heading the Danish section of the OSS, discussed with senior intelligence officers of the Second Tactical Air Force how to deal a similar blow to Gestapo headquarters at Shellhus in Copenhagen. The operation was codenamed *Carthage*.

The extent of the threat facing the Danish resistance became apparent during preparations for the raid. The Copenhagen Gestapo had made three important captures – a leading contact for many of the resistance groups, the leader of the underground army in the immediate area, and a resistant who was a vital liaison with the underground press. Such a triple disaster made *Carthage* a pressing necessity. Eighteen Mosquitos were assigned, their pilots briefed that they were to bomb the base of Shellhus, avoiding where possible the upper floor which housed the prisoners.

On 21 March 1945, the aircraft, with their Mustang fighter escorts, took off in tolerable weather conditions. At ll:14 a.m., the bombs of the three aircraft in the first wave homed in precisely on the bottom floor of Shellhus. The bombs of the fourth, however, struck a tall light pole and crashed onto Frederiksberg Alle, near the Jeanne d'Arc Catholic School for Children. Eighty-six pupils were killed, including forty-two who had been huddled in a cellar shelter area, and eighteen adults. Casualties in Shellhus itself were lighter. The thirty-five dead included nine Danish prisoners housed on the top floor and twenty-six Gestapo employees who had been caught lower down. By malign chance, the Gestapo dead did not include the Shellhus leaders: SS-Gruppenführer Gunther Pancke, Gestapo chief Karl Heinz Hoffmann, or his chief aide Otto Bovensiepen. All were unexpectedly away from their offices, attending a funeral.

Even so, *Carthage* was greeted enthusiastically by the resistance who sent the message to London, "City wild with excitement about Shellhus bombing. Reliable sources maintain thirty Danish patriot hostages were liberated, among them two leaders. Warmest congratulations." Survivors among the Gestapo attempted immediately to rebuild their secret files and dossiers, but it was too late.

In Norway, the Nazis held on tenaciously, even though they knew that defeat could not be far off. Reichskommissar Terboven, with the police chief Wilhelm Rediess, retired to Skaugum, the luxury residence commandeered from Crown Prince Olaf. Both men were cool realists. Terboven knew that he would have no chance of avoiding the death penalty. As for Rediess, his over-all responsibility for the acts of torture and murder committed by his police during the occupation was sufficient to condemn him.

What followed had elements of black comedy. While troops were instructed to make ready explosive charges, both men proceeded to become steadily drunk. Rediess, his courage sufficiently fuelled, was the first to seize a pistol and shoot himself. Terboven dragged the body out to his personal bunker in the gardens, then lit the fuse of a waiting explosive charge. A fragment of concrete, covered with bits of bloody flesh, was eventually carried away.

Jonas Lie, the Norwegian Minister of Police and head of the Norwegian SS, made a fruitless attempt with weak forces to recapture police headquarters at

Hans Albert Rauter.

Rauter was shot and wounded by the Dutch resistance group Binnenlandse Strijdkrachten (Dutch Interior) while they were trying to commandeer an Army vehicle in order to steal food.

Mollergaten 19 in Oslo. When that failed, he retreated to a farm in a suburb of Olso, digging himself into a bunker plentifully stocked with arms, ammunition, and cases of liquour. When he was surrounded with superior numbers of the Milorg resistance, he too shot himself.

Dr Karl Schoengarth, Commander of the Sicherheitspolizei in the Netherlands, was also addicted to alcoholic oblivion. He did not, however, commit suicide. As the subordinate of both Hanns Albin Rauter, the Höehere SS und Polizeiführer Nordwest, and of Lages, the head of the Amsterdam branch of the Sipo, Schoengarth had been fully occupied in implementing Hitler's so-called Niedermachungsbefehl, the instruction to the police to execute publicly any Todeskandidaten (death candidates) who were members of the resistance.

By the end of this first few months of 1945, the Dutch hoped that they had experienced the worst of the terror. But a single incident was to lead to a bloodbath without parallel. On the night of 6-7 March 1945, members of the resistance organization Binnenlandse Strijdkrachten (Dutch Interior) shot and badly wounded the country's police tormentor, Hanns Albin Rauter. The assault on Rauter had been unintended; the resistants had merely wanted to seize an army vehicle to hijack food intended for the Wehrmacht. The attack was swiftly avenged by the firing squads of the Orpo. The definition of Todeskandidaten was widened to include, not simply resistance members, but, in the words of Schoengarth, who had taken over from the injured Rauter, "looters and curfew breakers."

At his trial by the Dutch after the war, Rauter, who was still suffering from the effects of his injuries, protested that he had implored both Seyss-Inquart and Schoengarth to refrain from reprisals. He was not believed and went to the gallows on 25 March 1949. Schoengarth was also executed. It was alleged at his trial by a British court that a shooting on 8 March of 117 Dutch citizens was on a direct order from Himmler. Telegrams between the RSHA and the German authorities in the Netherlands though, contained no record of contact between the Reichsführer and Schoengarth. The conclusion of the court was that Schoengarth had instituted a terror programme solely on his own initiative and without higher authority.

As the situation in Germany worsened, Himmler stepped up his traitorous activities to bring the war in the west to an end. Himmler had meetings with Count Folke Bernadotte, the Vice-President of the Swedish Red Cross. At first, Himmler was cautious, beginning with such concessions as seeing to the release of prisoners, but flinching at out-and-out betrayal of his Führer. Eventually Himmler began to justify even this to himself: historical necessity might dictate the parting with Hitler, but would this matter if he (Heinrich Himmler) was designated the natural successor? Naturally, the war in the east would have to continue. Bernadotte was asked to transmit this proposal to the Swedish government for conveying in turn to General Eisenhower.

Such a scheme was, of course, preposterous. Himmler was not, however, to remain secure in his delusions. Not only were his proposals rejected out of hand by the Allies but their substance reached the Reuters news service in Washington which lost no time in broadcasting them to the world.

The news was picked up on Stockholm Radio by one of Goebbels' staff who passed it at once to Martin Bormann, who even at this juncture had not lost a lifetime's habit of intrigue. Hitler, according to the testimony of surviving witnesses, notably the celebrated aviatrix Hannah Reitsch who was one of the last visitors to the bunker, received the news at the same time as a hurricane of Russian shells was blowing-in the walls of the Chancellery above. In these grotesque circumstances, Hitler's eruption was terrible to behold. Reitsch described him as raging like a madman, thrusting the text of the message into the hands of everyone he met, as if seeking confirmation of the truth. He screamed out that his longest serving colleague – der treue Heinrich – had dealt him the cruellest blow of all.

Hitler's self pity turned to a lust for blood. He seized on the absence from the bunker of SS-Obergruppenführer Hermann Fegelein, the brother-in-law of his long time mistress Eva Braun. Fegelein, who had acted as liaison between Himmler and Hitler and who had made twice-daily visits to the bunker for military briefings, had planned to go into hiding with a woman. He was dragged back to the bunker and handed over to Heinrich Müller for what was probably the Gestapo's last assignment. Hanna Reitsch, who left the bunker late on Saturday 28 April, confirmed later to an American journalist, James O'Donnell, that Fegelein had been executed.

Reitsch flew out of the Berlin bunker amid explosions and a sea of flames with orders from Hitler to arrest the errant Reichsführer-SS at Plon, on the Baltic coast some 200 miles northwest of Berlin. Reitsch was accompanied by General Robert Ritter von Greim, (upgraded to Generalfeldmarschall in Hitler's final promotion) who had been stranded, badly wounded, in the bunker. At Plon, the couple found an uneasy power balance in force between Admiral Karl Dönitz, Commander-in-Chief of the northern armies, and Himmler, head of the SS and police. Himmler still had a formidable SS entourage in tow and it would have been impossible to effect an arrest. Besides, at this

At his trial after the War, Rauter still shows signs of the injuries he received at the hands of the resistance. He was sentenced to death and died on the gallows on 25 March 1949.

Hermann Fegelein, brother-in-law of Hitler's mistress, Eva Braun. Fegelein was handed over to Müller for interrogation and was probably the last victim executed by the Gestapo.

Admiral Karl Dönitz, Commander-in-Chief of the Northern Armies, with Albert Speer, the Armaments Minister.

Martin Bormann, the "Iago of the bunker," remained close to Hitler during those final days beneath the Reichschancellery.

point, Dönitz took it for granted that the Reichsführer would be Hitler's successor – and so, of course, did Himmler himself.

It was not until late 30 April that a signal from Bormann in the bunker informed Dönitz that he, and not Himmler, was the designated successor. The tone was evasive. Bormann did not even reveal that Hitler had died by his own hand at 3:30 that same afternoon. In his memoirs, Dönitz claimed to have received another message which said, "New treason afoot. According enemy broadcasts Himmler offered capitulation via Sweden. Führer expects you to deal with all traitors fast as lightning and hard as steel. Bormann."

With the Third Reich on the edge of disintegration, Dönitz was quick to disassociate himself from the taint of Himmler in any forthcoming "administration." To Himmler he wrote:

Dear Herr Reichsminister – In view of the present situation I have decided to dispense with your further assistance as Reichsminister of the Interior and member of the Reich Government, as Commander-in-Chief of the Reserve Army, and as Chief of the Police. I now regard all your offices as abolished. I thank you for the service you have given to the Reich."

It is not known whether Himmler ever received this message; a copy was found unsigned in Dönitz's desk, following the arrest and imprisonment of his rump government on 23 May 1945.

After the German capitulation fifteen days earlier, Himmler's powers of decision, never profound, had deserted him completely. The former Reichsführer had reverted to his status of a generation before: that of eccentric political vagabond. Bereft of any purpose or direction, he drove aimlessly around the countryside where he slept rough, finally setting off on foot with his secretary and adjutant. Over five days, they tramped slowly south through Neuhaus to Bremervorde where they were stopped at an Army control point. After questioning, Himmler, who finally gave up the struggle, was taken to Second Army headquarters at Luneburg where he was stripped and searched.

As it turned out, Himmler had managed to secrete a potassium cyanide vial in a cavity of his gums. When a second British intelligence officer arrived from Montgomery's headquarters on 23 May and instructed a medical officer to examine the prisoner's mouth, Himmler bit on the vial and was dead in twelve minutes despite frantic attempts to revive him. The former Reichsführer-SS and Chief of the German Police and Gestapo, General of the Order of Teutonic Knights, and self-proclaimed reincarnation of the Saxon King, Henry the Fowler, was baled in an army blanket, secured with camouflage netting and telephone wire. Then he was tipped into the back of a truck and driven to Luneburg Heath where a grave, destined to be unmarked, was dug for him.

After the German capitulation, Himmler drove aimlessly around the countryside before setting off on foot with his secretary and adjutant. Finally stopped at an Army control point, Himmler was taken to Second Army headquarters at Luneburg.

On 23 May, British Intelligence agents arrived at Luneburg to interview Himmler. Himmler bit on a hidden vial of potassium cyanide and was dead within twelve minutes. He was unceremoniously wrapped in an Army blanket and taken by truck for burial on Luneburg Heath, where a shallow grave was dug for him.

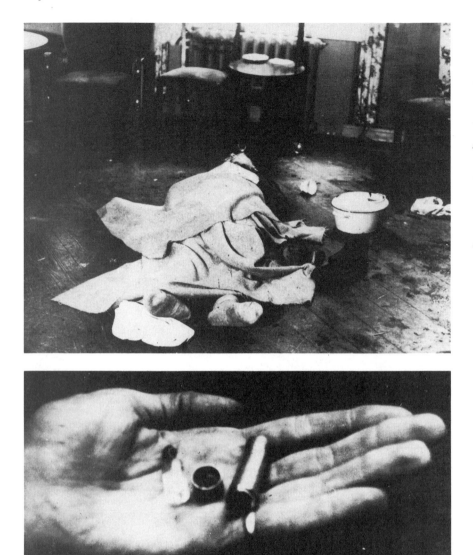

Some seventeen months later, at 4:00 a.m. on 16 October 1946, the body of Hermann Göring, the former Reichsmarschall, also set out on its last journey. But this was to a crematorium – and made aboard a 2-ton truck, followed by a jeep filled with picked American guards and a machine gun. Göring had for company the bodies of those who, two hours before, had perished as war criminals on the gallows of Nuremberg jail. Göring's corpse, however, bore no marks of death by strangulation. He, too, had succeeded in concealing poison – just how in a high security prison remained his secret and he had the last laugh on his captors.

During the Nuremberg trial, Göring had struck a combative, frequently aggressive pose, on occasions scoring notable points off a badly rattled, under-briefed prosecution. Where Himmler had progressively blotted out the real

Above: *In the same
woods near where
Himmler was buried,
the Allies discovered
the remains of hundreds
of bodies, victims of the
retreating Nazis.*

Left: *Thirty-two years
later, British sergeants
Ray Weston and Bill
Ottery at the spot where
they buried the former
Reichsführer-SS.*

world by contemplation of racial fantasies, Göring had taken refuge in a luxurious life-style and blatant neglect of his offices. He had admitted that he no longer cared and, in the words of Albert Speer, the Armaments Minister, "had sunk into his lethargy, and for good."

Nevertheless, Göring had not forgotten that by Führer decrees he was designated to replace Hitler should the latter become incapacitated or, in the event of Hitler's death, to replace him. Göring had dug out the decrees, satisfied himself as to their provisions, then on 23 April 1945 dashed off a telegram to Hitler, which contained the sentence: "If no reply is received by 10 o' clock tonight, I shall take it for granted that you have lost your freedom of action, and shall consider the decree as fulfilled."

Such a move proved a disastrous miscalculation. Hitler was beside himself, having been persuaded by the insinuating Bormann, the Iago of the bunker, that this amounted to a coup. Göring was promptly stripped of his offices and his Luftwaffe post given to Ritter von Greim. Göring was also placed under house arrest by embarrassed SS men but managed to despatch envoys on his behalf to the nearest American troops. There, still seeing himself as Hitler's

Hermann Göring, designated to succeed Hitler by decree, was finally put under house arrest on Hitler's orders by embarrassed SS men.

plenipotentiary, he submitted to captivity. But his attempts to ingratiate himself and to treat "man to man" with Eisenhower were total failures.

Ernst Kaltenbrunner – "that ugly vast hulk of a man" – who had seen the SS
as an instrument for attaining elite status, was the other senior Nazi directly
linked to the Gestapo to stand in the Nuremberg dock. Göring, by virtue of a
formidable personality, had presented a front of genial braggadocio. The vast,
grim-faced Kaltenbrunner, on the other hand, had broken down in tears when
served his indictment, moaning that no one would defend him and that he
would not receive a fair trial. In a moment of childish defiance, he protested,
"I have only done my duty as an intelligence organ. I refuse to serve as an
ersatz for Himmler!"

Confronted with the number of decrees he had personally signed, together
with directives issued from central or local Gestapo offices, Kaltenbrunner
either disowned them or branded them the responsibility of Himmler or
Müller. His defence was that he had been appointed chief of the RSHA solely
to reorganize the Reich's political intelligence service.

As a defence it was ludicrous. One chilling example of Kaltenbrunner's
decrees had been an order to Eichmann that Hungarian Jews were to be
marched on foot over 120 miles to the Strasshof detention camp near Vienna.
The marches of 35,000 Jews had begun from Budapest on 20 October 1944 in
vile conditions of rain, sleet, and snow. The Jews had lacked clothing, food,
and adequate footwear. Several thousand had collapsed or been shot on the
way.

*Dönitz giving evidence
at the Nuremberg trials
in October 1946. Sitting
in the front below him is
Göring, with Hess to his
left. Kaltenbrunner is
fifth from the left.
Top row: Third from
right is Albert Speer;
fourth from right is
Arthur Seyss-Inquart.*

A break during proceedings. As he awaited the verdict Göring said, "If I am to die, I wish to face a firing squad in Berlin and die like a soldier."

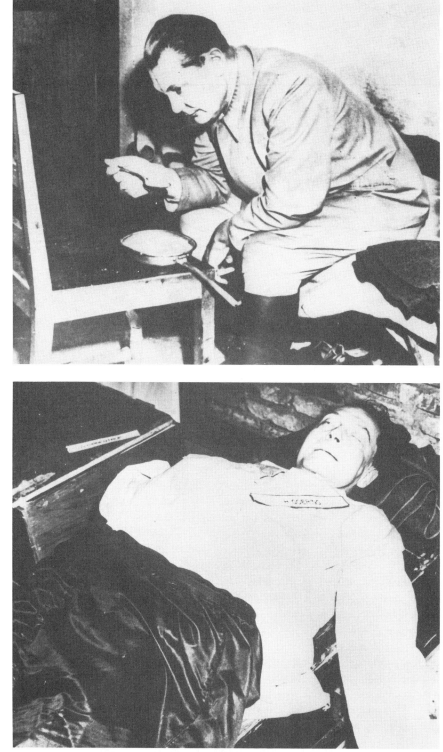

Hermann Göring gives evidence at his trial.

Like Himmler, Göring had secreted a poison vial and thus escaped the fate of so many of those on trial at Nuremberg who were hanged as war criminals.

The court had scant sympathy for Kaltenbrunner's monotonous abrogations of responsibility. The judges pronounced his guilt on counts 3 and 4 of the indictment (war crimes and crimes against humanity) and sentenced him to death. Kaltenbrunner, who was nearly seven feet tall, ascended the scaffold on 15 October 1946. Reportedly, he took fifteen minutes to die on the end of the rope.

By now the war had long come home to the Gestapo. On 3 February 1945, Gestapo headquarters in Berlin had been severely damaged. Artillery and tank bombardment in the final days of the war increased the destruction. From 26 April, Soviet troops under the command of General Vasili Chuikov advanced from the Landwehr Canal at Hallesches Tor towards the government quarter. Defensive positions were held rigidly in Koethenerstrasse and Prinz Albrechtstrasse. It was all useless; after further severe fighting in the Wilhelmstrasse, the commandant of the city of Berlin surrendered finally on 2 May 1945.

When it was over, Prinz Albrechtstrasse 8, together with the adjoining Martin-Gropius building, were found to have been gutted by fire, although structurally still intact.

The Gestapo continued to operate in the shell of its home, devoid of water or electricity, until shortly before the surrender. On the night of 23/24 April, most of those still held in confinement were marched to a war-ravaged site nearby and shot. When the cells were finally liberated, only six inmates were still alive.

At around 3:30 p.m. on 30 April, Hitler and Eva Braun withdrew into the study of the bunker where the Führer took his own life with a heavy 7.65 mm Walther and Eva Braun bit down on a poisoned capsule. By then the complicated edifice of the Gestapo had disappeared. And with it, incidentally, had vanished the sour, brutal, Heinrich Müller, who had been seen in Hitler's company as late as the end of April. In his memoirs, Walter Schellenberg claimed to have unearthed evidence that Müller had long established contact with the Russian Secret Service and had crossed to his new masters. Many who had set out with high hopes of working their passage with the Soviets found that their lot was incarceration in a labour camp. But, according to Schellenberg, a German officer who had been a prisoner of war in Russia claimed in 1950 to have seen Müller in Moscow two years before.

Rudolf Diels, the man who had started it all, actually ended up by outwitting the Gestapo itself, dodging the meat hooks and the piano wire which, given his suspected involvement in the assassination plot against Hitler, would almost certainly have choked the life out of this born survivor. After the war, Diels went back to the rôle which he always played best – that of loyal civil servant. He was killed in a hunting accident in 1957.

Rudolf Diels. A born survivor who had been head of the Berlin Gestapo. He returned to the civil service after the War. Diels was killed in a hunting accident in 1957.

To the intense relief of the German collective conscience, the terrible associations of the old site of Gestapo headquarters began to fade from memory, probably helped by the East German renaming of Prinz Albrechtstrasse as Niederkirchnerstrasse in honour of a Communist resistance fighter who had been murdered by the SS. Relieved also were those not inconsiderable numbers of former Gestapo, SS, and RSHA personnel who had escaped criminal prosecution and who, as the years passed, felt it was safe to relax. For two of them, at least, relaxation was to prove misplaced.

The most notorious of them long felt secure in Argentina under the alias of Otto Henniger. False civilian papers under that name had enabled the head of the Jewish section of the Gestapo and the RSHA to emigrate to South America and to assume yet another alias, Ricardo Klement. It was not until 1960 that Adolf Eichmann was tracked down by Israeli agents and captured in a daring Commando action in the heart of Argentinian territory.

Encased in a glass booth in the courtroom of Beit Ha'am – the House of the People – in Jerusalem, the bespectacled Eichmann looked every inch the bureaucrat and hyper-efficient desk man who, fifteen years before, his comparatively junior rank of Obersturmbannführer notwithstanding, had been one of the most powerful men of the Third Reich. The extent of that power had been strikingly demonstrated in the winter of 1944 when he had been sent to Budapest to assume control of the Hungarian "Jewish problem." Hungary at that time was the only Axis-ruled country still enjoying political independence and whose 800,000 Jews had experienced relative peace. Eichmann changed all that with sinister muscle, arriving in Budapest with a specially selected *Sondereinsatzkommando* (Special Duty Commando) brought from Mauthausen and which, with the help of the Hungarian police, had the task of rounding up the Jews for deportation to Auschwitz. The process was facilitated by Hungary's Regent Ferenc Szalasi, a fanatical anti-Semite and leader of the Fascist Arrow Cross, a puppet whose strings were being pulled vigorously by another zealous SS acolyte, Reich Plenipotentiary Edmund Veesenmayer. Then had come a threat to Eichmann's authority: Himmler was then in the throes of his negotiations with the Allies and ordered the cessation of the extermination programme. An order by Eichmann for the transportation of 1500 Jews was countermanded and a train sent back. Eichmann, abetted by Kaltenbrunner, was not to be deflected. He managed to collect the same 1500 Jews and smuggle them out secretly.

In her book, *The War Against The Jews 1933-1945*, Lucy Dawidowicz, two of whose family perished in the Warsaw Ghetto and in Treblinka, states that up until 4 April 1945 when Hungary was finally free of the Nazis, "over 450,000 Jews, seventy per cent of the Jews of Greater Hungary, were deported, were murdered or died under German occupation. Within the boundaries of lesser (pre-1938) Hungary, about half the Jews were annihilated."

In the dock on trial for his life, Eichmann's demeanour was marked with the same administrative pedantry and neatness which had characterized the running of his bureaucracy of genocide ensuring the efficient transportation of thousands, ultimately millions, to Treblinka, Maidanek, Buchenwald, Auschwitz. His confession under intense interrogation in Israel was characteristically full and factual; it ran to some 3,500 pages. Adolf Eichmann was found guilty and hanged at Ramle on 31 May 1962.

Eichmann's arraignment was followed down the years by numerous other trials for war crimes, but probably none were accompanied by the high drama leading to the 1987 sentence of life imprisonment on the "Butcher of Lyon" – Klaus Barbie. Barbie had attempted to cloak the past under the alias of Klaus Altmann, but had been brought back from a long period of sanctuary in Bolivia.

Even before the trial began in Lyon, Barbie was made to confront his former victims. One May morning in 1983, the gates of St Joseph's prison

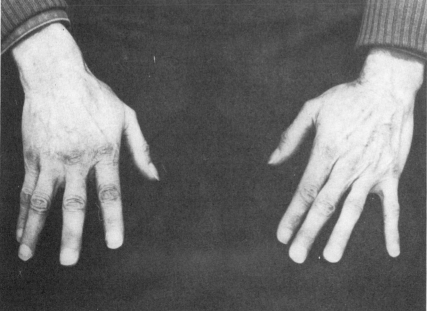

Left: *The neatly maincured hands of a mass murderer.*

Right: *Partisans are rounded up in a Budapest street. Their fate was execution.*

Below right: *Hungarian victims of the* Einsatzgruppen *are disinterred from a Jewish cemetery in Budapest. More than half of Hungary's Jewish population perished during the Nazi occupation.*

Above: *Sign at the entrance to the Budapest Ghetto warns non-Jews not to enter. Ghettoes such as this were a by-product of the notorious Wannsee conference.*

Scenes from the Terezin ghetto, a few miles outside Prague, which housed Czechoslovakian Jews. For those who protested there were (above) the solitary confinement cells and (below) constant surveillance amidst primitive conditions.

Above: *A drawing by Milos Bajic whilst a prisoner in a concentration camp.*

swung open and in a five-second flurry of noise and speed a van with motorcycle outriders hurtled out into the rush hour traffic. As the van tore across the town for two miles at more than fifty mph, the handcuffed figure inside was rocked back and forth, his white hair tossed. The destination for Barbie was the Montluc fortress across the Rhone, where thousands had been tortured, maimed, and killed at his instigation.

Within Montluc, Barbie was brought face-to-face in a four hour confrontation with an eighty-two year old woman who had been on the last prisoners' convoy from Lyon to Auschwitz in 1944. The move was designed to illustrate the insistence of the authorities that the trial should be preceded by painstaking investigations of Barbie's alleged crimes, a reconstruction as far as possible of events that occured during the Nazi occupation of France. The unnamed elderly woman was said to have witnessed some of the worst excesses of the Gestapo in Lyon. The trial, it was keenly felt, should not merely be designed for vengeance but be a factual record of Gestapo excesses and cruelty as practised by one man, a final closing of the book.

Raw nerves, however, remained exposed in prosperous, bourgeois Lyon until the handcuffs were clapped on seventy-three year old Barbie and he was finally led away to start his life sentence. The spectre of collaboration had stalked Lyon. In some households there had been sleepless nights from bad consciences and even worse memories. At café tables, Barbie and his reign of terror was either discussed frankly or delicately avoided. Those with the bad consciences need not have worried: there was no naming of resistance traitors at the trial. No one is likely ever to know for certain who betrayed Jean Moulin. Nor was Moulin's murder the single event which made Barbie's name so infamous.

In the Rhone Assize Court, the public prosecutor, Pierre Truche, estimated that Barbie had been responsible for the deportation of 842 people to the concentration camps, of whom at least 373 were known to have died. Truche asked: "What assize court has ever had to deal with such a total?" Of that total fifty-two were children – forty-four of them sent to the gas chambers from the children's home at Izieu. This was the crime which provided a motivating force for the famous Nazi hunters, French Jewish lawyer Serge Klarsfeld, whose own father was gassed at Auschwitz, and his German-born Protestant wife, Beate, to track Barbie down and lead the long campaign for his forced return.

With the bulk of Gestapo records dispersed or destroyed why, it was inevitably asked, bother to put one old man on trial after so long a time? After all, it could be argued that Klaus Barbie was no Eichmann, no assistant architect of the Final Solution, but a cog in Himmler's machine who never rose above Obersturmführer in the SD. There were thousands like him operating all over occupied Europe, many of whom escaped justice altogether. Why should *he* be singled out?

It can be argued that in Lyon at least it had been possible to bring justice to the memory of the children of Izieu and to the legend of Jean Moulin, one of the greatest of French resistance heroes, Moulin's widow Renée, a frail septuagenarian, who was said to have celebrated in champagne the arrest of "the Butcher of Lyon."

Left: *Klaus Barbie, "The Butcher of Lyon," at his war crimes trial in 1987. He was sentenced to life imprisonment and died in prison in 1991.*

Below: *Witnesses against Barbie still bear the scars of Gestapo interrogation.*

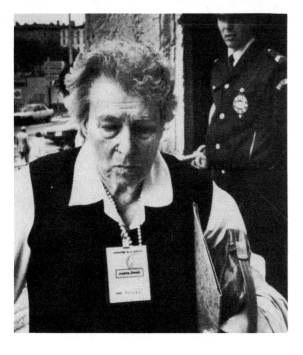

Barbie's family spoke of an apparently devoted husband and a father who had been inconsolable after the death of a son. Yet there was also the survivor of Barbie's tortures who was there to testify, "He loved to play God," recalling the Gestapo chief's devotion to cruelty and in inflicting pain. As for the shrunken nonentity on trial in the Lyon court, he put up no defiant defence and, indeed, for much of the proceedings insisted on withdrawing from the dock altogether.

Klaus Barbie died in prison on 23 September 1991. Few cared to remember a figure who had been notorious nearly two generations ago. But what the Gestapo did in Lyon was nevertheless on record. Justice, despite the passage of time, had touched a man whose crimes had proved too monstrous to ignore.

World War II cartoon depicting the Dutch veiw of the Nazis conscripting men for forced labour.

The
Gestapo
Today

During the winter of 1990 an exhibition of the life of Bismarck and the unification of 19th Century Germany which was held in the Martin Gropius building in what was formerly East Berlin, drew large crowds. Nearby another exhibition of German history was being held – one of a very different kind and which had to do, not with the pride and triumph of one empire, but the defeat and shame of another.

The second less publicized event, called the Topography of Terror, was held, appropriately enough, on the site of the Gestapo building on Prinz Albrechtstrasse, which it is planned to preserve as a museum. This exhibition covered the history of the Gestapo and SS, based mainly on enlarged documents and photographs. Indeed, it could have done little else – all that remains of the structure of the building are the submerged walls of a few cells and the cellars for a kitchen and supply building. Upstairs had once been the offices inhabited not just by Gestapo men of movie myth – leather-coated, snap-brim hatted sadists, storming into the houses of Jews and forcing them into gas chambers – but by the pen-pushers, the family men who mowed suburban lawns on Sundays as a break from dictating memos and signing requisitions and generally behaving like civil servants.

To many of the new generation in post-Soviet, post-Communist, East Berlin, the site of the former Gestapo headquarters, where a section of the Berlin Wall leads to the former Checkpoint Charlie seemed something of an irrelevance in a city that faces a fair share of the problems of the 1990s. Nevertheless the area does occasionally deliver up disconcerting reminders of the past of Prinz Albrechtstrasse.

During the excavation of the ruins in 1987, a number of photographs were found, including one of an attractive young couple, Harro Schulze-Boysen, a grandson of the First World War Admiral von Tirpitz, and Schulze-Boysen's wife, Libertas, who had both held key positions in the resistance group which the Gestapo had called Rote Kapelle (Red Orchestra). While employed in the Reich Air Ministry, Schulze-Boysen had transmitted military information to the Soviet Union and indulged in other anti-Nazi activities. After his arrest on 30 August 1942, he had been taken to the Prinz Albrechtstrasse where he was interrogated and tortured until sentenced to death on 19 December. Three days later, he was executed at Plotzensee prison.

Lest we forget. Right:
*The torture chamber in
Breendonk, preserved
as a memorial.*
Below: *Iron shackles
still in place.*

Libertas, arrested later, was also executed at Plotzensee – begging "spare my
young life" as she was rushed screaming to the guillotine.

Not all the surviving reminders of the Gestapo in Berlin are quite so grim.
Opened as a museum is the Wilhelmine lakeside suburban villa at Am Grossen
Wannsee 56-58, which had been used until 1943 as a recreational centre for
SD personnel. Here, on 20 January 1942, Heydrich had hosted the so-called
Wannsee Konferenz to review the achievements of the anti-Jewish pogrom
and to plot its future. In these innocuous and pleasant surroundings, Heydrich,
like any company chairman, had poured out reassuring statistics to his audience: more than 500,000 Jews had at that time already been murdered in the
Baltics, Belorussia, and the Ukraine. The Wannsee meeting had then gone on
to invest plans for the "Final Solution to the Jewish Question" in the bureaucratic obscurantism so beloved of the SS.

To enter the villa in the 1990s is to encounter a time warp. After lengthy
restoration and renovation, the ground floor is essentially as it was when the

meeting was held in the dining room and the cognac flowed. Under glass on a table in the centre of the room is the only surviving copy of the notorious conference protocol as transcribed by Adolf Eichmann. But the villa these days is more than a cold museum. A permanent exhibition traces modern persecution of Jewry: from the influence of anti-Semitic literature in pre-Nazi Germany, through the barring of Jews from everyday life, to physical persecution and deportation – policies which were broadened to encompass Jews in any country under German occupation. The instruments of such a policy are also detailed at Wannsee – the massacres and the extermination camps whose activities were only stemmed by liberation.

Merely being in the house is a sobering experience for any visitor. As Heinz Galinski, the chairman of the Jewish Council of Germany and of the Berlin Jewish community, put it: "In this house, on 20 January 1942, one of civilisation's thresholds was breached, an abyss of barbarity yawned that changed mankind's view of itself. What happened after the Wannsee Conference, as a consequence of its decisions, laid bare the inhumanity of which man is capable."

The tentacles of the Gestapo extended far into the occupied countries. Another victim of the round-up of Rote Kapelle had been Johann Wenzel, who had worked for the spy network in Belgium and, with other members of the espionage circle, had undergone torture at Breendonk concentration camp situated mid-way between Antwerp and Brussels. Breendonk, where the Belgian Gestapo consigned many of its victims, still stands, complete with torture chamber, firing squad execution posts, and gallows But these days the grim hulk is called the Fort Breendonk National Memorial; it also has urns containing the ashes of victims from Dachau, Auschwitz, Mauthausen, Ravensbruck, and Maidanek.

If Prinz Albrechtstrasse, the Wannsee villa, and Breendonk serve as reminders of State Police bureaucracy and the attendant murder and terror, other remaining traces of the Gestapo point up with great poignancy the merciless assault by its agents on the innocent. At Prinsengracht 263 in Amsterdam can be found the Anne Frankhuis where for two years and one month the young Jewess wrote her diary until the Gestapo action of 4 August 1944. On the walls of Anne's room, her cut-outs from teenage magazines and the pin-up photographs of favourite movie stars stand preserved in the former secret annexe, abandoned on the day they came to take her away.

But not all traces of the Gestapo in Europe seem like monuments to the dead. In the early postwar years little changed in the village of Lidice near Prague: there was only a mass grave, above which was a towering wooden cross with a circling halo of barbed wire. To construct anything from the past was impossible: sappers and members of the Reich's uniformed labour units had levelled the destroyed houses, cut down the trees, removed all trails and roads and ensured that the entire area was made untraceable under a covering of soil.

Today, the survivors of the horrific massacre of 10 June 1942 live with their descendants in a new Lidice, alongside fields where the old village once stood. Above the entrance of the two-storeyed school building is the inscription "School My Happiness." There were originally ninety-nine children at

In Prague, at the renamed Church of St Cyril and Methodius on Ressel Street. Through this vent the Nazis pumped water and tear gas to flush out the parachutists. The ledge below the vent is scattered with flowers and messages left by visitors from all over the world.

Lidice; only sixteen could be traced after the war. Hints of the past now are the outlines of the church foundations – and the cross marking the farmyard where the men were shot.

The intention of Hitler to blast the name of Lidice from the face of the earth was a conspicuous failure. News of the crime shocked the world, particularly in Britain from where the assassins of Reinhard Heydrich had originally set out. The mining area of Stoke-on-Trent in the English Midlands began the British "Lidice Shall Live" Committee and implemented plans to rebuild the village as a model mining community.

A competition among architects for the reconstruction of Lidice was announced; keys to the first homes were handed over at Christmas 1949. In addition, a Garden of Peace and Friendship, on the slopes of the valley, opened on Sunday 19 June 1955. Banks of flowers and wreathes hid the ruins of the foundations of the old mining village while the red roofs of the new houses stood out in the bright morning sunshine.

A full half century after the atrocity committed by the Germans, the region of Lidice faced a new threat of destruction, this time from ecological pollution and industrial damage. An appeal was launched from Britain by the Lidice 50th Anniversary Committee to raise money to plant avenues of trees in and around the village, an area of severe pollution. It was a potent gesture of faith in both rebirth and survival – elements which the Nazis had intended to destroy utterly for their revenge of Heydrich's death.

For the Gestapo itself, however, there was to be no rebirth and no survival. All over the Reich and the occupied countries at the war's end, Allied bombers

The Children of Lidice. A sculptural group by the Czechoslovakian artist, Marie Uchytilova, which took twenty years to complete. The work represents the eighty-two Lidice children who fell victim to Nazi brutality. The statue is dedicated to the 13,000,000 children who perished in World War II. Marie Uchytilova died in 1989.

Above: *The women of Lidice. Here the women of Lidice learn the fate of their fathers, husbands, brothers, and sons when they return to Lidice after the War. Until then, they had dared to hope.*

had wrought devastation in camps, block houses, offices, and anywhere else where the Gestapo had operated. No longer did interrogation rooms in Berlin's Prinz Albrechtstrasse or Prague's grim, black-faced Petsche Palace, where poor Ata Moravec was tortured until he could bear no more, resound to the screams of its victims.

Almost as terrifying as the instruments of torture which the Gestapo had employed had been the bulky dossiers which had housed the intimate secrets of millions. When Soviet troops reached Prinz Albrechtstrasse 8, for example, they had come across a jumbled but otherwise complete card index of all "suspect Berliners." Many of these records had been destroyed by the invaders.

But not quite all the paper went up in flames through carpet bombing or was snatched away by the wind on muddy roads or slipped from convoys of abandoned trucks or was hastily destroyed by the Germans themselves. More than enough precisely phrased memoranda survived to confront war criminals brought to justice or to confound apologist historians for Nazism.

The Document Centre in Berlin, for example, holds an entire shelf of reports of mopping up operations by *Einsatzgruppen* alone. This in itself helps provide ample evidence of the consummate evil of dictatorship and of the bullying arm of any secret police apparatus which seeks to enforce it.

The warnings are portents for the future.

Maria Dolezalova, one of the Lidice children sent to Germany for 'Germanization,' is reunited with her mother after the War.

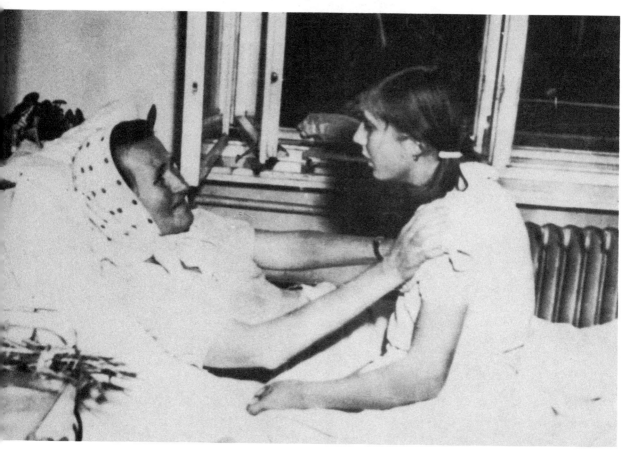

The
Survivors

During the course of my researches for this book, I
interviewed men and women in a number of countries who
had encounters with the Gestapo. Many of them suffered
mental and physical torture, but they spoke of often appalling
experiences without anger or bitterness. Indeed, there were
instances of rueful humour – Paul "Yogi" Mayer, for instance,
met Reinhard Heydrich by mistake!

These survivors stand as witnesses to the truth about the
Gestapo and its methods. The testimonies which follow are as
near as possible faithful transcriptions of what was actually
said. The text is tailored only by the dictates of space. I would
like to dedicate this book to the survivors I met – indeed, to
the victims of Gestapo tyranny everywhere and to
those who remember them.

Rupert Butler.
London 1992.

*The woodcut on page 204 shows Lidice before
the War; page 227 shows the new Lidice after its
reconstruction. Reprinted by kind permission of
the Orbis Press Agency, Prague.*

Marcel Baiwir

Twenty-three year old Belgian MARCEL BAIWIR came from a family with a long tradition of dissidence, to the extent that the whole Baiwir family had been placed on a 'wanted' list by the Gestapo. At the funeral in Liege of Marcel Baiwir's mother, the Gestapo sprang a trap.

"It was not even possible to pay our last respects to my mother at the graveside. As the family followed the funeral cortege, the Germans arrived. The military presence, of course, was obvious – toting machine guns even as the coffin was being lowered into the earth. And then there was the Gestapo, moving in for their arrests, snatching my brother-in-law and nephew. My uncle Reel was taken to the concentration camp at Breendonk and from there to the notorious slave labour camp of Neuengamme in the Elbe marshes. None survived."

Marcel Baiwir fled from Liege to Brussels with his wife, Berthe.

"We posed not as husband and wife, but as lovers. This gave me cover for visiting the house clandestinely. It probably would have been a safe enough arrangement but for an Estonian woman across the corridor. We discovered later that she had been having an affair with a member of the Geheime Feld Polizei, attached to the Abwehr. There is no doubt that she betrayed us. One night, in bed, we were terrified by the blinding beam of a searchlight which had been placed in a house opposite. Soon the Germans were breaking down the door, piling in and leaping on us, beating me continually with pistol butts. Then we were both dragged downstairs and crammed into separate cars.

"But I was only too conscious that, initially, we were lucky to have been picked up, not by the Gestapo on this occasion, but by the GFP, even if they did rough me up a bit. Liaison between Gestapo and GFP was not good; the Field Police didn't have a file on me or knowledge of my activities as a saboteur. Our precious Estonian betrayer had heard me addressed by Berthe as 'Marcel', but other visitors to the house had used a cover name which had aroused the woman's suspicions. The GFP had absolutely nothing on Berthe and no reason to detain her, so she was released.

"I was paraded before a group of prisoners, each of whom was asked if he could identify me. All of them flatly denied even having heard of me except the very last man of all. I tried to bluff it out, saying of course he didn't know me, that he was mistaken. But it was no use. My cover was blown. They interrogated in the classic Gestapo manner – beginning by bellowing at me, then working themselves into increasingly violent rages. Then one of them would adopt a kindly tone, apologizing for the manners of his colleague and inviting my co-operation. It didn't work and it was then that the beatings began. I was made to kneel down and my back soon turned dark blue under a steady regime of beatings.

"All torture sessions were carefully arranged so that certain picked prisoners would be sure to hear a victim's screams. That made them more amenable when their turn came. I can remember praying for two things: that the beating would stop and that I would not involuntarily relieve myself in front of my torturers. That was the ultimate humiliation, the lack of dignity.

"I managed to stay silent for three days and they gave up. They could have had me shot, I suppose. Instead, they behaved like good bureaucrats. They persuaded themselves that, since most of my activities had been in Liege, it was only proper that Liege should deal with me from then on. So they sent me home.

"That early arrest by the GFP helped a lot; they didn't have the right papers! Gestapo arrest straight away would assuredly have meant an early death for both of us. For that respite, I shall always be grateful."

Jozef Garlinski

In Poland, the underground was known as the Home Army (Armia Krajowa) and it was responsible to the Polish Government in exile in London. Many young Poles fled abroad to fight – some, like twenty-nine year old JOZEF GARLINSKI, chose to stay behind and carry on the fight there.

"My job was to protect Home Army headquarters from the Secret State Police which in Warsaw was directly under SS-Hauptsturmführer Alfred Spilker, head of the *Sonderkommando Warschau* (Warsaw).

"If people were arrested by Spilker's men, I, through a network of some 300 agents, had to try and make contact, or at least to find out what had happened to them. Had they perhaps suffered a sudden heart attack? Had they died and been taken to the mortuary? My agents were in place to consult records and report back.

"If one of our people had been arrested by the Kripo rather than the Gestapo their prospects were brighter. It was easier, you see, to bribe a member of the Kripo and buy someone's release. With the political policemen, the Sipo and the Gestapo, it was also sometimes possible to bribe them, but very dangerous. A man in the hands of the Gestapo was not only in peril but he represented a threat to the entire Home Army. Had he been tortured under interrogation? If so, could he have talked? What did he know?

"Security within the Home Army was elaborate. I lived at a number of different addresses under different aliases since the use of real names was out of the question. Each block of flats had the local equivalent of the Gestapo Blockwart as it existed in Germany. Spies were everywhere. Indeed, my own arrest came about through betrayal by an old school friend.

"Luckily, my Home Army connection remained concealed because the Gestapo made a costly mistake. When I was picked up, it was getting late in the day. They locked me straightaway in a cell, intending to deal with me the following morning. One of the first rules of secret police interrogation is that you waste no time in getting information out of a prisoner, no matter how late it is. The Russian NKVD, for example, would never had made such a slip.

"Left in a cell overnight, I took advantage of the situation, knowing what I must do. That was to get rid of the papers I was carrying which gave me a false identity. My captors, you see, had already addressed me as 'Garlinski' but I was tolerably certain that they had no proof of my connection with the Home Army since I never used my real name in my work, even with closest colleagues. If I had been carrying *false* documents my connection with the underground would have been obvious. I managed to destroy the incriminating papers overnight. As it turned out, a fresh surprise awaited me next morning. Two Gestapo carried out the interrogation, flanked by a large man in uniform and a sulky, dark, curly-haired civilian. The first question was surprising, 'Why have you got a false Christian name on your identity card? You are Tadeusz and not Jozef.'

"It turned out that Tadeusz Garlinski worked in a factory making radio sets for the underground and that he was also a wanted man. It soon became obvious to me that the Gestapo had confused the two Garlinskis. I said stubbornly, 'I am Jozef Garlinski.' The result was fifteen blows of a hide whip, followed by the sneering question, 'Well, how do you feel now, Mr Engineer?'

"I stuck rigidly to the truth and the result was more beatings in just about every part of my body. But a sense of the ridiculous came to my rescue and helped me to bear it all. Here I was being beaten so that I should confess that my authentic papers were forged, that I was not myself!

"They then sent me to Birkenau, which was part of Auschwitz. Even here I was still at the whim of the Warsaw Gestapo. All so-called political prisoners were. My greatest nightmare was my Gestapo file – there were 100,000 files on prisoners in Auschwitz alone. Was someone else back home betraying me? Had the Gestapo found evidence at last to connect me with the Home Army? If such things had happened the Gestapo might have sent some order like, 'Keep this man in a penal company for two years and then hang him.' The camp commandant would have carried out the order without question."

Somehow Jozef Garlinski survived the war. Following Auschwitz's disbandment and his removal to the notorious Neunengamme concentration camp, he hovered between life and death, stricken with typhus in a Halle hospital, but by then a free man. It was not until his recovery that he was able to contact a friend of his wife's at a camp for women soldiers of the Home Army at Darmstadt and learn that she was alive and living in London. Here husband and wife were finally reunited.

Paul Levy

Young PAUL LEVY, a Professor in statistics at the Institut des Hautes Etudes de Belgique in Brussels and a news journalist for the National Radio Station, could have had a quiet war. Indeed, his first contact with the German occupation forces in May 1940 was deceptively mild. It was made clear to him with courteous firmness that, naturally under the new order of things, his present radio job had ceased to exist.

"Then came a polite invitation from the German head of Belgium Broadcasting, suggesting that I reapply for my old job. It was obvious that if I did so and was accepted I would have to toe the Party line and become nothing but a tool for Nazi propaganda. I refused. The Germans were less polite after that."

One of the two men who came to the professor's apartment was a noticeably arrogant plainclothes Gestapo official, while the other wore SD uniform. Arrest and transportation to the prison of St Gilles was immediate, the aggressive Untersturmführer Humbert promising, 'We'll be back here to turn the place over,' It was to prove a frustrating experience for them.

Paul Levy explained, "Like reporters the world over, I had too many files and too much paper but they found nothing that would remotely implicate me. That was scarcely surprising because there was really nothing to find. They fell back on hours of lengthy interrogation, both at St Gilles and at Gestapo headquarters in the Avenue Louise. They were not very subtle and there was an air of desperation about their efforts, including a few incidents which on reflection took on shades of black comedy.

"They questioned me about my early youth, the time before I was a professor. I happened to mention that I had been a student of international studies for a time in Geneva. One of them snapped, 'Under whom?' 'Under Professor Zimmerman of Oxford,' I told him. The man was triumphant. Here at last was something to go on. He pounced, 'Ah, he was surely a Freemason?' I managed to keep a straight face, saying blandly, 'I really have no idea.' He tried yet again, 'Come on, with that name he was surely a Jew?'

"When this received no response he began frantically rummaging through a pile of my papers. He waved a letter in my face from the famous Professor Gallup, the pioneer of opinion polls whose work at that time was poorly known on the Continent; since my speciality at the university was statistics, I had written to him for some information. But it was not the contents of the letter or indeed Gallup, that interested the man from the Gestapo. The letter was signed by a certain Esther Schwarzstein, one of Gallup's secretaries. The man was nearly delirious by this time, 'Ah, she is a *Jew*.' I replied reasonably enough that I did not know, since I had never met her.

"By now, I was getting the measure of these men. They were not very intelligent, very much prisoners of a Nazi mentality that saw Jews and Freemasons everywhere. They had nothing they could actually pin on me."

After further questioning, Levy was sent to Breendonk concentration camp, where, "although the camp was run by the SS, the influence of the Gestapo was still there, notably inside the cells where they would plant informers. My release after one year could only have been at the whim of the Gestapo who had the say over the length of incarceration. Release of prisoners was often quite arbitrary. There were no conditions attached to mine – provided I reported regularly to the Avenue Louise. Of course, the Gestapo had the power of re-arrest as well. I soon realized they were on yet another tack when they mentioned to me casually that, since I had made contacts, I could still be of use to them. In other words, I was invited to collaborate.

"There was the implied threat: if I refused I could find myself back in Breendonk. It would surely only be a matter of time. I vowed to get out."

Shortly afterwards, Paul Levy paid his last visit to the Avenue Louise. He went home and sent his family to unoccupied France where they were to survive the war. He himself via the underground network found his way to London through France, Spain, Portugal, and Gibraltar.

Kira Solovieff

As one of three daughters of an expatriate professional white Russian violinist from pre-Revolutionary St Petersburg, KIRA SOLOVIEFF was an unlikely recruit for the Communist Party and for anti-Nazi resistance in Brussels.

"One of my contacts in the resistance was a maid who worked in the house of a senior government official in the Brussels district of Schaebeek who was known to be a German sympathizer who received SS and Gestapo in his house. Although I had no proof, there has never been any doubt in my mind that this woman betrayed me and that was why the Gestapo knew where to find me.

"At the Avenue Louise and in St Gilles prison I told my interrogators nothing. This, I should say, was not because I had no information to give. I knew plenty. The Communist Party had entrusted me specifically with the task of finding comrades who would shelter members of the resistance. Now in Gestapo custody, I was in a position to destroy the underground. Instead I preferred to tire out my interrogators. They questioned me for hours and hours. I think they were only too relieved to send me to the concentration camp at Breendonk.

"On arrival at Breendonk, I was taken to a room which I learnt later had been the site of a powder magazine; it had been carefully bricked up and transformed into a torture chamber. This was under the supervision of the Gestapo. There I had to undress and with my hands behind my back was hoisted from the ground by rope and pulley. The beating with leather truncheons started. They went about their work slowly. They wanted to know things, you see. So five or six blows would be delivered, then they would let me down. When it was clear that I was not going to talk, they would start again. But I managed to persuade them I knew little. After it was over, there was no respite in a cell. Breendonk was a camp for men and there was no accommodation for women. I had to pass my nights lying on a bench.

"From there, I was sent to Ravensbruck. I was determined to survive and decided on a bold gamble. On arrival I was asked my profession and I promptly said that I was a qualified nurse. It was an appalling risk because I had not a scrap of medical knowledge.

"Incredibly it worked, and because of one woman's laziness. This was the one genuine German nurse I encountered in my time there. She found that I could speak English which she was anxious to practise. She had no intention whatever of doing any work and left it all to me. I was furnished with an arm band that gave me some freedom of movement within the camp. One of my duties was to issue certificates on behalf of women who were too ill to work and who were kept in separate compounds. I found that it was a way of saving at least some lives and the authorities seemed to respect my judgement.

"But the day inevitably came when the Commandant went through the inordinately long lists of the sick and tore them up in front of me. There then followed a beating. After that, there was nothing further I could do to save these women.

"Every so often a covered truck or wagon would appear in the camp. We soon learnt that it was used for torture sessions and we were told that on these occasions the Gestapo was responsible and not the staff of the camp."

Alfred Hausser

ALFRED HAUSSER, a young unemployed metallurgist from Stuttgart, was an active anti-fascist. His resistance activities resulted in him going underground. When the Stuttgart Gestapo began making mass arrests, he fled to Chemnitz, in Saxony.

"As I was to discover, liaison between the various offices of the Gestapo and Kripo across the Reich was extremely efficient. By late December they'd tracked me down to Chemnitz. When they hauled me in I used my cover name and told the usual lies. But they just smiled and marched me to the outside of one cell where I was made to peer through the spyhole. The cell was jammed with a lot of my fellow resistants and I realized that we must all have been closely tracked over many months. I was told, 'It's really useless of you to tell us any more lies. We have got all your friends.'

"So I decided on different tactics. Instead of covering up my identity and that of my organization I answered all those questions I reckoned they would have discovered subsequently through their own investigations. I kept quiet, of course, about things of which I felt sure they had no knowledge and which could have endangered the organization. It developed, willy-nilly, into a sort of game. There were times when I would throw them a morsel of information which disconcerted them when I volunteered it. But I had to calculate carefully. One wrong answer could jeopardize the entire movement.

"One detail puzzled my interrogators particularly. A man who comes from the Stuttgart part of Germany has a very distinctive accent which would be extremely difficult to conceal. But my regional intonation happened to be very slight. The Gestapo men were hoping desperately that they had hooked a big fish who perhaps operated out of Berlin and was more important than a mere provincial dissident.

"Gestapo operatives, you see, were paid like old-time bounty hunters; the bigger the catch, the bigger the pay-off. I'm afraid that I was to turn out a severe disappointment to them, robbing them of their pot of gold.

"Still they refused to give up. They sent for a speech expert who listened to me and pronounced, 'This man is telling the truth.' Seeing their bounty money slipping away, my questioners tried again. They had me photographed and fingerprinted and my details sent to Stuttgart. Their next move was to find my mother and get her to confirm that I was in fact who I claimed to be. After that, they gave up. I had a big advantage over them now. They tended to believe most of what I said, even the lies.

"Their interrogation methods relied heavily on the so-called 'sweet and sour;' gentle sessions of questioning would be followed by hectoring and bullying. A favourite line was, 'You're going on trial and we'll be giving our testimony. Tell us what we want to know and we'll make things easy for you.' Many people fell for that appeal which was generally made after hours of questioning. I didn't because I knew very well that those specimens never made life easy for anybody and certainly not in court. At first I thought they had very little on me. But it didn't do to underestimate the thoroughness of the

Gestapo and you can take it from me that they were very thorough indeed. Their organization – and of course, their network of informers – was second to none.

"There was one incidence of this I remember very well. I had visited a certain house on a certain date and had ridden away on a bicycle. One of the Gestapo said, 'I followed you, but you were too fast. I couldn't keep up.' I remembered the incident and realized that it had taken place weeks before my arrest. So obviously there had been long-term surveillance."

Hausser was held in custody by the Gestapo for nineteen months after which he was bundled without explanation into the back of a car and driven to an arraignment before the Völksgericht (Peoples' Court). "I remember August 1936 particularly because the Olympic Games were going on in Berlin. I was taken from Gestapo headquarters to a chamber decorated with three large Swastika banners and busts of Frederick the Great and the Führer. I faced a long table where there sat two professional judges and five others selected from among Party officials and the SS.

"My attention was riveted by the documents on the desk – or, rather, by one particular document on the pile. It was a leaflet stating that the Reich's main armaments combine of Krupp was engaged in producing munitions of war.

"One of the judges waved it and demanded, 'Who wrote this? Who was responsible?' If I had told him, the result would have been catastrophic for one small resistance cell of around a dozen people. It was they who had done the typing and setting, had run off the copies clandestinely, and then, of course, distributed the leaflets. There could be only one course. Acquittals by the People's Court were rare. I would be found guilty anyway. I told the court that I was the only one involved. The sentence was right in the tradition of the harshness of the People's Court: fifteen years followed by a further ten years of loss of civil rights."

Eugen Kessler

In March 1933, twenty-one year old painter and decorator EUGEN KESSLER was living in Munich. Although essentially apolitical, he was opposed to the Nazis and distributed some leaflets for the Communists because "they were the strongest opposition group." Eventually, "someone just talked too much in the wrong place." He was arrested by the Gestapo and taken to the Munich headquarters of the Gestapo at Wittlesbach Palace.

"They'd picked up a friend of mine as well and they put the two of us face-to-face, asking me if I knew anything about illegal leaflets. I said with an air of injured innocence, 'Who is talking about illegal leaflets,' as if no sane person could seriously believe that leaflets could actually be *illegal*. The result was a fist crashing into my face and the cell door slamming shut. I learnt later that they were debating whether to send me to Dachau then and there but, first, there were more beatings and more questions. I lied that I knew nothing about leaflets, legal or otherwise, and certainly hadn't distributed any. I had three interrogators.

"Since I was young and full of self-assurance as well as being angry, I didn't hesitate to be cheeky and provoke all of them in turn. It was dangerous, of course, but by that time it made no difference. They told me that there had been a meeting of some sort of council of the Gestapo at the Wittlesbach and that they were sending me to Dachau."

The Gestapo did nót run the prison camps but maintained a close presence in all of them. This could be discerned by the activities of the political department (the so-called Politische Abteilung) with offices near the camp's main gate. Although nominally under the commandant's orders, the political section was a Gestapo cell watching not only the behaviour of prisoners, but also that of SS personnel. This was where the fate of the prisoners was decided and where "the enforced interrogations" were held. It was also a well organized intelligence cell seeking to uncover clandestine activities, such as political meetings, the formation of resistance centres, escape plans, and attempts to contact the outside world. Prisoners who acted as informers for the Politische Abteilung were rewarded with privileges.

Kessler continued, "I later learnt that I had been sent to Dachau, not as a punishment, but to await punishment – to be held at the pleasure of the Gestapo until my trial. The camp authorities brought me the news eventually that all charges laid against me at the Wittlesbach Palace had been dismissed. Obviously they regarded me as being of no importance. But, presumably, just for the hell of it, the Gestapo directed that I was to be held for one more year. I reckon that I was lucky. At least I was put to the work I knew best – painting the camp buildings."

Kessler's release did not come until September 1937, long enough to have been eyewitness to one of Dachau's most sadistic commandants, SS-Oberführer Hans Loritz. It was Loritz who was responsible for introducing to Dachau one of its most appalling tortures with the blessing of the Politische Abteilung. This was the so-called Baum (tree) or Pfahl (pole) treatment, applied on fixed days twice a week. The victim had his hands tied behind his back and was attached by the wrist to an eight-foot post to which hooks had been fitted. After climbing onto a stool, which was then kicked away, the man remained suspended with his feet clear of the ground for up to two hours. An added refinement was to make the body swing and flog it in the process. The sudden drop caused broken joints and, even when there were no permanent effects, a victim could not use his arms for weeks afterwards.

Kessler served his sentence, but then the Gestapo apparently lost all interest in him. After his release he was required to do nothing more onerous than report regularly to a police station. Fate, however, seems to have had the last laugh on young Kessler. At the start of the war he found himself drafted into the Wehrmacht and sent to the Russian front. But as a survivor of both Gestapo interrogation and confinement in Dachau he counted himself among the more fortunate ones.

Maria Radecka

Nineteen year old waitress, MARIA RADECKA, was a patriot who served the Polish Home Army as a courier – first against the Soviets, then against the Germans. Eventually, she was betrayed by another courier.

"That was why at 2:00 a.m. on 17 July 1943, four Lithuanian police came to arrest me at my aunt's apartment in Vilnius where I was living. One of my first reactions was relief. At least I was going to be in the hands of collaborating Lithuanians. It was sometimes possible to bribe them, an altogether riskier proposition with the Germans, although they too had their price.

"One of the favourite hobbies of the police was getting young girls to dress and undress in front of them. At least, this lot let me get dressed in my aunt's bedroom. They took me to Gestapo headquarters which of course was in the control of the Germans. It wasn't far away but they hemmed me in with armed guards who threatened to shoot me if I as much as thought of escaping. I replied coolly that of course I would not think of escaping. Plainly, my arrest was a mistake and I would welcome the chance to sort things out.

"If I thought that was going to be done by bluffing I was sadly mistaken. Obersturmführer Schmidt of the SD took away my handbag and put me in a small, stuffy cell. I scarcely noticed, though, because I was too busy putting resistance training to work.

"One of the first rules was that if you spoke or understood German you mustn't show it. What you desperately needed was time to get a cover story together. I did that by demanding an interpreter. Since they wanted information they were scarcely in a position to refuse. The other rule while facing Gestapo interrogation was *never* to lose one's temper. A lost temper could lead to loss of nerve and judgement which is precisely what they wanted. Indeed, once during questions, one of my interrogators said something that infuriated me. I blazed with anger. But when I saw the look of triumph on his face, I decided that I would not give him that satisfaction again. So from then on I was very meek, whatever the provocation. That enabled me to keep my nerve and there was no risk of my blurting out some indiscretion in high heat. It was galling but it was worth it.

"All this was a prelude to three weeks in the stinking underground cells of Ofiarma Street. Conditions were appalling. Cockroaches dropped from the ceilings. There was no contact with the outside world. I was not allowed to receive food parcels. I had, for the moment at least, ceased to exist.

"Throughout this time I was interrogated for periods of up to four or five hours. The questions were always the same. And the reaction to my replies was always, 'That is not what has been said about you in Warsaw. We shall take you there and then you will be sent to Auschwitz.'

"However, where the Gestapo did send me was the dreadful prison of Luk-iszki. We were packed twenty to a cell. The food was very poor but at least we were allowed food parcels every week. The humiliation otherwise was abso-lute. Prisoners had to go to the toilet in the full view of the guards. What's more, toilet visits were only allowed at 5:00 a.m. and 5:00 p.m.

"You could only ever outwit the Gestapo by cunning. The attempt to humil-iate the resistants by putting us in with thieves and prostitutes came to nothing thanks to one of my cellmates, Basia Dudycz. The Germans had sentenced her to death, but this was commuted, thanks to judicious bribery.

"Basia was a survivor. Her idea was to put a particularly aggressive crimi-nal prisoner in charge of our cell. The woman we selected was so pleased with the 'honour' that she kept everyone in the cell in order.

"Everywhere, though, there was the spectre of death. You were constantly reminded of it by the graffiti on the cell walls where prisoners had scrawled details of their torture and, in the last hours of their lives, the date and time of executions. Friday was the worst day of all. That was when the executions were carried out, not just of political prisoners but of ordinary criminals who had been convicted of stealing German property. The cell door would be flung open and the warders and wardesses would enter the cell with a list of names. They were Lithuanians and they relished their work. After someone had been taken away for execution, none of the other prisoners had much of an appetite.

"A cardinal rule for dealing with the Gestapo was to trust no one. And that meant *no one*. There was indignation when I warned about giving confession to the Lithuanian prison chaplain. I was more cynical than devout and even the most intelligent political prisoners argued that a man who had been ordained would not break the seal of confession. I was right, though. The man *was* a Gestapo agent."

Wolfgang Szepansky

WOLFGANG SZEPANSKY, an artist of Polish-Latvian stock was living in Berlin in 1933. "My home was in the suburb of Mariendorf. About 11.00 p.m. I was awakened by the sound of shooting. I looked down into the street and there was this lorry-load of Nazis emptying their rifles into a bar. Just for the hell of it, I suppose.

"I think that incident acted as adrenaline. It certainly brought out the devil in me. The very next day on a wall in the Kreuzberg district I scrawled the words DOWN WITH HITLER. COMMUNISM LIVES. THE RED FRONT. As it was to turn out, as well as scrawling such a childish slogan in the first place, I had made an even more serious blunder. I thought I had chosen a place which couldn't be seen. But either someone I knew spied me from buildings opposite or I talked too much later on. Either way, the result was a car with an escort to take me to Prinz Albrechtstrasse.

"A very small Gestapo operative greeted my arrival at Prinz Albrechtstrasse with a swift kick to my stomach. Then I was marched upstairs and told to stand against a wall where, in the company of some fifteen other detainees, I remained all through the night and all the next day without any food or being allowed to go to the toilet.

"Every so often a Gestapo man would go down the line slapping faces which was a subtle form of torture because the victim – who, incidentally, had not even been questioned on his supposed crime – was never actually rendered unconscious. It became essential to stand upright. If you fell forward then you would be knocked back into a standing position with further blows.

"Eventually we were bundled into cars and driven to the Columbiahaus jail; from there we were shuffled to 'the Alex,' a grim Gothic-looking structure situated south of Alexanderplatz which many also nicknamed 'Grey Misery.'

"By now I was so tired that I thought I might as well give them something, so I admitted that I had painted slogans. Disconcertingly, their reaction was to let me go – but without my bicycle, my watch, or my money. A few weeks later, I received notification from the Public Prosecutor that I was to stand trial for being a member of an illegal banned organization, the Red Front. At first, I was puzzled. I certainly hadn't belonged to anything called the Red Front. Then I remembered the words scrawled on the wall at Kreuzberg. I realized that if the Gestapo got hold of me they would beat me until I confessed membership of the Red Front. If I didn't oblige they would concoct evidence for the court, anyway. It was plainly time to get out.

"I therefore decided to risk a train journey to Holland. I got a job with a Communist newspaper packing up copies for sending into Germany. One day the door was flung open and this voice bellowed: "GESTAPO!" I merely stood and grinned, suspecting a colleague with a rarified sense of humour. My visitor, who was in plain clothes, began examining the papers, snapping out questions like, 'What are you doing here? Where are these papers going?' I decided to play along with this charade, trying to look serious as part of the act. Then he left, slamming the door behind him. I learnt the truth a few days later. My visitor *had* been a Gestapo agent all right, an infiltrator of Communist groups who had decided to break cover and frighten the truth out of us.

"Eventually, I was to be interned by the Dutch and sent back to Germany straight into the arms of the Berlin Gestapo.

"Their questions this time were about what I had been doing in Holland and why I had gone there. In the hope of getting them off my back, I began spinning them tales. But they were skilled interrogators. I would have one session of questions from them. Then they would send me back to my cell for perhaps two weeks before summoning me again for more questions. By then I was thoroughly confused, not remembering what I'd told them the last time.

"The final interrogation was conducted in a large room full of people scribbling and typing furiously. This was stage management designed to intimidate. You asked yourself, 'Are they typing *my* testimony?'. This time there were no beatings up, no physical violence. They were in no hurry and were prepared to get whatever they wanted through a succession of probing interviews. Then came the morning when I was taken back to my cell and told I was going into protective custody (Schutzhaft). There wasn't any time limit on Schutzhaft. As it turned out, this meant Sachsenhausen, one of the worst of the early concentration camps."

Bora Pavlovic

Yugoslavia was invaded by the Germans, Italians, Hungarians, and Bulgarians in 1941. An independent fascist Croatia was set up whose strong arm was the bloodthirsty Ustachi. The Ustachi had a grim record of torture and cruelty, especially of Jews and Communists. In the city of Sabac, Jews and Serbs were massacred in the streets as a reprisal against an attack on a German patrol. Other Jews were then rounded up and forced to hang the corpses from lampposts, after which they had to remove the corpses and take them away in rubbish trucks.

BORA PAVLOVIC, a retired dentist now living in Belgrade, experienced at first hand what the Ustachi could do to Communists.

"I was with a twenty strong partisan unit, a complete cross section of young workers and students. I had been an open Communist sympathizer from being very young and never made any secret of my allegiance. In August 1943, the partisan bands were fighting both Germans and Ustachi near Progar, on the banks of the river Sava. It was some seventeen miles from Belgrade and under Croatian rule. The enemy cornered us in Progar and when they opened up I was wounded. There was no way in which we could have survived a pitched battle so everyone scattered. I was isolated and hid in the reeds of the Obed marshes. With the quicksands nearby, it was not exactly a kind hiding place for a man fleeing for his life! They sent in their snarling and biting dogs who soon rooted me out from near the quicksands so there had been a double danger.

"The Ustachi dragged me to a tree and I realized that their intention was to hang me. They threw a rope around the branch, made a noose, and stuck my head in it. They tightened the rope, hauling me up off the ground so that my feet dangled and it felt as if life was being squeezed out of me.

"Mercifully, the rope snapped. I fell to the ground at which a Ustachi took a knife from his boot and made ready to finish me off. He was stopped by this German officer who said something like, 'We in the Army don't kill people twice.' I realized that my death, when it came, would be at the hands of the Germans. But they didn't seem in a hurry to kill me and I was dragged away and turned over to Gestapo headquarters in Belgrade. It was a large place on four floors with a staff, I suppose, of about 400 Germans under SS-Gruppen-führer Meisner.

"I was beaten up again and again on the head and in the stomach by Meisner's thugs. I became indifferent to my surroundings, to time, and even to pain. There came a point when the beatings no longer hurt, and I could only *hear* the blows which seemed to come from very far away, like echoes.

"And, of course, there were the questions, the endless questions, asked by several Gestapo men working in relays. ' What had I been doing in the reeds of the Obed marshes?' 'Did I belong to the resistance?' 'Who were my friends?' I denied everything. This was not out of bravery, you understand, but because I knew that if I admitted anything, not only would I have betrayed names, but they would have delighted in beating me further before shooting me.

"As it was they sent me to the concentration camp at Banjica which was near Belgrade. If you were a prisoner of the Gestapo in that place, there was no prospect of a quick execution. They delighted in prolonged torture which resulted in slow death, even of women and children. There were other camps, of course, but it simplified the bureaucracy to put all the death tally down to Banjica. By the end of the war the total death toll recorded there was around 80,000.

"After four months at Banjica, I was deported to Austria. My time there was only a respite from further beatings and hunger. All the time I had a wound on my neck from the bungled hanging. I always kept the collar of my jacket up with a piece of wire around it because in a camp like Mauthausen to be even suspected of illness or infirmity meant death. I knew that if any of the guards noticed the wound, I would have been sent to the hospital where there were doctors who would have finished me off.

"I remained in Mauthausen as Prisoner Number 106923 until April 1945, when the camp was cut off from Berlin by Allied troops. I weighed only thirty-eight kilos at liberation and was registered as fifty percent disabled."

Paul Mayer

Rhinelander PAUL ("YOGI") MAYER, was a young Jew and sports teacher who had four encounters with the Gestapo, three of them in Prinz Albrechtstrasse:

"I studied in Berlin and later at Frankfurt university from which I was expelled for having my student card marked with the infamous 'J.' I was later appointed youth officer to the Reichsbund Judischer Front Soldaten (Jewish Ex-servicemen's League) and coach to their sports organization which at that time enjoyed President von Hindenburg's protection. I also edited the sports pages of their weekly paper, *Der Schild*. I had to send the proofs to the Gestapo-controlled censor. Anything that was not approved of was 'liquidated' with a blue pencil. When the proofs were returned too late for me to fill in the space, I simply left them blank. That led to my dismissal.

My first encounter with the Gestapo was when I had been visitlng Rexington in the Black Forest which had a population that was nearly one third Jewish. I spoke on the problems of young Jews in Germany. I noticed two strangers who entered the room and it was obvious that they were Gestapo. A few days later I was called to Prinz Albrechtstrasse where I encountered an official named Kuchmann who insisted that during my speech I had made anti-Government remarks. I told him I had been well aware of the two Gestapo men and that it would have been extremely foolish to make the remarks he attributed to me. I was let off but the Gestapo was not finished with me.

"Months later I was summoned back to Gestapo headquarters. This time I had, along with some non-Jews, attended a meeting arranged by the Prussian Professor Hans Joachim Schoeps, whose main interests werc religion and philosophy. When charged again that we had discussed political matters and had made certain observations, I had to refuse these allegations. I asked him who had reported us. Kuchmann replied, 'Adolf Eichmann.' I then remembered a man unknown to us who had lntroduced himself at the meeting and had professed interest in what we were dlscussing and who obviously had put us on our guard.

"My third and most worrying encounter with the Gestapo was a letter which arrived at my home in Berlin carrying the notorious return address of 8 Prinz Albrechtstrasse. The letter read:

> Based on paragraph one of the laws published by the Reich President for the Protection of the German People and State from 28 February 1933, published in the German Gazette under IS page 85, I herewith forbid you until further notice to act as a speaker in any public or closed meetings of any kind.
>
> Heydrich 5 April 1935.

"As my late father's firm had been confiscated, I depended at this time on my income as a sports teacher. I decided to go to Gestapo headquarters to ask if I could continue at least as a teacher.

"Number 8 Prinz Albrechtstrasse was a heavy and ponderous Wilhelmine building. Inside, it was dominated by a broad staircase which split to the right and left when it reached the first floor. There was a kind of guard post in the entrance hall staffed by SS men with steel helmets to whom every visitor had to report. I was wearing a trenchcoat and German sports badge so I must have looked different to the image they normally had of a Jew.

"When I said that I had a letter from the head of the Gestapo I was marched by two SS guards up the stairs to the first floor. I was then ushered into a red-carpeted room. Seated at a desk in front of a Swastika flag was a man writing. He made no attempt to acknowledge my presence. I waited and said, 'Good morning.' Disconcerted by the greeting, he raised his head and then I recognized him as Reinhard Heydrich. I had seen his picture in various publications and had also watched him in action as a well-known fencer.

"He looked at me with cold blue eyes and asked 'What do you want? How do you come to be here?' I handed over his letter and asked him whether it meant that I would also be forbidden to teach Physical Education. He replied tersely: 'No. . .but I must warn you. . .' The clear implication was that if I discussed the matter further or did not watch my future actions, I would have to face the consequences.

"That was the end of the interview. As I left, I heard him shouting over the telephone that the guards should report to him at once. I left as quickly as possible, aware that my personal encounter with Heydrich was actually a blunder by the guards who should have shoved me into the presence of some minor official. My affair had been too trivial for the admittance of a Jew into the presence of the head of the SD."

Miloslava Kalibova

When Czech patriots assassinated Reinhard Heydrich, Deputy and Acting Reich Protector of Bohemia-Moravia (the Czech part of Czechoslovakia), Hitler ordered that the mining village of Lidice be 'wiped from the face of the earth' in retaliation. With Gestapo help, this is precisely what occurred. The men of the village were shot, the women and children sent to concentration camps, pets were killed, even the graveyard was disinterred. The village was burnt to the ground and ploughed under. Even the name of the village was expunged from official records. Nevertheless, there *were* survivors. This is the story of MILOSLAVA KALIBOVA, one of those who came back.

"During the night of 9/10 June 1942, German soldiers surrounded Lidice and at about two o'clock in the morning we were woken and driven in the dark to the main square of the village. The men were separated from the women and children. They said we should take food to last for three days and any valuables if we wanted to. This was for an 'inspection' they said and then we would come back. We saw groups of the men passing down the main street of the village surrounded by soldiers. A group of soldiers came to our house and took the women and children to the schoolhouse and the men to the farm of the Horak family.

"At the schoolhouse there were two German soldiers in the corridor with two suitcases where we had to put all our valuables; earrings, rings, watches, money, and our savings account books. Then they assembled us with the children in the classroom and they checked us all against our police identity cards to make sure that everyone from the village was present. After the check trucks came and we were driven to the city of Kladno. It was exactly 6:00 a.m. when the sirens came on.

"We were located at the gymnasium hall of a secondary school in front of the Gestapo building in Kladno. I was with my mother, aunt, sister, and my cousin who was a boy. There was just straw on the floor and we lived in this place for three days. We were allowed to use the toilets. During these three days the main concern of the Germans was the thorough inspection of the children. Measuring their skulls, recording the colouring of their eyes and complexion. They asked the mothers about the illnesses the children had had and further details. We learned later that they were Gestapo men. The atmosphere in the room was very tragic. The eldest lady was eighty-eight years old and the youngest was only one. Weeping was heard all day. We didn't know anything about the men we had left behind at the village or what had happened to them. On the third day the Gestapo came into the hall. They shot their guns into the ceiling to make us afraid and said, 'You know what happened at Lidice and you will be sent to a camp with your children but, since the journey will take some time and you'll be going by the railway, the children will be transported by buses so that when you arrive at the place your children will be waiting for you there.' Then came the worst moment of all. Mothers had to give up their children. The children were crying. Some of them were pleading, 'Mummy, if you love me you cannot give me up.' When the children had been taken away we were rounded up and taken through absolutely empty streets to the Kladno railway station and transported to Ravensbruck. Before we were taken away, seven children under the age of one were also taken away. The mothers of the small children were told that they could stay with them for one night, then the children were sent to Prague and the mothers were sent first to Terezin and then after seven days finally on to Ravensbruck.

"At Ravensbruck we were met by women SS guards with alsatian dogs and carrying revolvers shouting, 'Out you get and into file.' All the time they were shouting and pushing us. On the entry to the camp was an inscription ARBEIT MACHT FREI! (Work makes Free). I remember that in front of me there were two women about forty years old carrying their mother on a chair. Their mother had suffered from rheumatism and had not been able to stand for over twenty years. We were assembled in a place in front of the camp 'hospital.' A window opened and a voice asked us in Czech, 'Where are you from?' 'From Lidice. Are our children here?' 'No, there are no children here whatsoever. This is a concentration camp.' That was actually the greatest shock. Especially for the women who had families. First the knowledge that they had lost their children, and secondly, the words 'concentration camp,' which meant 'the end station' to those who were condemned by the Germans.

"Throughout I tried to stay close to my mother and my aunt and my sister. We were then taken to a bathroom with showers and we had to strip which was another humiliation because old and young had to do the same and a soldier was walking amongst us. A shocking humiliation. They inspected hair. Some had their hair cut so short that they looked bald. We were given camp linen shirts, trousers, a dress, and a number. My number was 11789. The dress was striped and had a red triangle which meant political prisoner and a letter 'T' which meant Czech prisoner, followed by a number. We were then taken to Block 8, a wooden barracks. On one side of the room were tables and chairs and on the other side were iron bunk beds in three layers with straw mattresses and pillows. The atmosphere was extremely sad. There was much weeping and so many unanswered questions. 'Where are our children?' 'Where are our husbands and fathers?'

"Next morning we were made to get up at 4:30 a.m. We were taken to a meeting place, still without shoes, to see the torturing of some religious women who had refused to work for military purposes. Then we were classified for future jobs. The majority of us had to work with fur clothes taken from Jewish families. These were cut up and made into gloves for the soldiers. I myself with some others sewed concentration camp uniforms on electric machines. We worked twelve hour shifts either day or night, but even after a night shift we had to get up in the morning to be present at inspection. Our feet were so cold that we poured our morning coffee into a bucket to warm our feet up in it, otherwise we couldn't sleep. The work was extremely exhausting because we had to sew 220 heavy military coats in one day. It was conveyor belt production and there were only twenty-two of us. Each one of us had to make ten coats every day, including the lining, button holes, and the hem.

"In the spring of 1945, the Germans started to make selections among us. This changed the so-called 'work camp' into a liquidation camp. During selection women had to run a certain distance and those who were slow or grey-haired were fished out of the line with sticks by SS men and sent to the gas chambers attached to the camp. About 500 prisoners were murdered this way every day. This was sadly the fate of my aunt. That was one of the worst periods. We knew that the old and ill women were being killed and that after them it would be our turn.

"On 7 April 1945, two buses of the International Red Cross came to the camp. The gas chambers were closed down and some of the Norwegian and western prisoners were taken out. We expected to be liberated any day but the commander of the camp decided that only old and ill people could stay at the camp and that the rest of us must be evacuated.

"We marched for about three days with only three or four hours rest in forests or trenches, but after the third day we found that the guards had gone.

"We realized that we were saved but, of course, had no homes to go to. For our family, the sorrows and tragedies we lived through were multiplied by the fact that two generations were together and each of us suffered and felt the sorrow of the other. There was my mother, my aunt, my sister and myself. It is remarkable that my mother, sister, and myself came through it all. We knew not only families from the village, but school and workmates, and of course there were always the thoughts of our children and men who we had left behind and it wasn't until after the war that we knew what had become of them.

"Some 133,000 Czechoslovak prisoners passed through the gates of Ravensbruck and over 90,000 Czech Jews were murdered there."

The Internal structure of the 𝕽𝕾𝕳𝕬

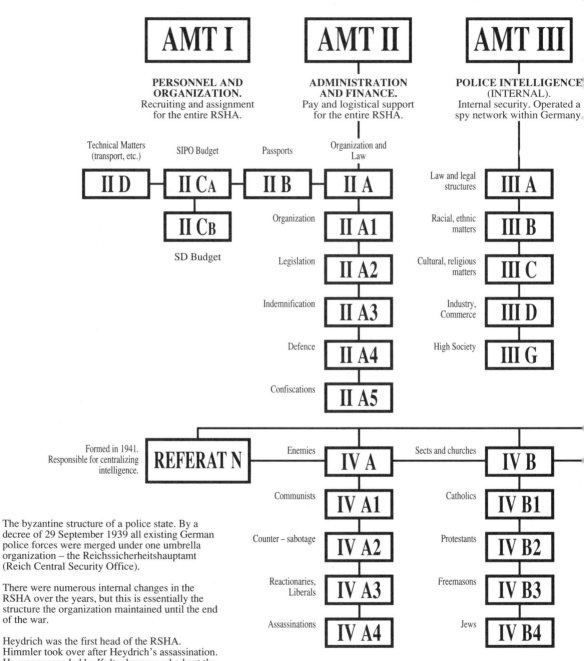

AMT I
PERSONNEL AND ORGANIZATION.
Recruiting and assignment for the entire RSHA.

AMT II
ADMINISTRATION AND FINANCE.
Pay and logistical support for the entire RSHA.

AMT III
POLICE INTELLIGENCE (INTERNAL).
Internal security. Operated a spy network within Germany.

Technical Matters (transport, etc.) — **II D**

SIPO Budget — **II CA**

II CB — SD Budget

Passports — **II B**

Organization and Law — **II A**

Organization — **II A1**

Legislation — **II A2**

Indemnification — **II A3**

Defence — **II A4**

Confiscations — **II A5**

Law and legal structures — **III A**

Racial, ethnic matters — **III B**

Cultural, religious matters — **III C**

Industry, Commerce — **III D**

High Society — **III G**

Formed in 1941. Responsible for centralizing intelligence. — **REFERAT N**

Enemies — **IV A**

Communists — **IV A1**

Counter – sabotage — **IV A2**

Reactionaries, Liberals — **IV A3**

Assassinations — **IV A4**

Sects and churches — **IV B**

Catholics — **IV B1**

Protestants — **IV B2**

Freemasons — **IV B3**

Jews — **IV B4**

The byzantine structure of a police state. By a decree of 29 September 1939 all existing German police forces were merged under one umbrella organization – the Reichssicherheitshauptamt (Reich Central Security Office).

There were numerous internal changes in the RSHA over the years, but this is essentially the structure the organization maintained until the end of the war.

Heydrich was the first head of the RSHA. Himmler took over after Heydrich's assassination. He was succeeded by Kaltenbrunner who kept the post to the end.

© Wordwright Books 1992

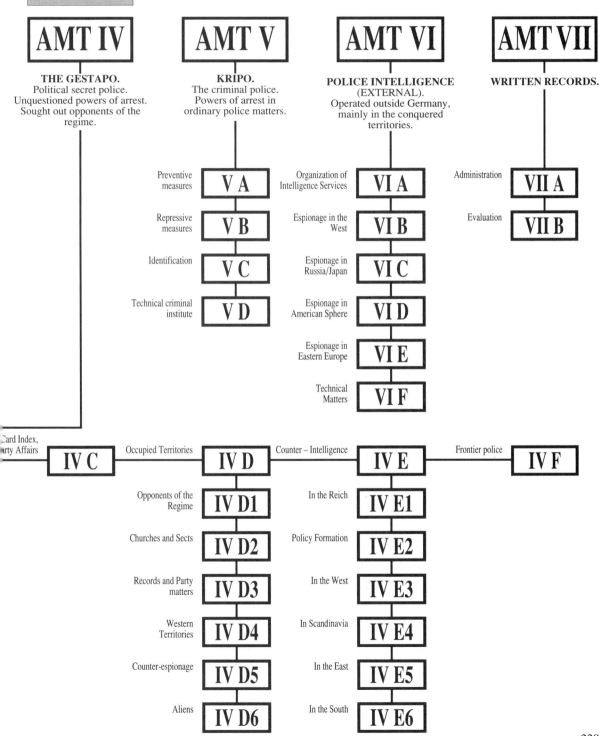

AMT IV

THE GESTAPO.
Political secret police.
Unquestioned powers of arrest.
Sought out opponents of the regime.

AMT V

KRIPO.
The criminal police.
Powers of arrest in ordinary police matters.

AMT VI

POLICE INTELLIGENCE (EXTERNAL).
Operated outside Germany, mainly in the conquered territories.

AMT VII

WRITTEN RECORDS.

	AMT V		AMT VI		AMT VII
Preventive measures	**V A**	Organization of Intelligence Services	**VI A**	Administration	**VII A**
Repressive measures	**V B**	Espionage in the West	**VI B**	Evaluation	**VII B**
Identification	**V C**	Espionage in Russia/Japan	**VI C**		
Technical criminal institute	**V D**	Espionage in American Sphere	**VI D**		
		Espionage in Eastern Europe	**VI E**		
		Technical Matters	**VI F**		

Card Index, Party Affairs	**IV C**	Occupied Territories	**IV D**	Counter – Intelligence	**IV E**	Frontier police	**IV F**
		Opponents of the Regime	**IV D1**	In the Reich	**IV E1**		
		Churches and Sects	**IV D2**	Policy Formation	**IV E2**		
		Records and Party matters	**IV D3**	In the West	**IV E3**		
		Western Territories	**IV D4**	In Scandinavia	**IV E4**		
		Counter-espionage	**IV D5**	In the East	**IV E5**		
		Aliens	**IV D6**	In the South	**IV E6**		

Glossary

Abwehr The central German military intelligence organization, headed by Admiral Wilhelm Canaris. Eventually absorbed into the RSHA.

Einsatzgruppen Mobile armed units of police, consisting of Sicherheitspolizei (Sipo), Sicherheitsdienst (SD), and Gestapo officials, used to attack and execute enemies in conquered territories. Split into units of up to 3,000 men each. Companies of the above were known as *Einsatzkommando*.

Endlösung The Final Solution. The planned wholesale destruction of European Jewry attempted by the Third Reich between 1941 and 1945. Although no written order for such a destruction is known to exist, Hitler wrote in *Mein Kampf* of a "race" to "destroy the weak to give place to the strong."

Gauleiter The supreme territorial or regional Nazi Party authority, employed in Germany and some annexed territories. The geographical units were termed *Gaue*, headed by Gauleiter (the term is singular and plural).

Hakenkreuz The Swastika or hooked cross, claimed by the Nazis to have originated in "Aryan mythology." In use in the days of the Freikorps, it was incorporated into Germany's new national flag from 1935, eventually appearing everywhere that the Nazis ruled.

Höhere SS-und Polizeifuhrer Supreme territorial or regional commander for all SS officers in addition to police officers within the territory or region. Responsible directly to Heinrich Himmler.

Ordnungspolizei Separate from the Gestapo and Criminal Police, the Orpo within Germany handled civil matters such as traffic, patrols, and routine police business. However, in the occupied territories — notably Poland and Russia — Orpo often had *Einsatzgruppen* rôles, including carrying out mass killings.

Reichsführer-SS Reich leader of the Schutzstaffel or SS — Heinrich Himmler. From 1936 on he also had the title "Chief of the German Police."

Reichsleiter Members(s) of an executive board of the Nazi Party, one of the best known of whom was Martin Bormann.

Reichssicherheitshauptamt Reich Security Main Office, created in 1939 as the "umbrella" organization incorporating all non-military intelligence agencies, including, of course, the Gestapo. Headed by Reinhard Heydrich and, after his assassination in 1942, by Ernst Kaltenbrunner from 30 January 1943.

Schutzhaft Protective custody under a law of 28 February 1933. Every type of opponent of the regime was subject to Schutzhaft: Jews, trade-unionists, and communists were followed by gypsies, homosexuals, petty criminals, and religious dissenters.

Schutzstaffel The SS, originally the personal guard of Adolf Hitler. Transformed by Himmler into a state within a state, an army within an army, the elite Black Guard.

Sicherheitsdienst The SD. On paper, at least, the SD was the intelligence organ of the Nazi Party, whereas the Gestapo was the Secret State Police. In fact, the two worked so closely together as to be at times indistinguishable. The SD laid a heavy emphasis on pursuing ideological and racial enemies.

Sicherheitspolizei Sipo or Security Police. Nominally – very nominally – part of the government and not the SS. In fact, they frequently worked hand-in-glove with the SD as a fusion of the various state political police and criminal police forces.

SS und Polizeiführer Sub-territorial commander(s) for all SS and police authorities within a given area. Subordinate to Higher SS and Police Leader(s) and to Himmler.

Sturmabteilung The SA. The Brownshirts. Originally, partly uniformed supporters, recruited in Munich by Ernst Rohm in 1921 to protect Nazi speakers. Emasculated during the Röhm purge of June 1934 – the Night of the Long Knives.

Volksgericht The People's Court. The dreaded court set up in Berlin to render quick verdicts against accused traitors of the Third Reich. Following the July 1944 attempt on Hitler's life, it sat almost without interruption into 1945.

Wannsee Conference A meeting held on 20 January 1942, in the Berlin suburb of Grossen-Wannsee that formalized the Final Solution, reviewed its achievements to date, and discussed ways of utilizing the vast labour pool of transported Jews. The occasion also gave Heydrich, who presided over the disparate gathering, a chance to emphasize his authority.

Gestapo Rank Comparison

British and US Army ranks are not exact equivalents to those of the SS.
The following table gives the nearest approximations:

German	British Army	US Army
Reichsführer-SS	—	
Oberstgruppenführer	General	General of the Army (5 stars)
Obergruppenführer	General	General (4 stars)
Gruppenführer	Lieutenant-General	Lieutenant-General (3 stars)
Brigadeführer	Major-General	Major-General (2 stars)
Oberführer	Brigadier	Brigadier-General (1 star)
Standartenführer	Colonel	Colonel
Obersturmbannführer	Lieutenant-Colonel	Lieutenant-Colonel
Sturmbannführer	Major	Major
Haupsturmführer	Captain	Captain
Obersturmführer	Lieutenant	First-Lieutenant
Untersturmführer	Second-Lieutenant	Second-Lieutenant
Sturmscharführer	Regimental Sergeant-Major	Warrant Officer
Hauptscharführer	Staff-Sergeant	Master-Sergeant
Oberscharführer	Sergeant	Technical-Sergeant
Scharführer	Lance-Sergeant	Staff-Sergeant
Unterscharführer	Corporal	Sergeant
Rottenführer	Lance-Corporal	Corporal
Sturmann-Mann	—	Private First Class
Anwarter	Private	Private

ACKNOWLEDGEMENTS

The preparation of a history of this kind inevitably requires the help and resources of many individuals and organizations. I should like to acknowledge the facilities granted me by Dr Gerhard Hirschfeld of the *Bibliothek fur Zeitgeschichte* in Stuttgart, and the staff of the *Staatsarchiv*, Ludwigsburg. Throughout my visit I had invaluable assistance from Uwe Siemers and Adriana Ritapal as interpreters and researchers.

At the Berlin Document Center, Dr David Marwell and his staff let me inspect, among other papers, the voluminous *Einsatzgruppen* files and other documents also held by the *Koblenz Bundesarchiv*. I was ably assisted in Berlin by Donna Alexander. In Munich, Douglas Bokovoy guided me to material held by the *Institute fur Zeitgeschichte*.

In Brussels, I consulted documents at the *Rijksinstituut voor Oorlogsdocumentatie*, while Wim Meyers granted me access to the *Centre de Recherches et d'Etudes Historiques de la Seconde Guerre Mondiale*. From Prague, Veronica Davis supplied much pertinent information on the assassination of Reinhard Heydrich and the rape of Lidice, a period of Nazi history already chronicled exhaustively by Dr Callum MacDonald, Senior Lecturer in History at the University of Warwick who patiently answered questions and clarified some details. In London, I drew on the unstinting help of the staffs of the Imperial War Museum, the Wiener Library, and the Public Records Office, while much additional advice and help was provided by Charles Messenger and Lilian Alweis.

Especial gratitude is due to those survivors of Gestapo brutality who, in Stuttgart, Munich, Berlin, Belgrade, Brussels, Lidice, and London, readily agreed to be interviewed, despite having to relive so many harrowing experiences. For guiding me to Polish and Lithuanian survivors in Britain I thank Romek Slimak, while Radomir Putnikovitch assisted with an interview in Belgrade and Joe Rose, MBE, then living in London, recalled for me the horrors of the personal Kristallnacht of he and his wife, Regina.

I should like to thank Dagmar Logan and Keri Owen who helped with the translation and Vicky Bryce who typed portions of the manuscript.

Very special thanks and admiration are due to my wife, Joyce, who organized my research and interview schedule, as well as interpreting in French and German, often under difficult circumstances.

Dr Richard Overy, Reader of History at King's College, London, and Terry Charman of the Department of Printed Books at the Imperial War Museum read the manuscript and made corrections and suggestions.

PICTURE ACKNOWLEDGEMENTS

Jacket: Barnaby's Picture Library, the Hulton Picture Company, Robert Hunt Library, Popperfoto.
AFF/AFS Amsterdam, the Netherlands: 146
Barnaby's Picture Library: 2, 23, 43, 56, 69, 85, 133 lower, 144, 196
Battle of Britain Prints International Limited: 185 lower
Berlin Document Center: 32, 72 lower
Bildarchiv Preussuscher Kulturbesitz, Berlin: 177, 191 lower right
CTK, Prague: 55, 120, 122 right, 123, 124, 125 lower, 126, 127, 129, 203 lower, 204
Camera Press: 13, 52, 54, 62, 82, 93, 100, 102, 106 upper right, 115, 118, 121 upper and lower,
    124, 129 lower right, 130, 131, 136, 161, 163 upper, 164, 167, 176 lower, 182 lower, 201
    upper, 202
Andreas Toscano del Banner: 159
Mary Evans Picture Library: 144
Express Newspapers Plc: 152 Ciaran Donnelly, 153
Hadtorteneti Muzeum Budapest: 192
The Hulton Picture Company: 19, 20, 26, 31, 40, 68 left, 72 upper, 87, 133, 187, 188 upper right
Robert Hunt Library: 13 left, 15, 16 upper, 17, 18, 21, 28 upper, 29, 30, 34, 37 upper left and
    right, 39, 41, 45, 47, 50, 51 upper, 57, 58, 63, 64, 67, 68 lower, 73, 76, 89, 94 left, 95, 97, 104
    lower, 106, 122 upper, 121 centre, 122 upper left, 137, 141, 149, 162 lower, 174, 188 lower,
    193 upper and lower, 233
Landesbildestelle Wurttemberg Stuttgart: 74
National Gedenkteken Breendonk: 200
Popperfoto: 15 right, 16 lower left & lower right, 27 lower, 28 lower left &
    lower right, 35, 37 lower, 42, 60, 65 upper right, 71, 75, 77,
    78, 79, 80, 81, 83, 84, 90, 92, 96, 101, 106 centre, 108, 109,
    113, 134, 151, 154, 155, 162 upper, 163 lower, 169, 173, 181
    lower, 182 upper right, 184 upper, 188 left, 191 upper right and
    left, 195
Rijksinstituut voor Oorlogsdocumentatie: 145, 178, 179, 180, 181 above
Uwe Siemers, Stuttgart: 157
Suddeutscher Verlag, Munchen: 158
Topham Picture Source: 27 upper, 44 right, 48, 51 lower, 53, 105, 106 lower,
    left, 124 upper two, 142, 176 upper, 186, jacket
Ullstein Bilderdienst Berlin: 25, 170, 171
Wannsee = Gedenkstatte Haus der Wannsee-Konferenz, Berlin: 111
Wiener Library: 65 lower, 189
Wordwright: 201

The publishers would like to thank the Survivors, individually and collectively, who entrusted to us the use of their treasured and often irreplaceable photographs: Marcel Baiwir, Miloslava Kalibova, Eugen Kessler, Paul MG Levy, Paul "Yogi" Mayer, Bora Pavlovic, Maria Radecka, and Wolfgang Szepansky. We should also like to thank Jozef Garlinski and his publishers Basil Blackwell for permission to reproduce the photograph from *The Survival of Love;* Milos Bajic, artist, who gave us kind permission to reproduce the drawing on page 193; and Orbis Press Agency, Prague, for the use of the woodcuts on pages 204 and 227 from their book *Lidice* by Ivan Ciganek.

Bibliography

I have consulted many of the following books as source material for my account of the Gestapo. Others are included as being of likely interest to students and the general reader on the evolution and history of the Nazi movement itself.

Aronson, Shlomo. *Reinhard Heydrich und Die Fruhgeschichte.* (Deutsche Verlag Anstalt, 1971)

Beattie, John. *Klaus Barbie; His Life and Career.* (Methuen, 1984)

Berben, Paul. *Dachau: 1933-45. The Official History.* (Comité International de Dachau, 1968)

Black, Peter R. *Ernst Kaltenbrunner.* (Princeton University Press, 1984)

Bower, Tom. *Klaus Barbie, Butcher of Lyon.* (Michael Joseph, 1984)

Bramstedt, E. K. *Dictatorship and Political Police.* (OUP, 1945)

Breitman, R. *The Architect of Genocide: Himmler and the Final Solution.* (The Bodley Head, 1991)

Brissand, Andre. *The Nazi Secret Service.* (Bodley Head, 1974)

Browning, Christopher R. *Fateful Months: Essays on the Emergence of the Final Solution.* (Holmes and Meier, 1985.)

Calid, Edouard. *Reinhard Heydrich.* (Military Heritage Press, 1985)

Conot, Robert E. *Justice at Nuremberg.* (Weidenfeld & Nicholson, 1983)

Crankshaw, E. *Gestapo.* (Putnam & Co, 1956)

Czech Ministry of Foreign Affairs. *Memorandum of the Czech Government on the Reign of terror in Bohemia and Moravia under the Reign of Reinhard Heydrich.* (1941)

Dawidowicz Lucy S. *The War Aqainst the Jews.* (Weidenfeld & Nicholson, 1975)

D'Alquin, Gunter. *Die SS.* (Junter und Dunnhaupt Verlag, 1939)

Denscher, Gunter. *Reinhard Heydrich: The Pursuit of Total Power.* (Orbis Publishing, 1981)

Dukes, Sir Paul. *An Epic of the Third Reich.* (Cassels, 1949)

Fest, Joachim. *Face of the Third Reich.* (Weidenfeld & Nicholson, 1963)

Frischauer, W. *Himmler.* (Odhams Press Ltd, 1953)

Gallo, Max. *The Night of the Long Knives.* (Harper & Row, 1972)

Garlinski, Jozef. *The Survival of Love, Memoirs of A Resistance Officer.* (Blackwell, 1991)

Gisevius, Hans Bernd.   *To the Bitter End.* (Jonathan Cape, 1948)

Graber, G. S.   *The Life and Times of Reinhard Heydrich.* (Robert Hale Ltd, 1980)

Grunfeld, Frederick F.   *A Social History of Germany and the Nazis 1918-1945.* (Weidenfeld & Nicholson, 1974)

Hansar, Richard.   *A Noble Treason: the Revolt of the Munich Students.* (Putnam, 1979)

Hausner, Gideon.   *Justice in Jerusalem.* (Nelson, 1967)

Hoffman, Peter.   *The History of the German Resistance, 1933-1945.* (Macdonald & Janes, 1977)

Hohne, Heinz.   *Canaris: Patriot im Zwielicht.* (C Bertelsmann Verlag Gmbh, 1976)

Hohne, Heinz.   *Der Orden unter dem Totenkopf.* (Verlag der Spiegel, 1966)

Irving, David.   *Göring.* (Macmillan, 1989)

Kochan, Lionel.   *Pogrom 10 November 1938.* (Andre Deutsch, 1957)

Krausnick Helmut, et al.   *Anatomy of the SS State.* (Collins, 1978)

MacDonald, Callum.   *The Killing of SS Obergruppenführer Reinhard Heydrich, 27 May 1942.* (Macmillan, 1989)

Manvell Roger & Fraenkel, H.   *Hermann Goering.* (Heineman, 1962)

Manvell, Roger & Fraenkel, H.   *The July Plot.* (Bodley Head, 1964)

Manvell, Roger & Fraenkel, H.   *The Hundred Days to Hitler.* (Dent, 1974)

Merson, Allen.   *Communist Resistance in Nazi Germany.* (Lawrence & Wishart, 1985)

Metcalfe, Philip.   *1933.* (Bantam Press, 1989)

Moczarski, K.   *Gespraeche mit dem Henker.* (Droste, Dusseldorf, 1978)

Molloy-Mason, Herbert.   *To Kill Hitler.* (Michael Joseph, 1979)

Morgan, Ted.   *An Uncertain Hour. 1940-1945.* (The Bodley Head, 1990)

Musmanno, Michael A.   *The Eichmann Commandos.* (Peter Davies, 1969)

Noakes Jeremy & Pridham, G. *Documents on Nazism, 1919-1935.* (Jonathan Cape, 1974)

O'Donnell, James. *The Berlin Bunker.* (J M Dent & Sons Ltd, 1979)

Overy, R. J. *Goering the "Iron Man".* (Routledge and Kegan Paul, 1984)

Padfield, Peter. *Himmler Reichsführer SS.* (Macmillan, 1990)

Pearlman, Moshe. *The Capture and Trial of Adolf Eichmann.* (Weidenfeld and Nicholson, 1963)

Petrow, Richard. *The Bitter Years. The Invasion and Occupation of Denmark and Norway.* (Hodder and Stoughton, 1974)

Peukert, J. K. *Inside Nazi Germany: Conformity, Opposition and Racism in Everyday Life.* (Penguin Books, 1989)

Polish Ministry of Information. *The German New Order in Poland.* (Hutchinson, 1942)

Reitlinger, Gerald. *The SS: Alibi of a Nation 1922-1945.* (William Heinemann, 1956)

Reynolds, Quentin et al. *Eichmann: Minister of Death.* (Cassell, 1960)

Ruerup, Reinhard (Editor). *Topography of Terror.* (Verlag Willmuth Arenhovel, 1989)

Schellenberg, Walter. *The Schellenberg Memoirs.* (Andre Deutsch, 1956)

von Schlabrendorff, Fabian. *They Almost Killed Hitler.* (1947)

Shirer, William J. *The Rise and Fall of the Third Reich.* (Secker & Warburg, 1977)

Simpson, Arnold E. *Why Hitler?* (Houghton Miffin, 1971)

Skorzeny, Otto. *Skorzeny's Special Missions.* (Robert Hale, 1957)

Smith, Bradley F. *Heinrich Himmler: A Nazi in the Making.* (Hoover Institution Press, 1974)

Tobias, Fritz. *The Reichstag Fire.* (Secker & Warburg, 1962)

Wheaton, Eliot B. *Prelude to Calamity.* (Victor Gollancz, 1969)

Wheeler-Bennett, John W. *The Nemesis of Power: The German Army in Politics 1918-1945.* (Macmillan, 1980)

Wighton, Charles. *Eichmann: His Career and Crimes.* (Odhams Press, 1961)

General Index

Because of the unusual complexity of
AN ILLUSTRATED HISTORY OF THE
GESTAPO, the Index has been divided
into three parts – a General Index plus
seperate indexes for Persons and Places.
We hope this will make the index more
accessible. In all three indexes, references
to photographs or captions are indicated
by boldface.